A BEGINNER'S GUIDE TO BETTER WORL

Ideas and Inspiration from the Zapatistas

Levi Gahman, Shelda-Jane Smith, Filiberto Penados, Nasha Mohamed, Johannah-Rae Reyes and Atiyah Mohamed

P

First published in Great Britain in 2022 by

Policy Press, an imprint of
Bristol University Press
University of Bristol
1-9 Old Park Hill
Bristol
BS2 8BB
UK
t: +44 (0)117 954 5940
e: bup-info@bristol.ac.uk

Details of international sales and distribution partners are available at
policy.bristoluniversitypress.co.uk

ISBN 978-1-4473-6213-5 hardcover
ISBN 978-1-4473-6215-9 paperback
ISBN 978-1-4473-6216-6 ePub
ISBN 978-1-4473-6217-3 ePdf

Cover design: NAM CHO
Front cover image: 'The Colors of Our Struggle' – mural by Gustavo Chávez Pavón and Mitzy Vergara Santiago in the Zapatista Caracol of Roberto Barrios (Chiapas, Mexico); photo credit: Autonomous Media
Bristol University Press and Policy Press use environmentally responsible print partners.
Printed in Great Britain by CMP, Poole

In contrast to those traditional stories that begin with
'Once upon a time',

Zapatista stories begin with 'There will be a time …'.

For the underdog

Contents

Contents

List of figures

Guilty parties (who agree that lead authorship, must it be ascribed or exist, is shared and interchangeable)

Levi Gahman is Lecturer at the University of Liverpool and remains a faculty affiliate with the University of the West Indies. He focuses on anti-colonial praxis, environmental defence and engaged movement research.

Atiyah Mohamed is an independent researcher, Spanish teacher, Geography tutor and local volunteer in Trinidad and Tobago. Her community service work focuses on homelessness and the underprivileged.

Nasha Mohamed is a University of the West Indies graduate and independent researcher from Trinidad and Tobago focusing on foreign languages (Spanish, French, Arabic) and postcolonial literature.

Filiberto Penados is a Maya activist-scholar focusing on Indigenous future-making. He is President of the Julian Cho Society and adviser to the Toledo Alcaldes Association and Belize National Indigenous Council.

Johannah-Rae Reyes is an intersectional feminist activist, currently working with Amnesty International, as well as Trinidad-based organisation CAISO and WOMANTRA. She has done advocacy work in Guyana and Mexico.

Shelda-Jane Smith is Lecturer at the University of Liverpool and has a focus on the social and political determinants of physical-mental health. She is also a community volunteer with the Merseyside Caribbean Centre.

Introduction: from liberal bystanding to emancipatory praxis

> Against death, we demand life.
> The Zapatista Army for National Liberation (EZLN)

Part I: Political education as historical necessity

Before we get started, and in order to be as upfront as possible about things, we must confess that this book is actually not about Zapatistas (believe it or not), but rather political education. That said, what better example of political education than the Zapatistas?

To begin, we need to address the current state of things. On this point, the world is undeniably in crisis and neither humanity nor Earth is safe. The coloniser's model of modernity, not to mention the global economy, has been in the making for over five hundred years and is operating, if not plundering, in full effect. The consequences include exploitation, repression, indifference, mass alienation and both human and non-human suffering, in addition to climate catastrophe and ecological ruin. We, collectively and the planet, are simultaneously confronted with the very real prospects of existential peril, environmental collapse, social anomie and spiritual death. All of these dynamics, when and if reflected on and considered seriously, raise a crucial two-fold question:

> Under what circumstances is continuing to live under such conditions our best option – and why are we accepting it?

Amid such a reality and as a response to this question, countless people and communities all over the world (as well as perhaps even you yourself) – who have not given up hope in the face of what is seemingly impending doom – are declaring 'Enough is enough!' or '¡Ya basta!', as the Zapatistas would say. Indeed, something's gotta give and things must change. But how?

On this front, well over half a century ago, the anti-colonial revolutionary Frantz Fanon (1963: 88) proclaimed in his ground-breaking book, *The wretched of the earth*, that 'the political education of the masses is now recognised as an historical necessity'. Fanon, who was from the Caribbean and was dying of leukaemia at the time, was passionately offering this assertion amidst a violent struggle for liberation while tending to the injured in Africa – Algeria, to be precise. Fanon was crying out for the wholesale transformation of the way that a racist and exploitative world had become (dis)organised and (mal)developed by colonial power, as well for a fundamental change in the ways we treat, care for and relate to each other as human beings. On these points, Fanon (1963: 239) writes:

> let us not pay tribute to Europe by creating states, institutions, and societies that draw their inspiration from it. Humanity expects other things from us than this grotesque and generally obscene emulation. ...
>
> For Europe, for ourselves, and for humanity, comrades, we must make a new start, develop new ways of thinking, and endeavour to create a *new humanity*. (Emphasis added)

In short, Fanon was pleading for the abolition of colonial and capitalist institutions, the democratic creation of inclusive alternatives and a revolutionary (transformed) version of humanity in which social relations between all would be defined by the mutual recognition of dignity and preservation of everyone's integrity. As any committed reader of Fanon will recognise, he had at once dedicated himself to collectivity and was calling for engaged, emancipatory praxis. Notably, while Fanon was primarily addressing the 'Third World' at the time, he saw everyone – regardless of race, colour, creed, gender or geography – as being included in, beneficiaries of and integral to the liberatory project of bringing about a 'new humanity'.

Fanon, a radical psychiatrist who diagnosed social structures and institutionalised norms as pathological (as opposed to individuals), was as much concerned with ending imperial domination and redeeming a divided and shattered world as he was with securing the material and psychological wellbeing of others. In pleading for a 'revolutionary humanism' and fighting for a world that would be liveable and safe for all, he recognised that political education, overtly *political*, was necessary for animating emancipatory politics and charting a course towards lasting freedom. In addressing education and critical thought, Fanon (1963: 237–8) states:

> let us flee this stagnation where dialectics has gradually turned into a logic of the status quo. Let us re-examine the question of humanity. Let us re-examine the question of cerebral reality and the collective sentiment of humanity in its entirety, whose affinities must be increased, whose connections must be diversified, and whose communications must be humanized again.

Fanon, who, not coincidentally, was a key inspiration for Paulo Freire's (2018) *Pedagogy of the oppressed* and development of the notion of 'critical consciousness' (a term we expand on later in the book), further recognised that there would be no end to the dehumanisation, suffering, oppression and division that was being wrought by colonial worldviews and capitalist social relations if societies did not prioritise political education, democratic participation and meaningful work. After having fought in wars against both the Nazis and White supremacist colonisers, and because of his experiences mending the physical and psychological wounds of those afflicted by racism, combat and exploitation, Fanon realised that education *could* provide a pathway out of violence and alienation, if it was explicitly political and praxis-oriented. Another point that merits underscoring is the emphasis Fanon placed on gender justice and redressing the enduring yet daily wrongs women face. On this issue, Fanon (1963: 163) states: 'Women will have exactly the same place as men, not only in the clauses of the constitution, but *in the life of every day*: at the factory, in the schools, and in the assemblies' (emphasis added). The pro-feminist politics and stance Fanon endorsed in an acutely male-dominated context and time when it was unpopular to do so is well worth repeating and foregrounding when discussing his ideas and contributions to revolutionary thought.

Like Fanon, and only two decades after his passing, the Zapatista Army of National Liberation (*Ejército Zapatista de Liberación Nacional*, EZLN) was clandestinely formed among the highland mists and humid jungles of the Mayan world in Chiapas, Mexico. In their rebellion 'Against neoliberalism, for humanity', the EZLN declared war on global capitalism by taking up arms against consolidated state power, racist exploitation and the driving forces of capital accumulation on 1 January 1994. On doing so, the Zapatistas called for '*un mundo donde quepan muchos mundos*' – 'a world where many worlds fit'. As Indigenous people, the Zapatistas were rising up to demand and struggle for an inclusive and democratic world that they, much like Fanon, felt should be characterised by dignity, peace and respect for difference – yet intolerant of repression, corruption, coercion and bystanding.

In their own words, the Zapatistas were both dreaming of and fighting for the dawn of a new day (Marcos, 2001):

> [W]e have come to wind the clock up to ensure the coming of a morning which is inclusive, accepting, and pluralistic and that, let it be said in passing, is the only possible morning.
>
> … for this is the dream that excites us as Indigenous people, as Mexicans, and, above all, as human beings. By our struggle we read the future that was planted yesterday, that is cultivated today, and that can only be harvested if we struggle, that is, if we dream.

Through dreaming and collective action, insurgents of the EZLN were seeking to unseat liberal-capitalist hegemony and sabotage the political and economic forces that were trying to homogenise society and turn people into obedient consumers with compliant minds. Their rebellion was an appeal to principle, integrity, shared ethics, accountability and prefigurative politics (van de Sande, 2015), that is, making radical dreams of a more just world come true. Their revolt also coincided with a powerful statement the Zapatistas continue to offer anyone who has been exploited or who is made to feel small or ashamed of because of who they are: *No están solos* – 'You are not alone'. We believe these convictions give us all something to think about – not to mention aspire to. Readers will be introduced to and will get to know the Zapatistas in far greater detail in the chapters to come.

Surviving society and the present moment

> It is time for our hearts to dance again, and for their sounds and rhythm to not be those of mourning and resignation.
>
> The Zapatistas

Around the same time the Zapatistas were organising their uprising, if not before, socialist feminists concerned with gender justice increasingly identified the domain of social reproduction, which is all the work that makes life possible (and a term we explain in more depth in Chapter 8), as a critical terrain on which to struggle for a better and more just world. In arguing that (re)valuing social reproduction was critical vis-à-vis building liveable worlds, autonomist-feminist Silvia Federici (2012, 3) states:

> it is through the day-to-day activities by means of which we produce our existence, that we can develop our capacity to cooperate and not only resist our dehumanization but learn to reconstruct the world as a space of nurturing, creativity, and care.

More recently, in late 2020, a year marred by a devastating pandemic, spikes in overt anti-Black violence, continued mass shootings, police brutality, state violence in both the Global North and Majority World/Global South, and repressive crackdowns of peasants, Indigenous people, Muslims, members of the working-class, women and transgender people – to name only a few – the co-hosts and producers of the podcast *Surviving Society*, Chantelle Lewis, Tissot Regis and George Ofori-Addo, shared with listeners the following 'Note on hope':

> It's been such a difficult year. We aren't going to use this message to spell out how challenging it has been for so many as we are not sure we have the words to do it justice. It's challenging to be hopeful in the current climate. In our daily conversations, we have been thinking about how hope can be understood in the year ahead. What might

hope look like in 2021? For us, whatever the solution; love, care and understanding will always form the basis of any action. *Surviving Society* remains committed to engaging critically with experts, activists and writers who are involved in seeking solutions to the issues of the day.

A key theme for us going into 2021 is solidarity. We feel that together we can achieve more. Through *collective action* lies the possibility of building a future for everyone.

Our very small contribution to hopeful possibilities in 2021 will continue to be the *democratisation of inclusive political education* which values and stands up for the most vulnerable and marginalised within society; creating more space for radical love and care to prevail. (Emphasis added)

Contrary to what Chantelle, Tissot and George modestly stated about not having the words to do justice to the catastrophic challenges of the contemporary moment, we feel their prose perfectly captured the dire realities at hand, as well as inspired hope.

What Fanon, the Zapatistas, socialist feminists of all stripes and *Surviving Society* alike have all identified, along with so many other deliberately silenced radical thinkers irrespective of their labels or affiliations, is that there is no time to waste regarding building solidarity across difference, engaging in collective action and co-creating politically conscious *and* caring societies. This urgency is due to the world's regrettable status quo of ongoing racial violence, class stratification, authoritarian governance, chauvinistic nationalisms, gender inequities, corporate domination, state negligence, liberal self-centrism, environmental destruction ... and the list goes on.

In brief, there is a pressing need to create critically conscious and compassionate societies that think more carefully and intentionally about what we are collectively (re)producing as a species and what realities (that is, *worlds*) we are sending each other into. Political education can get us there. Regrettably, mainstream (that is, neoliberal) education, which arguably remains colonial, is failing us on all fronts. Disconcertingly, this is occurring across the globe. The present state of things means people all over the planet continue to be denied material needs, meaningful work, dignified wages and democratic participation, as well as being increasingly severed from any sense of connection, self-efficacy, meaning, purpose and joy in life. This is as grim to reflect on as it is harrowing to try to survive – and we should all be outraged – in particular, because some realities (for example, Black, Indigenous, Disabled, Working-Class, Migrant, Queer) are designed to be worse than others (Taylor, 2016). While radical love, care and solidarity are the solution, we must also not forget that anger is a gift – and a precious one at that. We should not be afraid to wield it, albeit wisely, ethically and constructively. Here, we feel the Zapatistas have set a good example.

Accordingly, and in agreeing with the prescient appeals made by Fanon, the Zapatistas, countless feminists from all walks of life and the sentiments shared by the crew at *Surviving Society*, we have penned *A Beginner's Guide to Building Better Worlds*. The book represents our admittedly small and imperfect attempt to pay heed to Fanon's exigent appeal for political education and the Zapatistas' clarion call that the world be a better place and one in which all worlds/differences fit.

Liberal bystanding versus radical (collective) action

> We do not surrender, we do not sell out, and we do not give up.
>
> The EZLN

In addition to the goals stated here, another key aim we have with this text is to move beyond calls to be 'nice' well-intentioned individuals and moderates who hold liberal values and support reformist policies. Put differently, we want to cast light on and raise consciousness about the trappings and consequences of becoming liberal bystanders. While on the surface 'good intentions', liberal ideals, being 'moderate' and supporting reform might sound perfectly fine and reasonable, or even seem necessary in some instances, we remain quite suspicious of them, and feel all are extremely limited, if not dangerous, with respect to social transformation, ending structural inequalities and actually changing anything. This is due to the fact that all facilitate signalling virtue, symbolic acts, performative gestures and complicity with the status quo at the expense of being engaged in the taxing intellectual work that is collective struggle, solidarity-building, emancipatory praxis and radical change.

At this point, you may notice we use the term 'radical' quite often. It is important to clarify what we mean by this. 'Radical', for us, is not synonymous with either 'fanatical' or 'extremist', and we do not use it as a noun. Rather, we use 'radical' as an adjective to signify what it designated from its Latin origins, *radicalis*, meaning: 'of, relating to, or proceeding from the roots'. In short, when we use 'radical' as a modifier for the terms 'action', 'change', 'ideas', 'care', 'hope' or any other word, for that matter, it simply means from the (grass)roots, bottom-up, foundation or core of things. In some instances, radical action and change means resistance, dismantling and abolishing; in others, it means constructing, building and co-creating. While we have plenty of thoughts on these matters, we will leave it up to you to figure out what things need to be abolished and what things need to be built wherever you are.

Liberal bystanding, which poses a major threat to the wellbeing of both humanity and the planet, is effectively any instance in which we are complicit with or do not speak out or act against an unjust status quo. It is rooted in selfishness (liberal ideals) but comes in many forms: silence, indifference, cowardice, obliviousness, ignorance, defensive moves to innocence, self-absolution, or sometimes even malice and contempt. If you cannot be bothered with or are indifferent towards the suffering and struggles of others, then you are a liberal bystander. The same charge applies to those who remain silent and sneakily try to get away with or benefit from corruption, cheating or conflicts of interest. Regrettably, liberal bystanding is now not only widespread and banally unnoticed, but often surreptitiously promoted and cleverly rewarded; it is at once a pandemic, social pathology and individual affliction of sorts. As Mary Watkins and Helene Shulman (2008: 64) explain:

> In large-scale industrialized societies, it has been hardest to recognize, describe, and begin to address the pathologies of bystanding. These pathologies are often normalized. Their cultural roots are unacknowledged; their dynamics largely unexamined; and their societal function unnamed.
>
> For those raised in educational systems that stress individualism, it becomes difficult to formulate ideas about the way one's own social environment and those of others affect one's wellbeing. Many cannot imagine themselves speaking out publicly or rocking the boat by asking painful and difficult questions. Bystanders may have been taught that protest is ineffective, that authorities know better, that getting to the roots of unjust power is impossible, and that the systems that manufacture injustice and violence are beyond one's control. Bystanders avoid talking with others with different points of view that might challenge their normalized perspectives.

While the vast majority of people are not necessarily intentionally, directly or purposely involved in exploiting or damaging others and the Earth, we are all, regrettably, in one way or another, most likely complicit with social institutions, organisations, systems of power and instances of 'business as usual' that are. Present company included. This unfortunate caveat and reality aside, we all have the capacity to act.

For example, it is one thing to pay lip service to or tweet about creating better learning conditions for students, ending gender and racial pay gaps and making universities more diverse, inclusive and equitable places along lines of race, class, gender and ability; it is another to sacrifice time and pay, take to the streets, join a picket, be marked by unprincipled managers and shameless colleagues as troublemakers or misguided, and have your job or career comprised for supporting these convictions in practice. It is quite telling apropos liberal bystanding to see who breaks a strike or does not show up for a movement, be it for better schools, dignified working conditions, a decent pension, climate justice, the safety of women, LGBTQI rights, Black life or Indigenous lands.

Put differently, collectively organising against injustice or an oppressive institutionalised way of doing things is an assertion of agency and a political act, just as is hiding, bystanding, refusing to engage and going with the flow. Some people decide to collectively struggle together for others and the Earth, while others decide not to and focus primarily on themselves. In both instances, people are making choices that are revelatory about their character and integrity, and must own their decisions. Notably, institutions will reward you for your complicity with the status quo, as well as equally punish you for your dissent, even though they will not necessarily say or make it known that these are the reasons why you are either being respectively rewarded or punished. In many cases, those who decide to get involved and refuse to be liberal bystanders learn an invaluable lesson about the ways in which the status quo and institutions exact discipline, so we resist as actively as we can, but as passively as we must. Moving against a status quo comes with consequences and can indeed take a toll. Contrariwise, it is always interesting to see who is being rewarded for complicity and promoted for their talent at being domesticated yet chalk up this 'success' to individual hard/brilliant work. Despite the short-term rewards, there are devastating costs to liberal bystanding, both social and psycho-spiritual.

The costs and consequences of liberal bystanding

> Freedom isn't just the ability to decide what to do and do it.
> It's also taking responsibility for what you do and for the decisions you make.
>
> The Zapatistas

When it comes to the matter of ending structural inequalities, saving the planet and building better worlds, a crucial question arises. Namely, what is the purpose and role of education in all this? Of course students need to learn skills, be exposed to new information, find gainful employment and be able to socially reproduce themselves under capitalism. But is this all education should be put at the service of? To sit with this query earnestly, considering the ongoing global injustices at hand, reveals there is neither time nor space for university curricula that prioritise entrepreneurialism over political education. The same can be said for the metric fetishes, award cultures, self-centrism and rent-seeking edicts that pervade higher education.

At this juncture, to recuse oneself from collective action or absolve oneself from having to be engaged with communities is to forsake both others and the Earth. Because in light of the pervasive and explicit racist, classist, ableist and gender-based repression that continues to plague the world and neoliberal academia, the only real measure of 'impact' that matters vis-à-vis a university curriculum is the degree to which it equally includes, is relevant to, and is thoughtfully put in the service of communities-in-struggle (on their terms). This must be the work of our institutions, pedagogy, research agendas and education systems, regardless of career aspirations, and remains the challenge of our respective generations and geographies.

Notably, not everyone will agree with these sentiments. Some will even actively avoid, oppose, suppress or try to undermine them because of what they mean for them and their personal/professional ambitions. Here, the consequences of self-centrism and liberal bystanding begin to bear out. On this point, Watkins and Shulman (2008: 66–7) offer some deep insights into what the consequences of bystanding include, noting it develops 'its own symptoms and pathologies' and generates 'psychic wounds' and 'comparative neuroses'. Here we share part of Watkins and Shulman's (2008) list of effects, along with brief descriptions, as a means of warning readers what we are all in for if we opt in to liberal bystanding.

Firstly, Watkins and Shulman underscore how becoming a liberal subject and bystander leads to a 'severing of the self', which separates people from one another and prevents them from identifying as part of, finding solace in, and being accountable to a community or collective. On this point, they note (2008: 66):

> When one is thinking within an individualistic paradigm, development entails a progressive differentiation of self from other, and a corresponding strengthening of ego boundaries between self and other. Independence and self-sufficiency become laudable states, pushing interdependency and reliance on others into the realm of pathology. At the same time, the self that construes itself as independent can be unconsciously compliant to social expectations, rejecting connection to others who may speak what the severed self cannot say.

Another common fixation, if not obsession, that has emerged as a result of liberal ideology and capitalist social relations is a 'preoccupation with personal success' that is oblivious to or denies the role of structural forces, which is a compulsion and condition that comes with a host of adverse upshots that Watkins and Shulman (2008: 66) elaborate upon:

> When people are preoccupied by a sense of responsibility for their own successes and failures, they do not focus on the fact that the playing field is tilted. ... Failure to succeed that has a context of lack of adequate access to resources is seen as personal failure; just as success in a context of privilege is lauded as wholly personal and "deserved". The sense of inferiority or superiority that results is illusory, while the advantages and disadvantages that are amassed are not.

In speaking to the debilitating personal, psychological, and spiritual toll that liberal social relations and instances of bystanding come with, Watkins and Shulman (2008: 67) note that alienation and 'loneliness' readily emerge as typical outcomes:

> Comparative practices distance one from the possibility of authentic relation to others. The other is someone to be outdone or is the one who has outdone us. Security gained by fighting one's way to an elevated position vis-à-vis the other is paid for by isolation and loneliness. The workplace may become a site of potential self-elevation, rather than a potential community of unfolding relations. The insecure individualistic self who is intent on amassing resources for its own survival and enjoyment, on striving to aggrandize the self, paradoxically at the very same moment is impoverished through cutting the self off from multiple kinds of relations with self, others, and nature.

Lastly, in detailing the trappings of liberal bystanding and degree to which self-centrism, virtue-signalling, award cultures, attention-seeking behaviour, and self-promotion have all become accepted and expected aspects of liberal-capitalist 'common sense' and social relations, Watkins and Shulman (2008: 67) highlight how ego-centrism and narcissism are consequences:

> The compulsive drive for success that arises in a competitive culture does not secure peace of mind, inner security, or joy. On the contrary, a person indiscriminately and compulsively seeks praise, glory, and affirmation. ... In its quest for excessive admiration and glory, the drive to excel is split from the discernment of what is meaningful, abandoning the self's search for deeper life purpose, and cutting the self off from the vitality and spontaneity that lie available at the heart of meaning. The severed self recreates its own abandonment over and over again. Intense needs for admiration stand in where mutual relationships are absent.

Watkins and Shulman (2008) go on to list eight additional symptoms of bystanding, and while we have only shared an overview of four in very brief form here, we think this partial list illustrates quite well just how much is at stake. Notably, while bystanding obviously takes a personal and spiritual toll in the way of pathologies and neuroses, the social cost is equally, if not more, pernicious, in particular because of who are being abandoned and forgotten by liberal bystanders. As an intervention, we hope *A Beginner's Guide to Building Better Worlds* instils within readers the ability to recognise those moments in which they will be encouraged, compelled or even coerced by their institutions, managers, colleagues, peers, conventions or the status quo to passively bystand and will, like the Zapatistas, refuse.

Part II: Positionality and the politics/responsibilities of writing

> To be Zapatista does not mean to hide one's face, but rather, to show one's heart.
>
> The Zapatistas

As a diverse collective of authors writing from different positionalities and standpoints but with a shared voice throughout the text, we come from and represent Indigenous, Black, Muslim, Diasporic, Caribbean, Central American, Majority World/Global South, Global North and rural White settler backgrounds and histories. These are in addition to a plethora of other identities, subject positions, political leanings, affiliations and ancestors we remember, have affinities for and engender that are far too long to list. Incidentally, amidst our differences, we all come from working-class or working-poor backgrounds; are first-generation university graduates; and are not satisfied, to put it lightly, with the current state of things, in particular mainstream education (aside from, perhaps, public libraries).

Our combined time and experience with Zapatismo, in Zapatista *caracoles* (community centres), or with Zapatistas stems from following the movement for years and different direct encounters most of us have had with Zapatistas, as well as several treks some of us have made to Central America over the past decade. Our trips have been a result of responding to global calls issued by the Zapatistas for participation in different events, seminars and gatherings. On replying, we typically received an invitation and permission to attend as either a member of the autonomous media, a student or as a listener. Here, we should note that conducting formal 'research' in Zapatista territory is a multifaceted, complex, oft-not possible endeavour given they are targets of a state-sanctioned counterinsurgency, and approval for official research necessitates permission from a region's respective *Junta de Buen Gobierno* (Council of Good Government). Hence, in respecting the Zapatistas' privacy, autonomy and entitlement to 'ethnographic refusal' (Simpson, 2007), we have never sought permission to conduct formal ethnographic research. The first-hand observations, stories, testimonials and communication that appear in this book will thereby be what Zapatistas have allowed delegates and members of the independent media to record and share, or it will be sourced from materials, statements and communiqués the Zapatistas have released and made public. Readers will also notice instances of direct quotes from Zapatistas. These accounts draw from wide-ranging empirical scholarship conducted by scholars and writers who have sought and received permission from the *Juntas*.

Thus, while the majority of us have shared space and spent time with Zapatistas, visited different *caracoles*, camped in the countryside at a few different

Zapatista villages, learned about the movement in human rights/solidarity organisations, and have worked, played and spoken with a number of Maya rebels in person, we will not be quoting any of them directly in this book, unless, again, it is from a gathering, event or conversation we were invited to in which consent was volunteered or granted (for example, *La Escuelita, Homage to Galeano, Worldwide Festival of Resistances and Rebellions, Critical Thought versus the Capitalist Hydra, Comparte por la Humanidad, Conciensas por la Humanidad, Journey for Life*).[1] Our personal and political approach to what we have participated in, seen and been exposed to in Zapatista territory and beyond, in short, has been to enthusiastically attend gatherings to which we have been invited and subsequently share information and stories on the terms and preferences of the Zapatistas, if permission is granted. Otherwise, to put it simply, we just let them be. Some stories are not ours to tell.

In the interest of addressing critiques that the information Zapatistas disseminate about the movement is biased and filtered, we would respond by querying what narrative or information released by any group, organisation or institution, be it a state organisation or otherwise, is ever unbiased, non-filtered, objective or politically neutral? Moreover, and to their credit, the Zapatistas are plausibly one of the most hospitable, welcoming, open and transparent rebel movements the world has seen (Zibechi, 2013), relatively speaking, of course, and to the degree that it does not compromise their own safety and wellbeing. There are several activists, academics and journalists who have carried out formal research in-and-with Zapatista communities over the past three decades (Gilly, 1997; Harvey, 1998; Stephen, 2002; Speed and Forbis, 2005; Cerda Garcia, 2006; Ramírez et al, 2008; Hernández Castillo, 2010; Baronnet et al, 2011; Rosset and Martínez-Torres, 2012; Altamirano-Jiménez, 2013; Klein, 2015; Mora, 2017; Marcos, 2014). Many of these researchers are guided by anti-extractive politics and authorised by Zapatista communities. This vibrant body of literature has not only been instructive and insightful for us collectively, but also provides rich and consensual details of what select processes and realities are like within certain communities. Thus, given that first-hand accounts, grounded scholarship and ethnographic fieldwork has indeed been approved and carried out in Zapatista territory in some circumstances, we are relying on it, in addition to our own qualified and differential experiences, as empirical evidence.

Admittedly, and a point in need of reiteration (de Leeuw and Hunt, 2018), is that academics have an extensive (colonial) track record of 'researching, analysing and studying' Indigenous people and the conditions they face. Such fraught undertakings are dangerous because they can further subject already besieged groups to more acute forms of exposure, racial tokenisation, extraction and expropriation. In many cases, research of this form and function is carried out by the most well-meaning of researchers, yet still results in reassertions of (neo)colonial power and erasures, mutings, distortions and plagiarisms of

Indigenous voices and knowledges.[2] It is with these complexities in mind that we suggest probing the Zapatistas as a clinical case study or fetishised ethnography would be committing an act of epistemological violence against them. Thus, we write not with the purpose of placing the Zapatistas under an analytical academic microscope, but to share their approach to resistance, collective organising, social reproduction and emancipatory praxis as of result of having been inspired by the movement ourselves. Another motive behind drafting this book is to propose that the politics, practices, principles and praxis of the Zapatistas might be something to consider embracing within our own local geographies, communities and even universities.

Our aims, motivation and (dare we say it!) agenda

> It is time to fight, we need to fight because we cannot stand this situation any longer.
>
> Comandanta Ana María (1994)

For context, from our vantage point, education-as-we-know-it is failing students, societies and the planet. With specific respect to higher/further education, we would contend that if any given university wants to create 'global citizens' or 'decolonise' (a claim we remain deeply suspicious of), then it must do so critically and concretely. We want this text to be a catalyst for doing precisely that. Our primary goal with the book, thus, is to prompt inspiration and hope in readers by raising awareness about the revolutionary politics and emancipatory praxis of the Zapatistas.

More specifically, we want the book to offer radical alternatives to staid ways of thinking about education, politics, society, the environment, knowledge production and the world's most pressing global challenges. Here, we feel the Zapatistas are a movement to look to for said radical alternatives. The unfortunate fact of the matter remains that neither governments nor corporations are responsive to the actual needs of the masses, with many being actively violent towards them. It is up to us to work out collective responses. Accordingly, by providing an overview of concepts and tangible examples of movement praxis (Cox, 2017), collective action and mutual aid, we hope this book will encourage readers to 'be a Zapatista, wherever they are'. For us, 'being a Zapatista wherever you are', a phrase we cannot take credit for, is a whimsical way of saying we would like you to see yourselves as co-creators and shapers of the societies, cultures, communities and even institutions you are part of.

In addition, the book aspires to disrupt the neoliberal status quo of higher education by arming readers with crucial insights about theories of social change in conjunction with glimpses of praxis and alternatives in Zapatista territory. We feel these are necessary towards: (1) becoming more inquisitive and solidaristic actors; (2) questioning institutionalised authority and holding taken-for-granted systems of power to the fire; and (3) co-constructing a better, more just and convivial world – or rather, *worlds* – given the varying realities faced by so many people across the globe. We also want the book to appeal to students, activists, organisers and any interested parties who recognise or are simply curious about the value of political education, radical thought and collective action. Here, we would contend that being politically conscious, aware of what social reproduction is and learning that people have the capacity to collectively act and change things (if not the obligation) is vital towards any given reader's formal or informal education and development of critical thinking skills.

Indeed, while you may not be interested in capitalism, capitalism is interested in you. For us, fashioning students into 'good' neoliberal subjects, teaching them to be 'respectable' and obedient consumers, encouraging them to become ambitious entrepreneurs, and framing 'success' as becoming a bourgeois 'global citizen' who is savvy at self-branding and accumulating possessions and clout is as socially dangerous as it is spiritually damaging. Any look at the world's rampant mental health crisis, regardless of geography or industry, but especially within universities, is evidence of this. Moreover, who is afforded the opportunities, life chances and privileges of being able to become a well-travelled 'global citizen' or charismatic entrepreneur? And, conversely, who is being globalised and gazed upon, or exploited and extracted from, in such arrangements?

Our critique here is not of good-natured and well-intentioned students who want to cautiously explore the world respectfully and who we wish to engage and be in solidarity with. Rather, our venom and ire are directed at neoliberal institutions, logics, managers and authority figures that we feel are doing a grave disservice not only to students, but also the whole of society, as a result of either deliberately suppressing or unwittingly stifling political education and collective action. Our sentiment, to be as candid as possible, is that if critical consciousness, engaged praxis and the pursuit of freedom for everyone is not a part of a curriculum, then it is not a curriculum worth having at all. Put bluntly, political education is our agenda and collective liberation the aim.

Despite what you can probably tell is our affinity for rocking the boat, upsetting the apple cart, pushing the envelope and not 'keeping our powder dry', as well as given our realisation that we might sound like militants or hard-liners at this point, we are writing and addressing readers, in particular, students, with as affable and genial a tone as possible. Our intent is neither to scold nor guilt-trip anyone into solidarity or moving against systems of domination. This rarely, if ever, works. We have all been struggling students and precarious workers before, some of us still even are, and recognise what students and workers from all walks of life are up against. Moreover, we individually and collectively continue to work through and re-examine our own ideas, core values and behaviours, as well as by no means thinking we either have or represent perfect or pure politics ourselves. Incidentally, we also do not consider ourselves 'experts' when it comes to building better worlds or bringing revolutionary humanism to fruition. In this regard, we are as much 'students' and 'beginners' as anyone else. If the charge is 'fallible subjects with a limited understanding of things', then we stand guilty. Ultimately, *A Beginner's Guide to Building Better Worlds* is the direct result of our collective observations and appraisals of the status quo in conjunction with the aforementioned convictions and sentiments. The book is not meant to be comprehensive of anything, but rather, provoke curiosity, encourage critical thinking, foster *structural* analyses and hopefully inspire readers to explore, discover and maybe even rebel and rage against the machine more – in addition to refusing to be liberal bystanders.

Broadly and with all that in mind, the book unfolds by addressing two interrelated areas of concern: (1) the suffering, despair and destruction wrought by colonial power and neoliberal capitalism; and (2) the inspiration, hope and alternatives offered by the Zapatistas. More precisely, the book covers content related to overcoming alienation and anguish via pluralistic solidarity and collective action. In doing so, we first introduce the Zapatistas before providing an analysis of neoliberalism and touching on what colonial worldviews and capitalist logics have and continue to produce within mainstream higher education and 'modernity'. We then offer some insight into resistance, dispossession and extraction, before discussing a series of topics and concepts we feel are generative regarding political education and critical consciousness. Then, based on our respective engagements with the Zapatistas and Zapatismo (the broad guiding principles associated with the Zapatistas), we share an overview of how the Zapatistas are constructing autonomy in the face of colonial-capitalist modernity and neoliberalism. In total, readers will receive a brief genealogy of the Zapatista rebellion and movement; an overview of the principles and spirit of Zapatismo; and exposure to how the Zapatistas are constructing autonomy, that is, building self-determined education, health and freedom via a commitment to democratic process, collective work, gender justice and mutual aid.

Structure, organisation and a word of caution

> Zapatismo is not a new political ideology or a rehash of old ideologies. ... It only serves as a bridge, to cross from one side, to the other. There are no universal recipes, lines, strategies, tactics, laws, rules, or slogans. There is only a desire – to build a better world, that is, a new world.
>
> The Zapatistas

The EZLN, the Zapatista uprising and the Zapatista communities at large have all been written about at length (Ramírez et al, 2008; Klein, 2015). Given the point of this book is to share with readers an array of their practices that we hope will spur further interest in the movement, ideas for alternatives and facilitate political education, we only offer a very brief summary of the rich history and deeply layered yet kaleidoscopic politics of the Zapatista resistance and construction of autonomy. That said, we caution against reading this book as a romanticisation of the Zapatista struggle or exercise in hagiography. While we feel what the Zapatistas are doing and creating is admirable, laudable and enlivening, we realise their resistance, fight and ancestors' histories are marked by pain, loss and needless suffering. We also understand that the movement is not infallible. Indeed, no one – or movement – is. Anyone who has paid close attention to the Zapatistas, listened to their words or spent any time movement-building, community organising or been in an activist collective themselves (that is, engaged in grounded politics) will know all too well that there is no perfect or pure model of resistance, organising or mobilising for change. Even so, in a world replete with persistent injustice, increasing despair and escalating retreats into cynicism, indifference and pessimism, it is important to make room for inspiration, upliftment and motivation. We feel the Zapatistas are a potent source of all these.

It is impossible for us to do the movement justice with only one book, and a more dedicated engagement with the Zapatistas is certainly in order, be it via reading or 'in real life'. Admittedly non-exhaustive, we want the chapters that follow to fuel your enthusiasm for future investigation, and even prompt some of you to question authority, disrupt orthodoxy, proclaim '¡Ya basta!' ('Enough is enough!') in the face of belligerent institutions and injustice in all forms – and demand the impossible. At the same time, we hope learning about the Zapatistas will enable you to discover how we can all work together to overcome hostile forces, transcend petty quarrels and personality conflicts, build solidarity across difference and co-create the inclusive cultures and dignified day-to-day realities everyone so very much deserves. To do so, we provide explanations of revolutionary ideas and radical approaches to neoliberalism, modernity, colonialism and race, critical consciousness, social reproduction, feminist ethics, holistic views on health, food sovereignty and decolonisation, among several other mystified and oft-elided terms.

Specifically, after being more thoroughly introduced to the Zapatistas and their history and politics in Chapter 2, the first half of the book expands on a host of concepts we feel are essential apropos political education and becoming more critically informed and discerning thinkers. Chapter 3 focuses largely on neoliberalism, with specific attention paid to health and education. It highlights how contemporary universities are inculcating the people who learn and work in them with neoliberal values and market-oriented subjectivities by advocating extreme individualism, self-centrism (protagonism), capitalist mentalities and consumerism. Chapter 4 offers a sharp genealogy and dissection of modernity, with a dedicated look at the struggles of Indigenous people, in particular the Zapatistas. Chapter 5 touches on the consequences of resisting exploitation, extraction and 'development', as well as the realities of environmental defenders and what movements like the Zapatistas offer us in the way of building alternatives and changing the world. Chapter 6 includes explicatory synopses of an eclectic constellation of terms and concepts we feel are essential to be aware of but are either being cunningly suppressed or senselessly side-lined in mainstream education.

The second part of the book offers readers vignettes of how the Zapatistas, who are arguably one the world's foremost examples of decolonisation and Fanon's notion of 'revolutionary humanism', are organising life in their neck of the woods. While situated in the latter half of the text, we feel this content should be featured in the matinee, so to speak. More expressly, Chapters 7, 8 and 9 all include details and accounts of how Zapatista communities are placing dignity, mutual aid, defiance, care, material-psychological wellbeing and selflessness at the heart of their social relations, education system, culture and economy. In Chapter 10 we end with a reflection of the current challenges at hand regarding universities, as well as our thoughts on some potential solutions, which draw directly from the spirit of Zapatismo. Cumulatively, these chapters provide readers with an overview of how the Zapatistas have prioritised political education, social reproduction, solidarity, collective action, democratic process and praxis in their resistance, movement and pursuit of health.[3] Overall, we want the book to be a gateway text that motivates readers to refuse liberal bystanding and contribute to collective action and radical change wherever you are, from the local to the global, that is relevant, inclusive and enduring.

In many ways, we also hope the pages that follow prove to be as subversive and unsettling as they are solidaristic and inspiring. Learning is effortful and can be uncomfortable, but it is growth. On this front, we are endeavouring to transgress scales, borders and credentials as a means of rousing hearts and minds to build critical mass and collectively mobilise, or at least see merit in doing so. The book represents our proposal to readers to find camaraderie with 'others'; see your own ideas, thoughts and contributions as worthy; confront the corrupt powers-that-be; and collectively and compassionately struggle for better realities, that is, *worlds* – 'whatever your calendar or geography', as the Zapatistas would say. In sum, *A Beginner's Guide to Building Better Worlds* is meant to be both a convivial read that lets readers know you are not alone, and a proposal aimed at inspiring open-minded students to refuse liberal bystanding, get involved in emancipatory praxis and struggle together – in whatever way you can. Importantly, our intention as authors is to reciprocate and do the same, so let us begin.

2

A world where many worlds fit

We're sorry for the inconvenience, but this is a revolution.

The EZLN

A '¡Ya basta!' heard around the world

The story of the Zapatistas is one of struggle, dignity and hope. It is an ongoing saga of collective resistance to over five hundred years of attempted imperial conquest and accumulation by dispossession justified by the racist denigration of Indigenous people and the repression of rural peasants in their fight for land and freedom. It is also nothing less than a revolutionary and poetic account of liberation, empathy and revolt, a movement characterised as much by pain, adversity and tears as it is by laughter, dancing and dreams. And for people of the Ch'ol, Tseltal, Tsotsil, Tojolabal, Mam and Zoque communities who make the decision to become a Zapatista, it is a story retold, reborn and rekindled each new day, with each new step.

The most well-known aspect of the Zapatista struggle involves the uprising of the EZLN (*Ejército Zapatista de Liberación Nacional* [Zapatista Army of National Liberation]) led in Chiapas, Mexico on 1 January 1994. At that time, the Zapatista announced themselves as a product of '500 years of struggle', which includes resistance to: enslavement during the Spanish conquest; Spain during Mexican independence; the imperialist aggression of the US; the intervention of the French Empire; and the dictatorship of Porfirio Díaz (EZLN, 1998; Dinerstein, 2015). In sum, the EZLN identified their rebellion as the continuation of a generation's-long history of resistance to and struggle against dispossession, exploitation and exclusion that can be traced back centuries (Gunderson, 2019). The latest iteration of these things was the 70-year rule of Mexico's *Partido Revolucionario Institucional* (PRI, Institutional Revolutionary Party) and the ensuing hegemony of neoliberalism.

Appropriately enough, the EZLN introduced themselves in spectacular fashion, by taking up arms against neoliberalism and a corrupt government on the day the North American Free Trade Agreement (NAFTA) went into effect. Their successful insurrection was the result of over a decade of clandestine organising throughout the Lacandon Jungle and Chiapas Highlands. Although they laid siege to capitalism and state power in 1994, the origin of the EZLN dates back to 17 November 1983, when three urban Mestizo and three Indigenous revolutionaries arrived in the mountains of the Mexican southeast to form a guerrilla army. Just over 10 years later, and after having been transformed by the Indigenous communities they encountered, on the dawn of New Year's Day, thousands of masked insurgents from the EZLN stepped out of the mist and the shadows to declare '¡Ya basta!' ('Enough is enough!') to the repression and misery that colonialism and capitalism had thrust upon them.

The stunning way they presented themselves to the Mexican government, as well as the world, saw them descend on several towns, cities, prisons and ruling-class landowners. In doing so, the EZLN liberated political prisoners, overtook military barracks, seized government offices and burnt administrative files that unfairly criminalised Indigenous people. In the rural countryside, Zapatista soldiers forced wealthy property-owners off the abusive plantation-like *encomiendas* that had been expropriated from Indigenous *campesinos* (peasants), and reclaimed stolen land that had been taken from their ancestors via historical and contemporary processes of enclosure and privatisation (JBG, 2013a).

The federal military responded with force by sending thousands of troops to Chiapas in order to try to suppress the Zapatistas. Hundreds died in the ensuing 12-day exchange of bullets, with a ceasefire commencing on 12 January 1994 (Ramírez et al, 2008). What followed thereafter was a series of peace negotiations that resulted in the San Andrés Accords of 1996 (Ross, 2000). These were made to ensure the Mexican state recognised Indigenous rights in the areas of land, culture, self-determination and respect. Despite signing the Accords, however, the federal government betrayed the peace process by failing to implement the changes in the constitution and refusing,

Figure 2.1: A sign in Zapatista territory that captures their definition of democracy and the spirit of their rebellion, which reads: 'You are in Zapatista territory, here the people lead and the government obeys'

outright, to uphold the commitments they had made in principle to the Zapatistas, not to mention all of Mexico's Indigenous people (Collier and Quaratiello, 2005).

Phases of the Zapatista resistance

Soriano González (2012) describes the Zapatista resistance and struggle as consisting of: phase one – war and negotiation with the Mexican government; phase two – rupture with the government and the construction of Zapatista de facto autonomy; and phase three – building relationships with progressive sectors of Mexican civil society and international sympathisers. While these phases do not follow a strict chronological order and include both elements of resisting power and building alternatives, they are useful in understanding the Zapatista struggle. What needs to be kept in mind is that phases two and three overlap considerably, and are presently ongoing. As noted, the armed conflict in 1994 only lasted 12 days. On 2 January 1994, the Mexican government ordered military intervention and was poised to crush the insurrection, but as a result of the Zapatistas' savvy and effective use of public relations, protests by civil society and international pressure by humanitarian groups, a ceasefire was declared 10 days later. The Zapatistas would later state, 'our word is our weapon'.

The EZLN then entered into a process of dialogue with the Mexican state mediated by Father Samuel Ruiz García, Bishop of the Diocese of San Cristóbal de las Casas. This dialogue produced the San Andrés Accords on the rights and culture of Indigenous people, which were aimed at recognising Indigenous rights and proposed systemic reforms. By the end of 1996, negotiations with the state for the implementation of the Accords collapsed as a result of government intransigence and a lack of political will. At that point, the Zapatistas decided to focus on building their autonomy (Oikonomakis, 2019). While abandoned by the state, Zapatista communities began implementing the substance of the Accords in their autonomous territories, later establishing what they call the *Juntas de Buen Gobierno* (Councils of Good Government) and *caracoles* (snails, which function as administrative centres), which are part of their communal system of governance. This work focused on constructing local economies, pursuing their notions of wellbeing, practicing grassroots participatory democracy, and, in short, constructing autonomy. All of this roughly marked the beginning of the second phase of their struggle. Ever since, writes Soriano González (2012: 397), the Zapatistas 'have followed their own path of political autonomy all while being watched over and harassed by both the military and paramilitary'.

Soriano González (2012) goes on to note that the *Sixth Declaration of the Selva Lacandona* (Lacandon Jungle), announced in November 2005, marked the beginning of the third phase of the Zapatista struggle. In this

Declaration, the Zapatistas explained that they rose up in arms because they had had enough of the rich and powerful exploiting, stealing, humiliating, imprisoning and killing people 'from below' with impunity, and that their struggle was for justice, democracy and freedom. They clarified that they were fighting not only for Indigenous people in Chiapas and the rest of Mexico, but for everyone throughout the entirety of the world (EZLN, 2005). In 'La Sexta' ('The Sixth'), as the Declaration is often referred to, they restated their desire:

> [T]o fight along with everyone who was humble and simple like ourselves, who was in great need and who suffered from exploitation and thievery by the rich and their bad government here, in our Mexico, and in other countries in the world.

During that time, the Zapatistas committed to building solidarity with international supporters and launched an invitation to other people to walk with them 'in something very great that is called Mexico, and something greater which is called the world' (EZLN, 2005).

Their most recent initiative, launched in 2020 (EZLN, 2020d, 2021), continues what Soriano González describes as the third phase, which reiterates the solidaristic essence and building of bridges that now defines the Zapatista struggle. In 2020, the Zapatistas announced that they were embarking on a journey to take their word far, a journey they have called 'La travesía por la vida', 'The journey for life' (EZLN, 2021). The first part of this journey has been dubbed 'The European chapter'. In April 2021, a team of mostly rebel women departed Chiapas for Europe, and, at the time of this writing, are currently en route. The mission, as the Zapatistas have described it, is to be 'a seed that seeks other seeds'; to share the journey of their struggle for autonomy and for life; to learn from others and support others; and ultimately, to build solidarity in the struggle for life.

Autonomy in the face of the hydra and colossus

> Our choice is not between war and peace but between life with dignity or without it.
>
> The EZLN

Since the 1994 uprising, the Zapatistas have been the target of physical violence, political repression and paramilitary aggression by the Mexican government and its army. This counterinsurgency, which includes unremitting martial surveillance, has been sanctioned by all levels of government (federal, state, municipal), and continues to attempt to fracture Indigenous communities in Chiapas by pitting them against one another.

The divide-and-conquer tactics employed by the state primarily include offering co-optive government 'assistance' packages (that is, payments and amenities) to the rural poor in Chiapas (largely Indigenous peasant farmers) in exchange for disavowing or sabotaging the Zapatistas' movement.

Remarkably, even when violence is lateral in form, the Zapatistas withhold from retaliating, maintain their steady focus on peace, and refer to *PRI'istas*[1] (those Indigenous people who remain loyal to the government by accepting payments or even assailing the Zapatistas) as their Indigenous 'brothers and sisters'. This stems from the Zapatistas' recognition that the source of the belligerence is *el mal gobierno* (the bad/evil government) and not necessarily other Indigenous community members who acquiesce to its coercion and seduction.

The Mexican government's bought-and-paid for interferences take the form of attacks on Zapatista communities, schools, health clinics and *milpas* (agroecological cornfields), as well as food, water and energy sources. Zapatistas have also been directly assaulted and murdered by the paramilitary. The Zapatistas' response to the counterinsurgency has been to maintain their steadfast conviction against ever becoming dependent on the state and its corporate overlords. Thus, the Zapatistas wholly refuse to accept any money or aid the government offers, and defiantly do so by referring to such buy-outs as *migajas* (crumbs) (Klein, 2015). Their decision to never accept government assistance is crucial to their resistance. This is because, despite the fact that at one point in time they took up arms against the government, the most powerful weapon the Zapatistas now wield in the face of neoliberal violence is neither guns nor bullets, but rather, their word and autonomy (Marcos, 2001; Ramírez et al, 2008).

The autonomy of the Zapatistas centres on decentralising and democratising power, collective work, iterative reflection, reciprocal offerings of dignity and developing a culture of conviviality, dissidence and respect (Callaban, 2005). Consequently, as they are not preoccupied with the accumulation of profit, individual status, private property or personal prestige, they are able to concentrate their energies and emotions on fortifying their communities. Notably, for the Zapatistas, community is a very precious thing. On this point, the Zapatistas move forward in their communities and resistance by constructing social relations centred on mutual aid, voluntary cooperation, participatory-democratic governance and horizontal popular assembly. These everyday revolutionary exercises of co-creating the society they desire are rooted in the 13 original demands they made on the dawn of their rebellion in the face of colonial-capitalist modernity, which included: land, housing, work, food, health, education, information, culture, independence, democracy, justice, liberty and peace.

For more context and a concise synopsis of neoliberalism as the Zapatistas see it, we can turn to their apt diagnosis of the world's neoliberal status quo, which they shared at the 2015 seminar, 'Critical thought in the face of the capitalist hydra' (EZLN, 2015a):

> Because it not just in one place or in one way that capitalism oppresses. It oppresses you if you're a woman. It oppresses you if you're a white-collar worker. It oppresses if you're a blue-collar worker. It oppresses if you're a *campesinos*. It oppresses if you're a young person. It oppresses you if you are a child. It oppresses you if you're a teacher. It oppresses you if you're a student. It oppresses you if you're an artist. It oppresses you if you think. It oppresses you if you are human, or plant, or water, or earth, or air, or animal.

Given the critical analysis, emancipatory politics and intellectual insights offered by the Zapatistas, we cannot help but be reminded of anarchist Peter Kropotkin's words (1975: 3), who, in 1880, stated: 'There are periods in the life of human society when revolution becomes an imperative necessity, when it proclaims itself as inevitable.' Furthermore, if earnestly considering what the Zapatistas' uprising against a capitalist state represents for the world in the face of the current neoliberal order of things, one cannot also help but see resonance in Kropotkin's (1975: 7) nearly prophetic words:

> But soon it became apparent that the established order has not the force one had supposed. One courageous act has sufficed to upset in a few days the entire governmental machinery, to make the colossus tremble.

From our vantage point, the Zapatistas, via imagination, courage and creativity, are at once providing us with confirmation that the established order and modern nation-state (the 'colossus') are as innately violent as they are anti-democratic, and that capitalist relations of all kinds (the 'hydra') are as inherently dehumanising and materially injurious as they are spiritually debilitating and environmentally destructive. Equally, they are also co-creating a political movement characterised by rebel art, poetics, encounter and revolutionary humanism. All one needs to do to experience this is have a look at any of the vibrant murals and colourful paintings that adorn their communities and *caracoles*, or participate in or read up on any of the invitations they have offered or gatherings they have held for international sympathisers.

In addition to taking neoliberalism to task, the Zapatistas, as we will see in the chapters to come, are also laying at humanity's feet evidence that heteropatriarchy has been wrong about women this whole time (Speed et al, 2006); that the world is equally enriched by and ought to be more queer (Zapatista Women, 2019); that the planet is neither a plantation nor a shopping mall; that underdogs can win; and that we can all – if collectively organised and taking care of each other – get free. More succinctly, what the Zapatistas are demonstrating is that building what they call 'a world where many worlds fit' ('un mundo donde quepan muchos mundos') from the ground up is indeed possible.

Zapatismo: 'everything for everyone, nothing for us'

Zapatismo, sometimes referred to as *neoZapatismo* due to the connection the Zapatistas have with the Mexican revolutionary Emiliano Zapata, is a new way of doing politics and the product of radical imaginaries rooted in Maya *cosmovision* (*worldviews*) (Khasnabish, 2011). For the purposes of this book, we conceptualise Zapatismo as the diverse, unique and dynamic ensemble of relational practices, principles and core values the Zapatistas engender and share, which serve to recognise the dignity and interdependence of all, welcoming a plurality of responses to injustices of all forms.[2] Alternatively, as a Zapatista education promoter once shared with us, Zapatismo is linked to the Tzotzil concept of *ichbail ta muk*, which roughly translates as 'respecting the greatness of and reciprocally enlarging our collective heart' (Fitzwater, 2019). The Zapatistas see themselves as a collective subject (represented tangibly when they don their masks in unison) and connected to and in solidarity with the struggles of others. Here, consider the words of Major Ana María of the EZLN, who, in speaking directly to solidaristic interdependence across difference at the First Intercontinental Encounter for Humanity and Against Neoliberalism in 1996, states: 'Behind our black mask, behind our armed voice, behind our unnameable name, behind what you see of us, behind this, *we are you*' (Marcos and de Leon, 2002: 103, emphasis added).

In addition to the these dynamics, Zapatismo is often described as being comprised of the following seven guiding principles:

1. *Obedecer y no mandar* (To obey, not command).
2. *Proponer y no imponer* (To propose, not impose).
3. *Representar y no suplantar* (To represent, not supplant).
4. *Convencer y no vencer* (To convince, not conquer).
5. *Construir y no destruir* (To construct, not destroy).
6. *Servir y no servirse* (To serve, not to serve oneself).
7. *Bajar y no subir* (To work 'from below', not seek to rise).

These convictions are at the foundation of what guides the praxis and everyday efforts of the Zapatistas. They are also the principles community members abide by in their approach to fortifying their movement, protecting their communities and constructing 'a world where many worlds fit'. Zapatismo is thus the practice of community, the expression of collective work and the acknowledgement of interconnectedness coupled with a constant process of self-reflexivity. What Zapatismo gives rise to in substance are radical possibilities for galvanising horizontal relationships that actively value care work and the mutual recognition of dignity.

Importantly, the spirit of Zapatismo is constituted in the concepts of time, space and relationality of Indigenous people, specifically, the historical and ever-evolving customs of the Maya. Zapatismo, in its regenerated and transformed state, is the convalescence of a millennia-old living Maya worldview rooted in communal praxis that has been recuperated and revitalised by the present-day Zapatistas. While the contemporary Zapatista movement began on 17 November 1983 and subsequently presented itself to the world on 1 January 1994, the principles listed are not new to the Zapatistas. And while the revolutionary prose, poetics and politics of the current Zapatistas often mirror that of autonomous Marxists, anarcho-communists, libertarian socialists, and, more recently transnational feminists and queer theorists, Indigenous *cosmovisión* and cultural practices comprise the heart of Zapatismo.

The EZLN's heavy Marxist leanings can be traced to the original politicised urban intellectuals who arrived in Chiapas in 1983 in order to build a revolutionary vanguard of armed guerrillas (Ramírez et al, 2008; Conant, 2010). What the university-educated hard-line socialists arriving in the early years of the EZLN did not expect (including the well-known Subcomandante Marcos, who now goes by the name Galeano) was to be philosophically 'conquered', so to speak. Meaning, the rigid Marxist-Leninist

Figure 2.2: A sign at the Zapatista caracol (regional administrative centre) of Oventik with a message illustrating the ethos of the movement: 'Everything for everyone, nothing for us'

doctrines they sought to impress on the rural Indigenous peasants ended up faltering because the urban intellectual rebels were trying to *impose* ideas on the communities, rather than step back and pay attention to the Indigenous voices within them (Ramírez et al, 2008; Conant, 2010). They simply needed to listen in order to learn how to survive the remote jungle and highlands of Chiapas, as well as to gain an understanding of the histories, worldviews, ways of being and rhythms of life of the Indigenous people they were encountering (Speed, 2005; Conant, 2010).

Emancipatory politics, actually existing democracy

The result was a foundation and structure of Maya philosophies infused with anti-capitalist analysis and the praxis of liberation of theology that were later injected with emancipatory perspectives surrounding the rights of women and eventually united with queer discourses of inclusion. Incidentally, over the course of their insurgency, the discourse of the Zapatistas has become increasingly more progressive, particularly regarding what many of us think of as women's rights, gender justice, Indigenous feminisms and gender nonconformity, as well as queer and transgender inclusion. In addition to learning to listen, the armed guerrillas also had to be taught by the Indigenous peasants what it meant to patiently organise 'from below' (from the heart/roots), while also engaging in an iterative process of self-reflection, horizontal discussion and reciprocal support.

As Stahler-Sholk (2019) notes about the alternative politics and democratic practices of the Zapatistas:

> They also banned political parties and party-electoral politics in their territories, favoring instead a more unifying process of participatory assemblies and rotating leadership from within the communities. In rejecting the framework of liberal-representative government, they asserted the right of indigenous peoples to govern themselves according to their customs and traditions (*usos y costumbres*), seeking to break the bonds of clientelistic control that had long characterized conventional politics in Mexico. They even kept networks of solidarity and nongovernmental organizations at arm's length, taking care to ensure that their external alliance strategy did not compromise the commitment to decentralized community decision-making.

This quotidian process of constructing autonomy 'from below' and moving forward while exercising discernment and self-reflection epitomises the strength, resiliency and enduring qualities of Zapatismo. This is reflected in the Zapatista duelling axiom of '*preguntando caminamos*' ('asking, we walk'), which is central to their struggle, their process of education and their efforts in decentralising power (Holloway, 2002b). On this point, as well as the Zapatistas' approach to power, Zibechi (2019: 209) summarises:

> [T]he Zapatistas have built *non-state power structures*, that is, structures inspired by the communities: assemblies in which all decisions are taken by consensus following long processes of discussion; rotation of representatives in order to ensure that hierarchies (present in any form of power) do not become frozen into a separate bureaucracy sitting above the community. The concept of *mandar obedeciendo*, or "leading by obeying", summarises the way in which the Zapatistas understand power. It is not a *power over* but a collective *power to* and a *power between*: respectively, "the unique potential of every person to shape his or her life and world" and "find common ground among different interests in order to build collective strength" (Miller et al, 2006, 6). The leaders do not have power: they are a kind of unpaid official who takes on the desire of society to appear as a single whole, where power is not separate from society – which implies that while power exists in all societies, it is not always coercive in form. (Clastres 1981, original emphasis)

In reflecting on the ways in which the Zapatistas are decentralising governance and democratically sharing power, we cannot help but think that our respective political leaders, university managers and bosses would do well to learn a thing or two from the Zapatistas.

Here, it is essential that we point out, as the Zapatistas do, that Zapatismo is not a model, a doctrine or a blueprint. The Zapatistas move forward in their resistance by 'proposing, not imposing', and in so doing would not suggest their way of doing things be forced on others. They also, from our experiences, are not so conceited to think that their ways of organising and praxis are better or more radical than anyone else's. Meaning, the Zapatistas do not push Zapatismo as an ideology or an 'answer'. The movement is ever careful and cautiously aware of the tensions, fractious relations and foreclosures of solidarity that ensue when a group, organisation or collective asserts their philosophies and ideas as perfect, pure or dogma (EZLN, 2015c). Put differently, the Zapatistas are not a sectarian vanguard, and there is patience and inclusivity built into their politics of solidarity, which mitigate lateral hostility and do not rely on a recourse to guilt. As one Zapatista education promoter expressly stated, the Zapatistas 'are not here to "*zapaticise*" or *command*, because once that starts to happen, we are dead'.

We feel similarly about Zapatismo, although admittedly do think it is one of the world's most advanced and evolved examples of emancipatory politics, revolutionary humanism and radical praxis. In turn, we feel stories and accounts of what the Zapatistas are building and represent should be

Figure 2.3: The Junta de Buen Gobierno (JBG, Council of Good Government) in Oventik, where visitors are welcomed. The JBGs are a key component of the Zapatistas' autonomous governance

both taken seriously and promoted far and wide. Thus, our intent with this book is not to aggressively impose/*zapaticise* or even define, categorise, classify or clinically analyse the Zapatistas per se. Rather, we are simply sharing our undoubtedly limited and partial understandings, interpretations and experiences with Zapatismo and Zapatistas in the hope that doing so may spark some readers to consider 'being Zapatistas, wherever you are'. In many ways, this is less of a book about the Zapatistas than it is testimony of how we have been inspired by the Zapatistas and Zapatismo. In turn, we feel compelled, if not obligated, to spread the word. This is perhaps fraught, and we might completely miss the mark. Nevertheless, and despite our imperfect efforts, it is our modest attempt to raise what we feel is vital life-giving awareness about what is possible, and what hope is to be had, via collectively organising 'from below'.

Principles, ethics and poetics 'from below'

It is clear that the Zapatistas do not wish to suggest that their path is the 'correct' path, much less the 'only' path. We must also be careful not to imply that their worldviews, methods and ways of organising can be haphazardly extracted from their context and immediately grafted onto other political settings and struggles. Having said that, we do feel that there are some important and indispensable lessons to be learned from the Zapatistas, in particular, their guiding principles and rebel poetics, which we have already mentioned in brief, and will return to throughout the rest of the book. In light of this, here we offer a concise overview of some of their more well-known adages, collective ethics and political-spiritual ethos.

'Preguntando caminamos' ('asking, we walk')

The Zapatista struggle is neither arrogant nor triumphalist. This is reflected in their statement '*Preguntando caminamos*' ('Asking, we walk'). It is based on the understanding that the road and path to freedom is made as we walk it, in whatever way one 'walks'. This axiom alludes to the fact that struggling for autonomy is forever marked by certain uncertainty, a determinate indeterminacy. Put differently, *preguntando caminamos* means 'having enough conviction to engage in action, yet enough doubt to remain open to change' (Penados, 1999). It is precisely in this sense that in knowing others we progress. Knowing others helps us to learn, be challenged and grow. The Zapatistas have been true of this as over the years they have convened gatherings and invited social movements, intellectuals, civil society, activists, artists and others to their territory to engage in dialogue and analysis of the realities they are respectively confronting. The Zapatistas have held these gatherings, festivals and 'little schools' to get to know others, to build solidarity, to subject their struggle to examination and to learn and grow. This is exactly the underlying goal of their recently announced 'Journey for life, the European chapter' in which Zapatista delegates will travel are travelling to Europe to 'meet with those who have invited us to discuss our shared histories, pain, rage, successes, and failures' (EZLN, 2021).

'Para todos todo, para nosotros nada' ('everything for everyone, nothing for us')

Humility, conviction and the notion of a collective subject are central to the Zapatista struggle. Meaning, when they speak of resistance and freedom they are not talking about individualistic struggles, self-centrism or vanity projects. Rather than seeing humanity as *homo economicus*, that is, 'economic man' who is framed as a 'rational' (selfish and self-promoting) individual, the Zapatistas propose an alternative conception of the subject rooted in *lekil kuxlejal*, a Tzeltal term that translates roughly as 'existing and living with dignity, collectively, through the reciprocal acknowledgment of our connectedness with each other and mutual interdependence' (Mora, 2017). Compassion and selflessness is captured in their expression '*Para todos todo, para nosotros nada*' ('Everything for everyone, nothing for us'). At the individual level, these concepts place a subject (for example, a person) in – and inextricably linked to – community. This type of intersubjective relationality recognises that the wellbeing of the individual lies in the wellbeing of the collective, which safeguards against disconnection, estrangement and alienation. Notably, it does not mean the wellbeing, uniqueness or even aspirations of individuals must be abandoned, but that wellbeing will be pursued in the context of the collective and as part of a community. It is clear the Zapatista struggle is not solely for their wellbeing either, but for the wellbeing of all, for example, 'behind these masks we are you'. Their resistance is not about increasing the profile, level or clout of the Zapatistas, but securing material and psychospiritual health for all. The 'nothing for us' clause of the maxim also signifies selflessness, revolutionary humility (which does not mean diffidence or timidity) and redemptive sacrifice, all of which we feel the Zapatistas engender and represent.

'Mandar obedeciendo' *('to lead by obeying')*

The Zapatista struggle emphasises the importance of starting and working 'from below' (the grassroots) and never forgetting that authority lies with those 'from below'. This is a call for inclusive, participatory and radical (from the roots) democracy. The Zapatista struggle is not the struggle of credentialed intellectuals, vanguard militias or individualistic cult of personality leaders. The Zapatistas place their faith in the collective. This is why Subcomandante Marcos (now Galeano), who is non-Indigenous, has the rank of 'sub-commander'. The real *comandantes*, that is, commanders, are the people and the communities. On this point, the Zapatistas have coined the expression '*Mandar obedeciendo*' ('To lead by obeying'). They have developed their *Juntas de Buen Gobierno* (Councils of Good Government) on this principle. Leadership positions and roles are framed as cargo to carry (*cargos*, that is, being charged with responsibilities), frequently rotated and in permanent consultation with the community. This is a system of participatory government that resonates with how governance is understood by other Maya communities-in-struggle, for example, the Maya in Belize (Penados, 2018). They refer to Maya leadership as being 'the eyes, ears, and mouth' of the community, and those who hold leadership positions in communities can be recalled if they are not responsive to the needs and desires of their respective communities. The Zapatista conception of leadership and autonomous governance goes well beyond Western governance, liberal representative democracy and electoral/partisan politics as it is oriented towards radical democratic processes that are marked by the permanent and effective participation of community members. The Zapatistas call for a kind of leadership that is neither egotistical nor vainglorious, but one that is characterised by patience, humility, presence, good faith, service and a capacity to listen.

'Lento, pero avanzo' *('slowly, but advancing')*

Since their genesis, the Zapatistas have used the expression '*Lento, pero avanzo*' ('Slowly, but advancing') and the image of the *caracol* (snail/shell) to signify the tempo and durability of their resistance, construction of autonomy and progress. The snail and shell signify several things:

1. Protection – the strength, sturdiness and resilience of the snail's shell;
2. A winding path – the spiral on the shell connotes that they are traveling down a meandering and inexact path and approach the idea of 'advancing' pluralistically; compare this with 'modern' conventional notions of 'history' and 'development' that are linear;
3. Being both open and solidaristic – the spiral represents 'coming and going' both 'inside and outside' and is symbolic of being welcoming to the world, others and the ideas of others, that is, not closing off or being sectarian (for example, in order to visit Zapatistas, international sympathisers literally first enter one of their now 12 *caracoles* or administrative centres);
4. Indigenous participatory governance and assembly – the shell is closely linked to the conch, which their Maya ancestors traditionally sounded to beckon community members to gatherings in which communal dialogue, listening and decision-making took place; an emphasis here is placed on listening and introspection given community members were listening for the conch, listening to each other and listening to the collective while reflecting on their own individual responses and contributions; and

Figure 2.4: A painting on a Zapatista clinic of a caracol (snail) with one of the philosophical adages of the movement: 'Lento, pero avanzo', which translates as 'Slowly, but advancing'

5. Going slow – the Zapatistas do not necessarily adhere to colonial, capitalist or modernity's 'time'; rather, they move forward deliberately, purposefully and methodically, but arrive where they need to be, much like a snail.

Ultimately, the Zapatistas define time, democracy and the pace of their movement on their own (Indigenous) terms, while also having each other's backs. The *caracol* evokes all this. Similarly, the phrase '*Lento, pero avanzo*' ('Slowly, but advancing') stems from their realisation that in order to endure, maintain the health of individuals and communities and flourish, their rhythms and processes need to progress in a gradual, measured, slow and solidaristic fashion, or 'at a snail's pace', as a Zapatista once told us. We feel we all might learn something from this.

The coloniser's model/neoliberal state of the world

Neoliberalism: a brief definition

Neoliberalism defies a singular definition in large part because of its broad application across a variety of social domains, scholarly disciplines, spatial dimensions, and as a result of what it produces economically, culturally and politically (Springer, 2016a). Despite the seemingly never-ending exercise that defining neoliberalism proves to be, the term is regularly used to signify the constellation of political-economic policies and social-cultural relations that have intensified the capitalist status quo during the post-Keynesian era, roughly after the Second World War (Marcos, 2001; Barnett, 2005). This period has largely been marked by escalations in economic liberalism (for example, Reaganomics, Thatcherism) and structural adjustment policies (for example, the Bretton Woods System, Washington Consensus, World Bank, International Monetary Fund [IMF], World Trade Organization [WTO]), along with a rise in socio-political theories promoting austerity, privatisation, deregulation and a purported 'opening up' of markets and borders (Cabezas et al, 2015).

The consequences of neoliberalism have been devastating across both the Global North and Majority World/Global South. Here, it is important to take note of the spatial dimensions, bordering regimes and territorial differentiations of neoliberalism (Walia, 2021). That is, both capitalist logics and policies play out differently in different places. While neoliberalism is certainly a driving force of displacement, deracination, dispossession and deterritorialisation, the ways in which it functions and accomplishes each of these things varies widely across space, scale and state. Meaning, geography matters, even if there are identifiable tendencies and patterns associated with how neoliberal capitalism extracts, exploits and alienates. Nevertheless, neoliberalism's economic and philosophical influences are founded on the convergence of two overarching beliefs:

1. That markets, competition and individualism be granted supremacy over all else.
2. That work, production, nature and time be commodified and measured in monetary terms.

Neoliberal thinkers omit or refute the existence and role of structural forces regarding injustice in favour of placing the culpability for widespread social ills like poverty, deprivation and mass alienation on individuals (Roy, 2004; Springer, 2016b). The past few decades have seen dramatic increases in neoliberal policies across the globe, which are now privatising social services, overturning hard-won civil rights and leading to more acute forms of dislocation, destitution and environmental destruction. More recently, critical voices have argued that, in addition to being a sophisticated set of highly managed economic policies, neoliberalism is also a discourse (Springer, Birch and MacLeavy, 2016). These perspectives consider neoliberalism to be an emergent mode of exercising power over society, economy and life via rhetoric and establishing a very narrow, capitalist-oriented Overton window. Many suggest that neoliberalism is reshaping cultural norms, subjectivities and establishing new taken-for-granted 'truths' through the imposition of responsiblisation, entrepreneurialism, auto-commoditisation and self-capitalisation.

Responsibilisation involves framing the structural conditions and realities that different individuals and groups are living under as the accumulative result of individual choices. This denies the role that varying social forces have in limiting and/or enabling both the disparate life chances and choices of people. In short, blame the individual, deny the structure. Relatedly, entrepreneurialism comprises the pressures people face to monetise and sell their capabilities, passions and desires towards the ends of financial self-capitalisation, the attainment of individual recognition, and just to be able to socially reproduce themselves and their families (Sparke, 2013). Auto-commoditisation is the process of transforming oneself into a marketable product or brand and being seen as an economic asset. This also involves viewing one's thoughts, time, capabilities and even presence as merchandisable skills that will eventually be sold in a given market (Robbins and Dowty, 2008). In this way, neoliberalism is theorised as a rationality that produces assemblages of individuals and corporations that are engaged in transactional relationships, which continually (re)construct and reproduce capitalism. The state's role in neoliberalism, rather than being put at the service of securing the welfare of people and ecosystems, is to grease the wheels of trade and promote the circulation of capital and consumerism. Consequently, people become data points and are forced to navigate capitalist social relations in precarity and isolation while being subjected to cutbacks in healthcare, slashings of public services and denials of their humanity that stem from the priority given to corporate welfare, financial 'growth' and economic 'development'.

Undoubtedly, neoliberalism is a force to be reckoned with. It is paramount to note that it is a logic, discourse and rationality that picks up where the colonial ideals of liberalism left off in order to persuade members of civil society to believe that individualism, competition, self-centrism, private property and profit-seeking are the natural state of things. Moreover, through the use of a panic-inducing threat of 'not being successful' in life, neoliberal rhetoric suggests human existence is rooted in the (capitalist) desires of gaining competitive advantages, accumulating possessions, hoarding wealth, laying claim to 'knowledge' and 'expertise' and wielding power over 'Others'. Neoliberal logic generates capitalist social relations by asserting that earth and land are commodities, and people who deserve to flourish in life will only do so by demonstrating market ambition, financial self-reliance and an entrepreneurial spirit. As members of civil society consent or are reluctantly forced to acquiesce to these ideals, social relations iteratively become fragmented, alienating, extractive and profit-centric – oftentimes in the most seemingly ordinary of ways and at the expense of others and the environment. If you have ever heard the phrase 'business as usual', you are familiar with neoliberalism. Indeed, while you might not be interested in capitalism, capitalism is interested in you. If any of this sounds alarming or like something colonisers would think, it is no coincidence.

Neoliberal ideals suffuse a multitude of social relations, practices and ways of being, becoming a significant aspect of a Western colonial model for organising life itself, and reflecting the epithet that 'coloniality is not over; it is all over' (Lopez-Calvo, 2016: 175). As we will see in the coming sections, it is through a regime-of-truth that is endorsed and promoted by the state and its institutions that people are persuaded to accept the world as nothing more than a market in which everything, and everyone, can be bought and sold. Essentially, the discourse of neoliberalism has changed the rules of the game, so to speak, so that in order to survive we all must play on capitalism and concentrated power's terms. For many, this reality is as chilling as it is anti-democratic, because the consequences of existing under neoliberalism are both materially and spiritually devastating. We now turn our attention to how this unfolds in economics, discourses of power and knowledge, global health, biopower and education.

Oblivion, Babylon and an economy of contempt

In the current moment, neoliberalism is status quo. This has been brought about by over half a century of existing capitalist economic systems becoming increasingly liberalised through policies of privatisation, deregulation and financialisation (Marcos, 2001; Harvey, 2007). Social relations and private life are also undergoing processes of neoliberalisation, so that while neoliberal economic programmes have been intensifying, so, too, have spurious narratives promoting the perceived benefits to be gained if an unregulated capitalist economy is seen through to its fruition (Springer, 2016b). One fundamental tenet espoused by neoliberal rhetoric argues that capitalism is natural and normal because a purportedly 'free market' is unbiased and objective, and that it will impartially decide who succeeds and who fails in life (Marcos, 2001).

Neoliberal reason also suggests that structural inequalities are neither systemic nor interconnected, but that the pervasive anguish being felt across the globe resulting from differing institutionalised oppressions is nothing more than the aggregate sum of discrete personal flaws and individual failings. To pour salt into the wound, the state apparatuses and administrations disseminating neoliberal ideals claim government spending on social services, civic welfare and the common good are excessive, unaffordable or unreasonable (Heynen et al, 2007). 'Wasteful' public expenditure and inherent personal shortcomings are then chalked up as the real problems, and used to rationalise social inequality and structural violence, which often coincide with arguments that frame economic redistribution as 'handouts for freeloaders who take advantage of the system'. Contempt for and disdain towards the poor and working-class are part-and-parcel of neoliberal thinking.

In turn, solutions to the widespread social ills that market-focused state bureaucracies have given rise to are conceived, condescendingly, as issues best remedied by 'dumb' or 'lazy' people 'pulling themselves up by their bootstraps'. Every economic system that generates and justifies exploitation, inequality and suffering needs its scapegoats. Neoliberal discourse thus does the work of defending neoliberal policies by offering duplicitous commentaries on, and ineffective remedies to, the very socially destructive problems it has created. The absurdity of this logic is aptly summed up by a popular satirical 'demotivational' poster in which a government building is pictured with the caption: 'If you think the problems we create are bad, just wait until you see our solutions.'

All this goes to show that analysing neoliberalism would almost be comedic and humorous if it were not so tragic and violent. Even given the contradictions, the rhetoric of neoliberalism is able to garner support for free enterprise by blaming the poor, working-class and marginalised for their suffering, while claiming its correcting edicts of entrepreneurialism, self-branding and auto-commodification will benefit everyone if only embraced by the 'uneducated' and 'unmotivated' (Loveday, 2018). Open markets, free trade, foreign direct investment and export processing zones, it is suggested, will grow profits for businesses all across the globe, which subsequently will allow revenue to 'trickle down' on the masses in the form of job creation and revenue to pay more wages (Mohanty, 2013). Notably, decades of both peer-reviewed evidence and lived experience illustrate that neither the jobs nor the wages 'trickle down' all that much, really at all, demonstrating just how big of a fiction, that is, a lie, trickle-down economics actually are (Marcos, 2005b; Chomsky, 2021). From a materialist perspective, neoliberalism is an economy of ego, greed and contempt.

Despite the inherent paradoxes permeating neoliberal discourse, its messages nevertheless are highly influential, albeit hollow. But once the logics, processes and policies of neoliberalism become normative and endorsed by states, members of society are then compelled, often with no other options, to monetise their passions and creativity in order to fit into highly specified yet restrictive arrangements of capitalist social relations. In brief, we are taught we need to be able to market and sell ourselves and to run our lives like businesses. Individuals are thereby forced to self-surveil and regulate their thoughts and behaviours so as to reify themselves as skillsets and commodities to be bought, sold and circulated within said global market.

Within universities this manifests itself as a battle between political education and 'employability'. While these two are not necessarily mutually exclusive, because everyone deserves gainful employment, meaningful work and a dignified wage, the neoliberal mandates (and managers) of most universities care very little about creating politically educated societies. These nearly inescapable circumstances are often the only limited choices people (and students) have in simply making a go of it. And a situation in which it is compulsory for people to discipline themselves − as well as exploit, domesticate and punish others − into becoming hyper-competitive and self-centric for the purposes of individual gain and reproducing capitalism is, as a Zapatista *votan* (teacher-guardian) once noted, '*olvido*' ('oblivion', that is, forgetting our humanity [EZLN, 2019]). This is Babylon, as you might hear in the Caribbean.

Ironically, being competitive, entrepreneurial and more 'bankable' than peers has become convention and something we are taught to achieve. The banality of neoliberal discourse is what allows its recursive practices to eviscerate society so imperceptibly. In time, the ideals of neoliberalism establish an existence that teaches members of civil society that repression, injustice and domination are the inevitable consequences of an imperfect, innately hierarchical, world. People then learn that conditions would be much worse if it were not for the ability of capitalism to reward individuals who are 'smart, strong, competitive enough' to rise to the top, which is a fiction. The natural state of life is not nasty, brutish and short, but it will be if we decide to make it that way. Plantations, prisons and heteropatriarchy are a choice, and the people and powers-that-be who want them to exist and profit from them have names.

Discourse, power, knowledge

Neoliberalism is seemingly inescapable, be it in the domain of the economic, political, cultural or psychological (Chomsky, 1999; Braedley and Luxton, 2010; Altamirano-Jiménez, 2013). At the global scale, it is intensifying debt-servicing, dependency and ecological decimation through the promulgation of austerity policies, the deregulation of industry and free trade agreements – all of which work in conjunction with each other to weaken the rights of labour, environments and communities alike (Springer, Birch and MacLeavy, 2016). On psychospiritual and subjective scales, the internalisation of neoliberal values are persuading people to believe that self-centrism and dog-eat-dog competition are the normal and ordinary conditions under which economies are developed and life is lived (Klein, 2016). Indeed, neoliberalism, along with the pathological individualism and subsequent alienation it generates, has become part of everyday life.

In the contemporary moment, neoliberal ideals have become embedded in constructions of 'knowledge' and exercises of power, as well as assertions of 'truth' and taken-for-granted 'common sense'. The ways in which power, knowledge and 'truth' function are complex, transitory and ephemeral. This is because power, knowledge and 'truth' are neither exercised in strictly top-down fashion and nor are they solely generated 'from below' or the grassroots. And while power, knowledge and 'truth are each associated with and reproduced by and within institutions, they also flow through and mutually constitute discourses. Like power and 'knowledge', discourses emanate diffusely while being context-dependent.

Discourses, which are (and shape) the ways we think and talk about the world, set boundaries and rules. These boundaries and rules seemingly emerge 'from both everywhere and nowhere' despite the fact that they are situated, mutable, and, most importantly, power-laden and productive. That is, discourses *produce* certain effects. On this point, one of the most important questions we can ask is not necessarily whether any given thing (for example, idea, discourse, institution, value, practice, policy) is 'good' or 'bad', but rather, 'what does it produce?'

Given the relational and fluctuating processes and productive effects that come with neoliberalism, it is thereby helpful to analyse it as a discourse (Springer, 2016b). In stating this, it is essential to recognise that despite the abstruse, concealed and spectral nature of how neoliberal discourse operates in day-to-day life, what it yields (read, 'produces') undeniably affects our lives, often viscerally so. It is therefore crucial to emphasise that the discursive practices of neoliberalism are both material and psychological in process and *product*, as well as emplaced in day-to-day life and felt by the body. For example, if you are taught from an early age that you must individually compete against everyone else, whether in an economy or an education system, and you do not 'win' in every instance, chances are you feel it, in more ways than one.

In turn, the prosaic manners in which the disciplinary mechanisms (for example, entrepreneurialism, responsibilisation, auto-commoditisation) of neoliberalism function often result in fractious relations and societal apathy, indifference, despair and widespread neglect with regard to the limited life chances and needs of others. The rules of (neoliberal) conduct are thereby (re)asserted and (re)affirmed in the most commonplace situations and serve to subtly impel members of society to atomise their patterns of thought and compartmentalise social interactions (Scharff, 2016). Regrettably, empathy has become a liability under liberal-capitalist social relations while ego and the drive to best others is seen as an asset. This is not a recipe for a healthy and flourishing society.

The products generated by neoliberalism run deep, and the adversity and hardship it creates is often seemingly ad hoc, arbitrary and haphazard. That said, the consequences of neoliberalism do have a classed, racist and gendered pattern and trend. Abject poverty, dismal living conditions, ongoing colonial violence, institutionalised racism, heteropatriarchal oppression, the ostracism of queer and gender non-conforming people, the invisibilisation of disabled people,[1] the exclusion of migrants/'foreigners' and the whole lot of society's grim ills are parcelled out and blamed on individuals or 'othered' groups (Mullaly, 2010). Their alleged culpability is then justified through interpellations of essentialist stereotypes and reductionist classifications. The universal message is clear – under neoliberalism, if you are working-class or cash-poor, you will suffer (some demographics more than others) as well as be blamed for it.

Consequently, social inequality and structural violence are deemed inveterate, ordinary or even non-existent because they are perceived to be the result of a lack of effort on the part of apathetic people who are thought not to have equipped themselves with the necessary skills required to thrive in a free market. In a sense, the projection of blame onto individual bodies and minority groups for the turmoil and trauma experienced by society may be neoliberalism's most effective accomplishment in privatisation to date. Put differently, if disaffiliating from the misery capitalism has caused, while accusing the poor and destitute of creating their own suffering, is not neoliberalism's greatest feat, it certainly is its most manipulatively sadistic one.

Social norms and discourses that convince people injured by capitalism that their wounds and suffering is self-inflicted and their own fault is a convenient disavowal for neoliberalism. This is because individualising structural violence allows the institutions and agents of neoliberalism to claim innocence by belabouring the irrefutably vapid cliché 'that's just the way it is'.

Global health under neoliberalism

More than simply an economic system, capitalism, and its latest more aggressive iteration, neoliberalism, organises our daily lives, activities, relations and ways of being (Hickel and Khan, 2012). The deleterious health impacts of capitalism have been widely documented, from Friedrich Engels' (1887) account of industrial labour in 19th-century England to contemporary analysis of the perverse consequences of global financialisaton and consumerism on disease outbreaks and healthcare systems (Waitzkin, 2018). One striking example includes World Bank instruments such as 'pandemic bonds' (that is, the Pandemic Emergency Financing Facility), first championed during the 2014–16 West Africa Ebola outbreak. These bonds provide opportunities for private wealth accumulation by enabling free market investing to be leveraged against global outbreaks (Erikson, 2019; The World Bank, 2020). However, the use of the pandemic bonds in 2020 faced criticism as the predetermined 'trigger criteria' – based on border crossing and virus growth rate – were not met quick enough, despite growing numbers of fatalities (Erikson, 2020). Rather than providing a quick, responsible and humanitarian response to the pandemic, this reflects a trend towards greater privatisation within global health, as investors stand to make gain a profit if the trigger criteria is not met and the funds are not released.

The coronavirus pandemic is a case in point for the entanglements of global health and capitalism. Forcing its way through circuits of global production, COVID-19 prompted an unparalleled economic crisis compounded by healthcare systems that had previously faced decades of austerity policies or privatisation, revealing huge holes in public health infrastructure. Consequently, Sell and Williams (2020) describe capitalism as an 'all-encompassing global pathology' disproportionately impacting the lives of the world's most poor. The EZLN point to this entanglement of capitalist socio-political structures and health, stating that:

> The COVID-19 pandemic demonstrated not only the vulnerabilities of human beings, but also the greed and stupidity of the national governments and their supposed opposition groups. The most basic, common-sense measures were discarded on the gamble that the pandemic would play out in a short timeframe. As the epidemic's timeline extended, numbers began to replace tragedies. Death became a statistic, lost amidst the noise of daily scandals and declarations in a dark contest of ridiculous nationalisms, playing with percentages like batting averages and earned runs to decide which team, or nation, is better or worse. (EZLN, 2020a)

With a renewed vigour, the pandemic reflected how structural violence operates locally and globally, exposing venerable inequalities of gender, race and class (Büyüm et al, 2020; McClure et al, 2020). Speaking on the disproportionate effects of COVID-19 on working-class Black and Latinx people, Executive Director of Women in Global Health (WGH),[2] Roopa Dhatt, noted that 'COVID-19 does not discriminate but societies do' (UN News, 2021). This has led to the unevenly distributed impacts of the virus to be labelled as 'the other pandemic', citing racism, poverty and food security among many other reasons for this systemic inequity (Gray et al, 2020).

As (at the point of writing) the virus is still in circulation, the 'success or failure' of various government responses remains to be seen. We do, however, have the opportunity to evaluate social and political systems that have exacerbated the mortalities and morbidities associated with COVID-19. The pandemic has exposed outdated assumptions while disrupting settled ways of being. When global capitalism stalled, the health crisis demonstrated that the work of producing and sustaining life, the lives of racialised and socio-economically poor populations are too often marginalised and undervalued (McClure et al, 2020). However, amidst these moments of deep global trauma there are also moments for social transformation. As we search for a 'new normal' (Anderson et al, 2021), we would do well to remember that 'crises are moments of potential change but the nature of their resolution is not given' (Hall and Massey, 2010: 55).

As severe as the pandemic may be, it is further compounded by crises of environmental breakdown and rampant social inequality (Lawrence and Laybourn-Langton, 2021). Our current reality shows that contemporary systems of global and public health are ill equipped to address the structural and slow violence wrought by the confluence of social, political and financial agendas (Nixon, 2011). Health practice (and research) requires integrated, holistic and anti-colonial approaches that are supported by communities, governments and institutions. Such an approach would address the complex interdependence of health on various factors including histories of imperialism, global financialisation, political decision-making and environmental and social policies. The global movement, Action to Decolonise Global Health (ActDGH), led by students and other professionals, is one step towards this vision; however, a more potent realisation of de-/anti-colonial healthcare is one that is currently in operation in the autonomous regions of Chiapas. In the face of these neoliberalising assaults on society, it then becomes crucial to determine how to respond to the discursive practices and disciplinary mechanisms of neoliberalism. We must therefore identify the sites, situations and institutions where neoliberal logics are disseminated in order to be able to unsettle the conventions and norms neoliberalism has generated.

Biopower and discipline

One concentrated and influential site sanctioning neoliberal ideals is the university. Higher education, across both the Global North and Majority World/Global South, has regrettably been co-opted and become complicit in producing and disciplining neoliberal subjects and training the consumerist 'good soldiers' of capitalist states (Weiner and Compton, 2008). In short, we are being domesticated. Just how this occurs is oftentimes as insidious as it is effective. In detailing the ways in which people are regulated and self-regulate as a result of both state power and social norms, Michel Foucault (2010) offers the useful concepts of governmentality and biopower. Governmentality is the rationale and way in which a given population or society is regulated and managed, as well as the ways in which it regulates and manages itself. Biopower, which is different from governmentality but a constituent part of it, is a dispersed mode of control and oft-diffuse means of manufacturing consent and obedience that is employed by the state to manage, surveil, administrate and either include or exclude differing populations in a given society (Foucault, 2008). Biopower, in brief, is the exercise of power and authority over life. It can take multiple forms, ranging from overt force, top-down authority, consenting compliance or veiled coercion. Biopower compels people to act, think, behave and 'be' in particular ways – ways that are amenable to the capitalist state, (neo)liberal ideals and the coloniser's model of the world that we currently inhabit.

Foucault (2008) elaborates on governmentality and the ordering and administering of society via biopower by noting that people are influenced by the presence of multiple and pervasive, yet oft-invisible and normalising 'gazes'. Society thereby becomes omni-panoptic, meaning that surveillance, self-regulation and the ways power is exercised over life unfolds in a multitude of ways that are dynamic, mutable and context-dependent. Biopower induces people to submit to (or contest) differing socially constructed and reproduced norms and cultural expectations. The ubiquitous monitoring and scrutiny of our lives, decisions, behaviours, desires and values is pervasive yet diffuse, with authority and power seemingly remaining immaterial and often things we internalise.

Biopower, and the state's edict to conform and obey, thereby comes from 'everywhere-but-nowhere', and recurrently functions as a regulatory apparatus that persuades people to either remain complicit with what norms and rules are being imposed on them or resist and act in disaccord with the processes of normalisation they find themselves exposed to (Foucault, 2008). Taking into consideration these dynamics of biopower and resistance allows us to see how state structures, its subjects and even our own subjectivities and personal agency all mutually influence and affect one another, as well as how people are (or resist) being moulded into 'docile bodies' based on the influence of state apparatuses like the education and judicial system and socially constructed hierarchies of difference.

For those of us who dare dissent, contest power, question authority or refuse to 'fall in line', in countless instances, the reality remains that we resist as actively as we can, but as passively as we must, because there are indeed consequences for refusing to submit or being a 'killjoy'. In turn, the only protection we have is acting collectively and having each other's backs, because individual rebelliousness, as important and necessary as it is, is not a pathway to liberation, and is ultimately useless if it does not contribute or lead to collective action.

Further elaborating on how biopower operates, Foucault (2008) notes power is not limited to state authority and 'a group of institutions and mechanisms that ensure the subservience of the citizens', but rather, it is constituted by the 'numerous and diverse techniques for achieving the subjugations of bodies and the control of populations'. He goes on to state that biopower is made up of the iterative exercises of regulation permeating all aspects of life, and suggests it has no observable core and is incapable of being located in a single, identifiable source (Foucault, 2008). Thus, for Foucault, biopower flows across-and-within societal institutions, cultural mores, calls for national unity and the widely held normative principles and core values found throughout varying societies. From this assessment, many of Foucault's conceptualisations regarding biopower closely resemble the thoughts and insights of dissenting non-state captured peasants and Indigenous populations who have been resisting (colonial) modernity and Western governance, authority, surveillance and state power for centuries.

Notably, race, or perhaps more appropriately, the ways in which certain people and groups are negatively racialised via state institutions/laws *and* social norms, is critical. In linking biopower to race and the liberal Western state, Foucault (2003: 256) elaborates:

> In a normalizing society, *race* or racism is the precondition that makes killing acceptable. When you have a normalizing society, you have a power which is, at least superficially, in the first instance, or in the first line a biopower, and *racism* is the indispensable precondition that allows someone to be killed, that allows others to be killed. Once the State functions in the biopower mode, racism alone can justify the murderous function of the State. (Emphasis added)

Thus, for students concerned with the dynamics of power, resistance and education, as well as the complex relationships between both, the notion of biopower is particularly useful. In bringing biopower into the foreground, as well as realising higher education is a place where liberal-capitalist and Western ideals are banally espoused, we can infer that universities are one of the many sites where domesticated yet competitive neoliberal subjects/subjectivities are forged (Baltodano, 2012). This is due to the variegating ways in which power, knowledge and regimes of 'truth' are circulated, altered and reaffirmed within universities, especially by the managers running them. Presently, on weighing the social and personal costs associated with entering an academic institution promoting the individualising tendencies, discourses and 'truths' of neoliberalism, the prospect of 'getting an education' is now somewhat of a trap. This is the reality of universities because many of the hegemonic 'knowledges' and core values being disseminated by mainstream education are colonial-capitalist-patriarchal in nature, as well as saturated with the ideals and rationalities of the market, that is, neoliberalism (Berman, 2012).

Death by a thousand cuts

If one listens to colleagues, friends or students working and learning in any given university, it will not take long to hear about feelings of acute anxiety, depression, worthlessness and paranoia, as well as stories of despair, misery, hopelessness, institutionalised racism, transphobia, rampant sexism, substance misuse and suicidal ideation, to name a few (Mountz et al, 2015; Peake and Mullings, 2017). The neoliberal university is contributing to degradations in mental health and erosions of emotional stability while elevating stress levels and anxiety for students, faculty and workers alike. This is all now a common occurrence in universities across the Global North and Majority World/Global South. Life, labouring and learning in the neoliberal university, dishearteningly, is now marked by suffering in silence, and has seemingly become a war of attrition – a proverbial death by a thousand cuts (Amsler and Motta, 2017).

One of the most disconcerting yet overlooked or deliberately sidelined products of the neoliberal university is how students are treated within it (Emejulu, 2017). Students face a demoralising barrage of emotional slings and arrows as part of their educational 'experience'. Learning now consists of rote memorisation; standardised tests; high-stakes exams; factory-like classroom settings; hierarchical competition among peers; and the accumulation of ruinous debt to afford rising tuition costs (Neary and Winn, 2009). Cramming for multiple exams and essays concentrated near the same due date and writing 'pleasing to the professor' academic papers that are tacitly expected to draw from an arguably staid, colonial and classist scholarly canon – which is largely behind corporate pay-walled journals – have all become commonplace. This is not to mention that it is not infrequent for students to be patronisingly scolded 'this is what you signed up for' if they speak out or stand up for themselves.

The prospect of expanding one's intellectual horizon functions with the general premise that students become entrepreneurial *homo economicus* (economic man) via competing for high marks, scholarships, recognition and awards of excellence in conjunction with paying substantial, ever-rising tuition fees to do so (Cantwell, 2016). Students must run this neoliberal gauntlet while simultaneously being pressured into enthusiastically performing the outlandishly absurd yet spectacularly mediocre bourgeois role of 'entrepreneur' or 'global citizen'. This pressure is often applied via a rhetoric of 'employability' and without critical reflection on the fact that certain privileged people in the world get to be entrepreneurs and 'global citizens', while others, often negatively racialised or working-class people, particularly those in the Majority World/Global South, are *globalised on* and made to suffer by entrepreneurs and citizenship (or a lack thereof). Freire (2018) warned us there would be dehumanising days like this.

Notably, students are generally expected to manage these oppressive aspects of higher education on their own, all the while being offered petty statements of indifference framing their stressful and nerve-wracking conditions as 'something everybody has to deal with'. In many cases, students must learn to cope with these conditions while simultaneously holding a job(s), providing/seeking childcare, perhaps coping with a disability, and trying to balance what is going on in their personal lives (Giroux, 2014). These normalised, fast-paced, anxiety-inducing mistreatments are nothing less than covert processes of individualisation that wreak havoc on the emotional stability and mental health of those who have to endure them (Hall and Bowles, 2016).

Here, the sheer number of 'wellbeing' weeks and mental health initiatives that are being mainstreamed by university administrations (Duffy et al, 2019), while well-intentioned, are indeed instructive about the degree to which managers recognise the inherent violence in the systems they are overseeing. The source of mental health injuries, the institution and its protocols, is elided, and the onus of getting healthy is offloaded onto students and workers themselves, who are pathologised and told to 'make time' – as if there is some sort of magic alchemy to perform that will 'make' time (Vostal, 2016). Students are forced to endure all this in order to simply gain an education that, distressingly, has been corrupted into nothing more than a credential that enables them to sell themselves on a market and become either a willing or reluctant functionary of capitalism.

There does remain hope in light of the lashings neoliberal education inflicts; despite the systemically destructive ways in which authority and the pressure to be productive on capitalism's terms flow through the academy's hierarchies, those who are suffering in universities can find each other and slow things down (Mountz et al, 2015), because encountering, relating to, taking care of each other and collectively saying 'Enough is enough!' in oppressive circumstances constitute acts of defiance in-and-of themselves. More candidly, in the face of neoliberalism and the ongoing coloniality of it all, mutual aid is resistance.

As Indigenous rebels, the Zapatistas astutely refer to state-sanctioned schools and universities as 'corrals of thought domestication'. This is due to the emphasis that government-legitimated institutions place on coercing students and faculty into becoming docile citizen-consumers (Barbosa and Sollano, 2014). The Zapatista response to the prospect of having to send their children into hostile learning environments and colonial-capitalist modernity was open-and-armed revolt (Oikonomakis, 2019; Weinberg and Weinberg, 2000). Their '¡*Ya basta!*' ('Enough is enough!') rallying cry 'woke up history' and allowed them to take back the land, dignity and type of *political education* of which they had been dispossessed and deprived.

Before directly discussing Zapatista education in more detail, it is paramount to point out that the ongoing project of their autonomy is the direct result of Indigenous people's self-determination, as well as their decision to engage in highly disciplined organising against a neocolonial and militarised elite (Mora, 2015). More pointedly, the Zapatistas sacrificed themselves to make the world a better and safer place (Earle and Simonelli, 2005). Fittingly, one of the most widely seen phrases scattered across the rebel territories of Chiapas, noted earlier, reads: '*Para todos todo, para nosotros nada*' ('Everything for everyone, nothing for us'). In the face of global entrepreneurial capitalism and neoliberal rationality, such a statement is as profound as it is humble. It explicitly foregrounds compassion, selflessness and heart, virtues the Zapatistas have arguably integrated into their autonomous education system.

4

Modernity-coloniality and Indigenous realities

In the face of challenges such as global poverty, structural inequality, increasing intolerance, climate change and the current existential threat we are contending with vis-á-vis sustaining life on our planet, three questions press themselves on humanity: (1) Are alternative futures possible? (2) What might these alternative futures look like? (3) How might we bring these alternative futures to fruition? We realise we are not unique in asking these questions, as countless communities from across both the Majority World/Global South and Global North have been grappling with them for generations. Even though they are very simple queries that many of us have pondered and engaged in conversations about at one point or another, they still are often quite overwhelming and depressing questions to think about. In many cases, responses to them often end with a deep sigh, silence and a sort of hopeless conclusion that the world cannot or will not be changed. Giving up on thinking through and finding answers to these questions, however, is not something we can afford to do.

In addition, the simplicity of these questions obscures their profundity – meaning, each query requires us to 'read the world', as Paulo Freire (2018) would put it, and to examine and interpret our realities/worlds to determine what it is that we are seeking alternatives to. So, while they perhaps seem like stock or even clichéd questions, they nevertheless remain 'generative themes' in a Freirean sense (2018) – meaning, they require us to both think and dream outside of the prevailing box, to imagine alternative paths, to engage in dialectics with others, and to refuse to succumb to hopelessness. In brief, they both challenge and require us to resist surrendering to despair and to practice radical hope. It is here, in developing answers to these questions and in holding on to radical hope, that we feel Indigenous struggles, whatever their geography, can teach us much.

Indigenous struggle as knowledge production

There are at least two reasons why we should consider Indigenous voices and experiences. First, Indigenous people have faced a long history of exploitation and violence, and continue to be among the most affected by global challenges such as climate change, poverty, inequality and intolerance. Be they in the Americas, Africa, Asia, Oceania or elsewhere, Indigenous people are among the world's most 'poor' (as loaded as a term as this is), excluded, forgotten and dismissed, which is a product of the ongoing colonial enterprise (for example, capitalism). This said, it is crucial to understand that Indigenous people are neither a monolith nor a uniform bloc, and they and their cultures must be neither essentialised nor viewed as static. Notably, however, Indigenous people's realities, whatever places they are situated in and no matter how varied and dynamic they are, are reflective of global reality.

In turn, the global challenges and status quo that we aim to change cannot be understood, that is, the world cannot be comprehensively 'read', without considering the experiences and voices of Indigenous people, whether they reside in the Americas, Africa, Asia or any other island or continent. In terms of feminist standpoint theory (Harding, 1992; Haraway, 2009), it is not possible to fully understand any given reality without considering the standpoint of the subjugated. Why are Indigenous people targeted, 'poor' and excluded? An answer to this question will reveal much about what the problems of the present-day global reality are. The history of Indigenous people is connected to our histories and worlds; their realities and worlds are connected to our realities and worlds.

Second, having said this, Indigenous people are not passive victims but rather, they are active agents who are confronting and challenging the political and economic forces that are shaping their realities. In addition, via their political agency and creativity, they are imagining and crafting alternatives. Indigenous movements are on the frontlines of asking and engaging the three questions posed at the outset of this chapter. In doing so, they are shedding light on the challenges we all confront, and shining a light on possible paths into liveable futures and more sustainable and just worlds. More importantly, the conviction and practice of *radical hope* of Indigenous movements, that a different world is possible, can serve as an inspiration. After all, the efforts of Indigenous people's movements to change their realities are connected to any efforts that others might make to change our realities. While not always recognised or cited, there is no shortage of knowledge produced by Indigenous struggle. A case in point, and perhaps the most well-known Indigenous movement, which you are now aware of and we elaborate on more in the chapters to come, are the Zapatistas.

Modernity/coloniality/decoloniality

To understand the broader implications of the Zapatista struggle and Zapatismo, we turn to the work of Latin American scholars inspired by the philosophy of liberation (Dussel, 1993, 1998), and who refer to themselves as the Modernity/Coloniality/Decoloniality (MCD) project (Mignolo, 2000; Quijano, 2000, 2007; Escobar, 2004 Maldonado-Torres, 2007). This work helps us to see how Indigenous realities and struggles are connected with the realities of those of us who live in other contexts. Understanding Indigenous struggles and their relevance for other contexts requires an understanding of colonialism. On this point, Corntassel and Bryce (2012: 87) note: 'When asked about living sustainably today, Indigenous people inevitably confront the ongoing legacies of colonialism that have disrupted their individual and community relationships with the natural world.'

The fact is that the global challenge of living sustainably and dealing with things like persistent racialism, inequality and dangerous climate change requires us to confront legacies of colonialism too. This is a central argument for the MCD group, as well as one we feel all universities should stress. Maldonado-Torres (2007) alludes to this when he points out that as 'modern subjects' we all live and breathe coloniality every day. Indigenous struggles help us understand the coloniality we breathe and live while simultaneously casting light on pathways out of it.

'Modernity', as it is conventionally defined, is generally associated with terms like rationality, individual freedom, science, technological advances, tolerance, liberal open-mindedness, secularism, 'progress' and universalism. Essentially, modernity is framed as a triumph over tradition, superstition, authority, narrow-mindedness and localism that opened an era of freedom and progress. It is usually seen as an exclusive, self-fuelled European achievement emerging with the Enlightenment that was later diffused across the rest of the world. For decolonial thinkers, however, modernity is the management of an uneven world system and power structure, with Europe at the centre. Far from being self-propelled by Europe, as Fanon (1963) notes, modernity was built on the backs of Europe's 'Others'. Far from 'universal', modernity is the burial of 'Others' (Dussel, 1994). Far from representing unequivocal progress and harmony, modernity has led us to a crisis of civilisation (Dussel, 1998). Essentially, modernity has a dark side – coloniality. Coloniality is the other side of the coin given there would be no modernity if not for colonial worldviews and power.

To speak of modernity is to speak of coloniality and vice versa, hence the term 'modernity-coloniality'. Coloniality (and modernity) is described by Quijano (2007) as a pattern of power that revolves around two axes, the fabrication and categorisation of biological difference and ethnic distinctions into racial hierarchies and the capture and subjugation of land and labour under a global capitalist system. This 'Empire of Money', as the EZLN has defined (colonial-capitalist) modernity, and the machinations of fanatical supremacist ego are what the Zapatistas revolted against. Indeed, modernity, and the colonial worldviews, capitalist logics and liberal ideology it is shaped by, undeniably, is in need of indictment. As Subcomandante Marcos (Marcos and de Leon, 2002) described modernity just after the turn of the millennium, it can arguably be summed up as: 'The long and lazy dream that *imposes* on everyone and everything – at the cost everyone and everything – injustice, inequality, lack of democracy' (emphasis added).

While what we offer in the sections to come seeks to broadly historicise modernity, our account is admittedly limited and more linear in structure than it ought to be – meaning, both history and modernity are incredibly messy, and neither can be fully recapped in a clean-and-crisp narrative in which one thing happens immediately after another, seemingly in perfect sequence. We understand some of the generalisations we offer in the next few sections are summaries more established academics would/will call the book out on or argue need to be expanded. Hence, our proviso to readers is that what follows is by no means the be-all-and-end-all regarding modernity, and more homework is certainly in order. That said, this text is aimed at introducing concepts, ideas, terms and trajectories that we feel are crucial to be aware of, and it is our hope that the partial explanations simply trigger the curiosity of readers who will later explore what they find intriguing and important in their own further readings.

A genealogy of modernity-coloniality

Modernity emerged with the 'exploration' (that is, enslavement economy of the Atlantic) and conquest of the Americas (Dussel, 2019). Notably, the Caribbean was ground zero. This is why the region is often referred as the 'crucible of modernity', as well as having such a rich history of anti-colonial resistance and formidable revolutionary thought. It was the conquest of the Americas, as well as Africa, Asia and Oceania, that facilitated the emergence of Europe as the 'centre' of modernity's geopolitical power complex. This centring of Europe, of course by European imperialists themselves, provided colonisers with a pretext for imagining Europe as the protagonist of history. What followed was a ravenous campaign of resource extraction, bondage and death, all of which were put at the service of allowing imperialist Europe to *globalise* its culture as a means to establish itself as a universal standard against which all Other people and places would be measured. It is in this sense that coloniality is constitutive of modernity and an integral and inseparable part of it (Cusicanqui, 2010).

Dussel (2019) argues that prior to 1492 Europe was a marginal area, or province, in the Old World. It was under siege by the Ottoman Empire, locked into a peripheral corner that lacked access to India and China (the source of much trade and imports), and did not even have all that much to sell. It is this reality that pushed Europe into the Atlantic in hopes of finding an alternative route to India. Instead of making it to India, however, European entrepreneur-colonisers landed in the Caribbean, all the while thinking they had reached the Indian subcontinent, hence the name the 'West Indies'.

The Americas thereby became the first lands to be invaded by Europe – its first colony, its first 'Other'. It is in this relationship that Europe used to construct itself as a 'modern' subject, the tip of the spear of 'civilisation' and the intrepid hero and narrator of History. In short, supremacism and ego unbound. On the other hand, it was from the lands and people of the Americas from which Europe extracted resources, minerals and labour as a means of fuelling the emergence of the 'modern' and global capitalist system that would allow Europe to cement itself as a metropole and font of imperial and racist aggression – 'God, gold and glory' were effectively imperialist Europe's banner words and rallying cry.

More specifically, modernity emerged with Spain and Portugal spearheading excursions into the Atlantic, making them the initial centre (Dussel, 1994). This early phase of modernity is critical in that it lays the foundation for Eurocentrism. The advancement and legitimation of supremacist ideologies as part of the project of modernity can be seen in the Valladolid Debate of the mid-1550s between Bartolomé de las Casas and Juan Ginés de Sepúlveda, who grappled with the question of what right Europe had for conquering the Indigenous people of the New World. For de las Casas, Europe did not have a right to enslave and dispossess Indigenous people. For de Sepúlveda, Indigenous people were not fully human, and by their 'nature' were thought to be brutish and barbaric. In turn, as they were not quite human, conquest and dispossession are justifiable.

The critical point here, writes Dussel (2019), is questioning the humanity of Indigenous people and Others, which occurred for no other reason than purportedly superior European subjects with rational Western logics thought of themselves as judge, jury and executioners vis-à-vis humanity. European subjectivity is afforded solidity and certitude by conquering 'the Other', whose humanity is doubted. Here, Dussel (1998) points out that the mentality of *'ego conquiro'* ('I conquer, therefore I am'), represented by the coloniser Hernan Cortez, is the precursor to the more widely known *'ego cogito'* ('I think, therefore I am') of René Descartes – meaning, it is the conquering of 'the Other' that provides European colonisers with a pretext to see themselves as rational subjects and enlightened thinkers endowed with reason.

'Others', in turn, are considered not quite human in relation to European subjects and placed at the bottom of a conveniently manufactured yet violent racial hierarchy. Their lands could then be pillaged and transmuted in 'private property' and bodies enslaved or eliminated, without repercussion. In fact, doing so was rewarded and came with great renown, which is why so many of our buildings, monuments and streets continue to glorify enslavers and imperialists. From then on, Europe became the model and centre of history, and its centrality and superiority – in the eyes of imperialists – must not be challenged, called into question or undermined. Ultimately, what all this illustrates is that the alleged rational and enlightened thought of Europe, ideals of liberalism and overall arrival of modernity are rooted in nothing other than authoritarian tendencies, racial worldviews and insular colonial mindsets. The negation and exploitation of Europe's 'Other', be they peasants in nearby fields or far-off 'exotic' places, became modernity's project and the core of the capitalist world system.

Modernity's advance, enclosure and dark side

In the late 15th and 16th centuries, the crisis of the feudal system gave rise to a new system of labour and land control defined largely by enclosure, which was and remains a key feature of colonialism/capitalism. In the feudal system, peasants were rooted to the land they were born in. They had to cultivate the land in order to sustain themselves and pay a form of rent to the feudal lords through goods produced or through labouring at the lord's manor (Dussel, 1998). Increases in the taxes that peasants had to pay and a shift from goods to money as payment led to peasant uprisings, which, while not entirely successful, led to greater flexibility (Dussel, 1998). On the one hand, peasants were no longer tied to the land but had increased mobility and the ability to sell their labour. On the other hand, better-off peasants could rent lands to cultivate for themselves and expand their operations by purchasing the now available labour. With this new acquired economic power they increased their political power and pressed for laws that enclosed common property, converting it into private property. This further limited the possibility of an autonomous s for other peasants and forced them into the sale of their labour. In effect, the emergent new subjectivity embodied by the better-off peasant turned entrepreneur will be elevated to the central historical actor, and the new system of labour and land control as the management system of the global system.

It is in what Dussel (1998) describes as the second stage of modernity, an industrial and purportedly 'enlightened' phase, that modernity will consolidate a global capitalist system as its management system – essentially, the system that will advance the centrality of Europe and the liberal reason of the Enlightenment and preceding Reformation. The second phase of modernity, argues Dussel (1998), is centred in countries like France, Germany and England. Dussel (2019) suggests that in order to manage the world-system, these tiny European states had to reduce complexity to create a simplified and efficient management system. This meant pro-market mindsets and the privileging of quantity over quality, as well as minimising variables related to the ethical, cultural, political and spiritual that would complicate the management of the world-system. That is, human nature, nature itself, human–nature relations and social relations must be simplified and divorced from each other.

In this new system of labour and land control nature became *de-sacralised* – meaning it was no longer seen to have value on its own, but was only viewed as valuable or productive through human use (Shiva, 2005). In Dussel's (1998) terms, no longer does nature have dignity and worthiness in-and-of itself, but rather, it is only viewed as capital, a means of production and baptised with monetary value. Land, nature and ecosystems, under colonial-capitalist worldviews, are mere objects and materials to be possessed, controlled and exploited. Knowledge, and the ways in which it is produced (epistemology), also become limited to that which emerges from Europe and Western science. Rather than from listening to, learning from and being in relationship with nature, knowledge under modernity was only legitimated if it could be proven empirically and linked to instrumental and insular notions of 'reason'.

In terms of being a subject (that is, fully human) as opposed to an object (that is, dehumanised), being recognised as human meant having to become 'White', bourgeois and often Christian. Those who did not pass the litmus test of Whiteness were negatively racialised, stripped of their 'subject'hood (that is, humanity), seen as objects (subhuman/empty), and relegated to what Fanon (1967) calls the 'zone of non-being'. Put differently, if a group or culture did not live up to or assimilate to bourgeois Whiteness, they were condemned, viewed as 'the damned' and deemed wretched. A pertinent question here forever remains: Who is doing the condemning here, and by whose authority are they damning Others? By contrast, European, White, upper-class 'subjects' were seen as rational possessive individuals who owed nothing to anyone, for European liberal subjectivity was individualistic and stood in opposition to identifying first as part of a community, collective subject or society. Liberal-colonial worldviews such as these, over a matter of only a few centuries, became commonplace. As Margaret Thatcher espoused (1987), 'there's no such thing as society. There are *individual* men and women and there are families' (emphasis added).

It is no coincidence that this type of (neo)liberal thinking has led to nothing other than mass alienation, anomie, fractured societies and spikes in anxiety, despair and nervous conditions. Indeed, liberal thought and modernity has always had its dark side: negatively racialising Others, White supremacist worldviews, enclosing and commoditising nature, consolidating power via the nation-state, enslavement and genocide, atomising and abandoning society, and the list goes on – in a word, coloniality For anti-colonial thinkers and movements committed to decolonisation, liberation and democracy, the task now at hand is overturning colonial-capitalist modernity and the world-system it has been developing for the past five hundred years. Just how we do this, however, is the crux of the issue. For a few ideas, insights and some inspiration, we feel the Zapatista struggle is arguably on the leading edge.

The Zapatista struggle

> Liberation will not fall like a miracle from the sky; we must construct it ourselves.
> So let's not wait, let us begin.
>
> The Zapatistas

In their declaration of war in 1994, the Zapatistas associate their resistance with the long historical struggle against an oppressive system that starts with European conquest and culminates with neoliberalism. In effect, they, as Indigenous people, articulate their struggle as a battle against (liberal-capitalist) modernity-coloniality, and what they are struggling for and against is made all the clearer in their subsequent communiqués and actions. The importance of Indigenous worldviews, ways of being and relating to each other and the Earth cannot be understated. In 'The Sixth Declaration' (EZLN, 2005), the Zapatistas, as Indigenous people, propose a struggle against neoliberalism and for humanity, a struggle for life and dignity. On the point of reigniting a struggle for dignity, John Holloway writes of the Zapatistas:

> Dignity, the refusal to accept humiliation and dehumanisation, the refusal to conform: dignity is the core of the Zapatistas' revolution of revolution. The idea of dignity has not been invented by the Zapatistas, but they have given it a prominence that it has never before possessed in revolutionary thought. When the Zapatistas rose, they planted the flag of dignity not just in the centre of the uprising in Chiapas, but in the centre of oppositional thought. (Holloway and Peláez, 1998: 160)

For the Zapatistas, capitalism is the centre of the world's exploitative system, which dominates the world and strips people of their dignity. In this system, capital is generated through the exploitation of labour and the theft and dispossession of land and resources. It is a system in which some have and others do not (haves versus have-nots); where those with power dictate and those without power must obey. It is also a system that represses, imprisons or disappears those who rebel with impunity. Capitalism converts everything into commodities: people, nature, culture, history and even conscience. It mystifies and obscures the exploitation of people and the planet by seducing us with merchandise and fashionable consumption. *Panem et circenses* redux,[1] with the state greasing the wheels. Capitalism is best understood as the type of economic system that demands perpetual 'growth' and is forever in need of more-and-more markets, products and consumers – hence, it seeks to convert the entire world into a strip mall. The Zapatistas understand capitalism to now be in an accelerated voracious phase – neoliberal globalisation. For the EZLN, neoliberalism is the idea, theory and plan of capitalism on steroids, going global. As such, neoliberalism has economic, political, military and cultural components.

Neoliberalism – which is in essence profit motives going global and overcoming their 'spatial fix' (Harvey, 2001) – leads to 'uneven geographical development' and destroys the countries it infects through extraction, exploitation and homogenisation. Meaning, cultures, languages, ecosystems, local economies, nature, alternative political systems and non-monetised ways of relating to each other 'from below' are targeted for elimination or reordered to benefit capital. In effect, neoliberalism's primary aim, as the Zapatistas see it, is to create one 'nation of money, of capital' that persecutes and marginalises any difference that does not fit into or serve capitalism's interests, as well as punishes anyone who does not want to live on capital's terms and conditions (EZLN, 2005). Notably, in a world of finite resources, perpetual growth is impossible, meaning that capitalism is effectively planetary homicide and humanity's way of committing collective suicide.

In the Zapatistas' letter communicating the launch of one of their latest initiatives, *La 'travesía por la vida'* ('The journey for life'), the essence of the Zapatistas' vision and struggle for 'a world where many worlds fit' is further clarified. Highlighting the diversity of those who are struggling for a better world, across the entire globe, they point to seven aspects that unite humanity across this diversity:

- The first is what they describe as the 'pains of the Earth': violence, against women, Indigenous people, negatively racialised 'others' and difference, as well as the exploitation, dispossession and destruction of nature.
- The second is that there is a system responsible for these 'pains' and the reality we are in – capitalism.
- Third, they recognise that this system, capitalism, cannot be reformed – it must be abolished.
- Fourth, a commitment to struggle, collectively, is required to end the 'pains of the Earth' and liberate humanity.
- Fifth, the struggle against the system is at once global as well as interconnected.
- Their sixth point reiterates their recognition of political agency 'from below' and the importance of respecting diversity and living in a pluralistic world. Here, they state: 'There are many worlds that live and fight within the world. And any pretence of homogeneity and hegemony threatens the essence of human being: freedom.'
- The seventh point they offer is the revolutionary possibilities that emerge from *listening*. On this point, the Zapatistas state:

The understanding that what allows us to move forward is not the intention to impose our gaze, our steps, companies, paths and destinations. What allows us to move forward *is the listening to* and the observation of the Other that, distinct and different, has the same vocation of freedom and justice. (Emphasis added)

These seven points capture the essence of the Zapatistas' understanding of what is at stake, what they struggle for and how they struggle. It is a struggle for life, both human and beyond human; it is a struggle for the diversity of life and cultures; it is a struggle for freedom, dignity and for a diversity of life and cultures. By extension, it is a struggle against a system and ongoing form of colonial modernity that negates life, which they understand as capitalism.

The Zapatistas understand the fight against capitalism, however, is not solely a matter of class struggle. They understand capitalism as a system that not only exploits and dispossesses, but that is also racist, sexist, ableist and intolerant of difference. For them, it is an extractive system that also objectifies the environment and desacralises nature, in fact, all life, and converts everything to merchandise – be it land, water, time, people, flora or fauna – everything must go and be bought and sold, given that is 'business as usual'. Moreover, the struggle they propose against capitalism, in turn, is not one oriented towards triumphalism or dominance, and nor does it aim to become hegemonic. The struggle the Zapatistas propose, conversely, is a journey for life that moves forward by listening and observing each other, with the ultimate goals being both the liberation and redemption of humanity, as well as the protection and safeguarding of the planet.

Figure 4.1: A mural on the side of a Zapatista school building with the phrase 'To exist is to resist' in English, Spanish and Tsotsil (one of the Mayan languages spoken in the region)

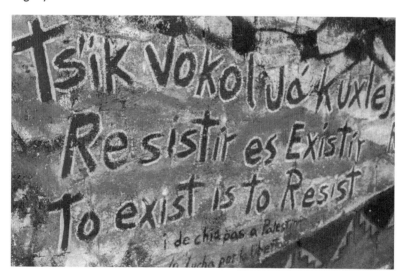

In many respects, then, the Zapatistas can be thought of as land defenders and water protectors who are engaged in the praxis of decolonisation, like countless other Indigenous activists and peasant movements across the world (EZLN, 2016b). As ironic as it may seem, the presence of rich biodiversity and abundant 'resources' in any given locale has been identified as one of the key factors resulting in the subsequent extraction from and 'underdevelopment' – and perhaps more accurately, ransacking – of numerous countries. Here, it is necessary to understand that the descriptors 'underdeveloped' and 'developing', when applied to the status of any given country or community, are unfair framings applied to places that have been targeted for exploitation.

Needless to say, capitalism has industrialised, expedited and normalised extraction to such a degree that it is now simply seen as an efficient and necessary ('common-sense') way of profiting from off of the alienation, monetisation and extraction of nature. As we move further into the 21st century and 'modernity', capitalism's colonising propensities, profit motives, growth imperatives and preferred extractive method of production, that is, dispossession qua 'development', is not slowing down, and continues to wreak havoc on myriad ecosystems, not to mention the climate. Regrettably, confronting extraction, the driving forces of accumulation, liberal–colonial worldviews and the consolidated power of the state – as the Zapatistas are doing – does not come without its own set of costs, consequences and reprisals.

5

Dispossession, extractivism and violence

> The understanding that a system is responsible for these pains. The executioner is an exploitative, patriarchal, pyramidal, racist, thievish, and criminal system: capitalism.
>
> The EZLN

To understand extractivism, it is essential to realise it is rooted in dispossession, has its historical origins in colonialism, and is now facilitated primarily by corporations and states. Extraction has traditionally and continues to be a hallmark of (neo)imperial domination and neoliberal policies (for example, 'cash crops', fossil fuels, minerals, biofuels, precious metals, water, livestock, timber/logging). Put simply, extractivism is a capitalistic method of acquiring wealth through the withdrawal of 'resources' or 'raw materials' from either 'conquered' (read, dispossessed) lands or territories that were encroached on, privatised and earmarked for commodification. After extraction, said resources and raw materials are transported for production, manufactured into value-added retail goods and shipped back to a respective metropole or placed on the global marketplace as stock suitable for consumption and disposal. Over centuries, the terms 'raw material' and 'natural/human resources' have been used and expanded to include privatising not only land, minerals and fossil fuels, but also fishing, farming, forestry and even humans. The punchy and all too exact axioms 'property is theft' and 'accumulation by dispossession' are each inextricably linked to the enclosure, privatisation and extraction of the commons, that is, the colonial enterprise and neoliberal capitalism. Unsurprisingly, the planet and all its inhabitants are suffering the consequences. Part of the Zapatista resistance is confronting this.

Because there is a massive imbalance between the amount of 'raw materials' being extracted over short periods of time and the brief period allowed to ecosystems to recuperate and replenish, the extractive industry is effectively cannibalising itself. The corporations and states that are endorsing and continuing to engage in extractivism also have little to no regard for the types of relationships and ways of being that Indigenous and peasant communities have with land and are beholden to. What results is the dismissal of any worldviews that do not align with liberal ideals and the prerogatives of entrepreneurial capitalism, which poses a major threat to rivers, soils, oceans, forests, plants, animals, the climate and humanity. The point so many people and communities who care about the planet and life on Earth keep reiterating is that it is impossible to pursue infinite growth in a world of finite resources – not that we should be thinking of the world as a repository of resources to be mined and merchandised in the first place. As long as economic growth and extractivist agendas, which are both often deceptively couched as 'development', go unchecked and continue to devour the commons, the world will continue to writhe and revolt in agony.

Paradoxically, countless professional (for example, liberal, 'well-intentioned', bourgeois) organisations (for example, NGOs, think-tanks, self-anointed 'socially responsible' corporations) and state entities that are purportedly engaged in 'development work' and efforts to abate or eliminate structural inequality, endemic poverty, social vulnerability and dangerous climate change – are not listening to the very people whom 'development' has historically and continues to land squarely on and smash (Choudry and Kapoor, 2013). From a liberal-capitalist perspective, this is logical, proof the system works just fine, and 'business as usual' (EZLN, 2015). However, for anyone harbouring sincere yearnings about the fruition of sustainable alternatives and viable practices that will cultivate, preserve and stimulate healthy ecosystems, social harmony, cultural vibrancy and planetary health, it is indeed a cruel irony that, by and large, the segments of society who are arguably the most experienced with all these, for example, Indigenous communities and the rural peasantry (Fanon, 1963), continue to go dismissed and ignored by mainstream institutions when it comes to discussions, theories and ideas related to sustainable development.

Unfortunately, the acquisition and accumulation of power, land and wealth via extraction, exploitation, desolation and bloodshed is a tale as old as time. As noted earlier, the onset of modernity and the industrialisation of production have each involved mayhem, annihilation and crimes against humanity. Over the long arc of history and at present, colonial-capitalism continues to evolve and take many forms. One long-standing capitalist practice related directly to extraction is land grabbing, an offence that transnational corporations, plantation firms and state governments are guilty of disproportionately committing the most. Consequently, agrarian communities, peasant farmers and environmental defenders are often faced with the ominous challenge of having to stand up to the driving forces of dispossession and extraction, as well as the violence initiated by those in power, be it a corporation or a state, that want such resistance to be eliminated. The Zapatistas, like a multitude of other Indigenous and Afrodescendant people whose lives, identities and relations are connected to land, are all too familiar with state-sponsored violence and corporate malfeasance. The Zapatista movement, since its inception, has been targeted for suppression and even eradication, which has meant their communities continue to experience abductions, assassinations, vandalism, slander, militarisation, counterinsurgency, derision, criminalisation and intimidation.

Land grabbing and environmental defence

Over recent years, land grabbing has emerged as a worldwide phenomenon that is growing in speed and scale as the convergence of multiple crises in global finance, the environment, food and energy has spawned significant reappraisal of land ownership. Partly resulting from a combination of globalisation, the liberalisation of land markets and the global increase in financial direct investments (Zoomers, 2010), land grabbing can be defined as a process of land acquisition made by wealthy actors – such as local elites, transnational corporations, private equity firms and national governments – that take control of large areas of land, including its minerals, water and other valuable resources, to aid the production of commodities for both global and domestic markets. Moreover, land grabbing is often characterised by low levels of transparency, and a lack of consultation with and respect for the rights of local communities living off the land.

Within contemporary cases of land grabbing, there is a significant North–South relationship that echoes the very same processes intrinsic to colonialism and imperialism. One of the key drivers of land grabbing is global capitalism, which, through increasing socio-economic inequality, greatly contributes to 'the dispossession and destruction of livelihoods that it causes for communities around the world' (Nyéléni Newsletter, 2020). The concentration of power into the hands of a few has, for too long, been a contentious issue; however, shifts in global capitalism since 2008/09 have resulted in new forms of extracting wealth and widened global inequality (Nyéléni Newsletter, 2020). Specifically, as countries shift from industrial capitalism, financialisation – referring to the increased size, power and importance of a country's financial sector relative to its overall economy and governing institutions (Palley, 2013; Durand, 2017) – has ushered in a multitude of novel financial instruments and motives, as well as transnational and domestic corporations that now have an ever-growing presence across many parts of society, including land governance. Furthermore, the rise of digital surveillance technologies, such as satellite imagery, drones and electronic databases, have assisted in a 'data grab' via land mapping, registration and governance (Fraser, 2019; Nyéléni Newsletter, 2020). The convergence of digital and financial technologies has transformed land and natural resources into quantifiable, globalised assets for governments and private sectors to claim. With shifts towards more capitalist-intensive and larger-scale agriculture (endorsed by the World Bank 2020), external agents have engaged in both dramatic and more gradual land acquisitions (Zoomers, 2010).

For Indigenous communities, land grabbing carries particular significance since communities often do not hold formal titles to their lands, and land rights are not protected by governments. Subsequently, Indigenous people's collective lands rights are often simply ignored by national governments. Notably, with accompanied deforestation and alterations to the biodiversity of their ancestral lands and territories, Indigenous communities are increasingly dispossessed of their ancestral lands and concurrently their key sources of livelihood. Additionally, many rural and Indigenous people have deep relationships with the land, giving it a particular meaning and significance. Holding such cultural and spiritual significance, land becomes more than something to own. This thereby leads to massive impacts on rural people due to the degree of connection with and dependence on these resources, and places a large amount of pressure on these resources. Similarly, land grabbing disrupts Indigenous systems of own-provisioning, cooperative relations (an alternative to monetary relations), self-sufficiency and traditional resource governance (Edelman, Oya, and Borras Jr, 2013).

Simultaneously, the importance of resources in such spaces also makes them key targets for what Harvey (2004) describes as 'accumulation by dispossession'. Thus, the grabbing of lands and resources in Indigenous territories is intensely violent, and related to either the displacement of rural people or their incorporation into new capitalist structures under highly adverse conditions (Edelman, Oya, and Borras Jr, 2013). Recently, mirroring the role of European imperial forces who profit from the extraction and destruction of the natural environment and the exploitation of Indigenous populations, government officials, extractive industries and transnational corporations in the Global South, like those from the Global North, also play a role in the growing phenomenon of land grabbing. The financialisation of land markets and the wealth it promises has ushered in a rising presence of authoritarian political regimes among countries in the Majority World with an emerging 'South–South' dynamic, which sees economically powerful Global South countries, such as Brazil, China and Qatar, engaging in efforts of land acquisition and dispossession. Such crimes remain hidden and ignored as those benefiting from such atrocities are often working together to conceal them.

Environmental defenders and others who resist such violations regularly experience violence, intimidation, threats against them and their families, harassment, discreditation and exposure to stigmatisation (Menton and Le Billon, 2021). And yet, the strong presence of anti environmentalism within the global economy has led to numerous crises including the extinction of biodiversity, food insecurity, absolute poverty, global warming and drastic climate change, to name but a few. Recognising these pertinent ecological issues, alongside protesting land degradation, and violence against Indigenous people and peasant farmers, is vital for exposing these issues and bringing them to wide public attention.

For too long these issues raised by environment defenders have been silenced or reframed to protect the ongoing machinations of global capitalism and authoritarian political interests. However, given many environmental defenders are Indigenous and hold worldviews that are commonly viewed as 'outmoded', 'underdeveloped' and 'silly' by state administrators, corporate officials and even some members of civil society, this means Indigenous people and peasants are especially vulnerable to land grabbing as they have historical relationships with traditional territories, are often based in isolated geographical locales, and tend to reside in areas that are rich in resources.

On the front lines: land defenders and water protectors

While it is sobering to reflect on, the work of safeguarding the environment (for example, being a land defender or water protector) from the driving forces of accumulation is one of the most dangerous vocations in the world. This is especially the case in the Global South, where environmental defenders who are opposing extractivism often face fatal consequences for the political work they are doing. Notably, Indigenous people and rural peasants are overrepresented in the ranks of environmental defence, as well as having to contend with the very real prospects of state-sponsored violence, character assassination, capture, and even being murdered. And while discussing the political violence and death environmental defenders face is a difficult and delicate topic, we feel it necessary to lay out the ways in which movements and community members like the Zapatistas are targeted, criminalised and sometimes even disappeared, so readers have a clear understanding of the gravity of the situation, as well as just how far capitalism, corporations and states are willing to go to dispossess land, accrue wealth and eliminate resistance. On this sensitive point, we provide a list of the most common repercussions and reprisals that environmental defenders face as a result of making the decision to protect their local territories, communities and relations.

Marginalisation and exclusion

Extractive industries and state officials frequently exclude local communities and environmental defenders from decision-making processes related to 'development' initiatives that affect their territories and resources. Moreover, when there are attempts at consultation, it is ordinarily with select individuals, and often bypasses established protocols and processes that Indigenous and/ or peasant communities may have been using for generations on end. It is also not uncommon for women to be left out of consultations altogether, even if said consultation is a fraught one done in bad faith (Tran et al, 2020). These actions contravene several human rights instruments, including both the United Nations' (UN) Declaration on Human Rights Defenders and the UN's Declaration on the Rights of Indigenous Peoples, which emphasises Indigenous people's right 'to participate in decision-making in matters which would affect their rights, through representatives chosen by themselves in accordance with their own procedures'. While international declarations and human rights instruments from supranational entities like the UN are useful on some fronts, they reproduce problematic and limited notions of liberal human rights that are deeply rooted in Western worldviews and Eurocentricism.

Environmental defenders can further be marginalised and undermined as a result of attacks on their character or through framing their political work as antagonistic and divisive (Birss, 2017). While these tactics are effective at ostracising water protectors and environmental activists across the board, they are especially devastating for women. This is because women, who perform a disproportionate amount of socially reproductive labour, are often accused of being 'bad mothers', unconcerned about families and unconcerned about 'traditional family values' and/or the stability of the family as a result of regressive norms that suggest a 'woman's place is in the home'. While the recourse to patriarchal respectability politics is obviously chauvinist, it can do untold damage to the efforts of women who are defending the environment and confronting capitalism. In short, activists, and in particular women, who are defending the environment are often shamed, scolded and reprimanded for the political work they do, with the upshots being exclusion, silencing and marginalisation (Tran et al, 2020).

Criminalisation and stigma

Criminalisation is a process wherein legitimate rights, such as participation in peaceful protests and demonstrations, are framed as illegal activities that can be punished through judicial systems (Bennett et al, 2015). Criminalisation is used to deter land defenders, water protectors and human rights activists from confronting corporate extractors, as well as being a punitive means through which Indigenous and peasant communities often have their traditional systems of governance and diplomacy delegitimised and dismissed. For decades now, both civil and criminal cases have been levied against environmental defenders by extractive companies, sometimes in collaboration with national–local authorities that aim to quell community opposition to extractive 'development' projects (López and Vértiz, 2015). The trumped-up charges frequently brought against environmental defenders can include, but are not limited to, terrorism, trespassing, obstructing justice, disturbing the peace and criminal property damage (Birss, 2017).

Stigmatisation goes hand in hand with criminalisation and is used to undermine the reputations and credibility of environmental defenders and their work. Discourses that stigmatise political activists are promoted via state officials and institutions, and can be found in both government broadcasting and corporate media. Some of the most common narratives Indigenous and peasant communities have levied against them are accusations that they oppose 'development' or 'national unity'. Criminalisation of this nature is a common tactic used against environmental defenders because, even if they are not threatened immediately with death, the prospect of imprisonment, being slandered and dragged through the courts can cause political activists to refrain from opposing extractivist companies and authoritarian states (Gahman et al, 2020). Character assassination is also transmitted and reproduced via news headlines and press releases that environmental defenders are unpatriotic extremists and 'anti-economic growth' (for example, consider the ways in which extractivist companies and officials endorse megaprojects as 'creating employment/jobs'). Defamation of this form can isolate and alienate environmental defenders from their own communities, as well as do severe reputational damage across the board.

Militarisation and intimidation

Environmental defenders are often readily classified as enemies of the state, meaning they can have both private and public 'security forces' deployed against them and their communities militarised (for example, placed under observation and patrolled by armed guards) (Menton and Le billon, 2021). Aside from being a means through which corporations purportedly 'protect' their interests (that is, profits), often with the support of the state, security forces are used to violate the rights of land defenders in a variety of ways including surveillance, threat, harassment, sexual violence and even killing. Additionally, private security forces and state-funded counterinsurgencies also try to infiltrate movements by forging personal relationships with local communities and movement activists as a way of gathering intel or emotional manipulation (Birss, 2017).

In some instances, however, corporations simply resort to naked violence. In fact, over the past decade, there have been thousands of reported murders and abductions of environmental defenders across the globe, and this is not accounting for those that have not been recorded (Glazebrook and Opoku, 2018). Furthermore, militarisation has gendered effects and can lead to an increase in gender-based and sexual violence given women are frequently targeted, as well as avoid reporting cases due to the fear of victim-blaming or being shamed (Tran et al, 2020). While harrowing to think about and seemingly ironic to focus on in a book that is ostensibly about hope, inspiration and overcoming injustice, the state violence and corporate-driven reprisals environmental defenders are subjected are nevertheless important to discuss, in part because we all need to be aware of the consequences of resistance, not to mention the threats to life and dignity that water protectors, land defenders and autonomous movements like the Zapatistas face.

Are alternative futures possible?

'The problem isn't getting to the destination but making the path. That is, if there is no path, one has to make it. That's the only way,' she [Defensa Zapatista] continued, brandishing a machete.

The EZLN

The Zapatistas recognise that 'changing the world is difficult, perhaps impossible', but refuse hopelessness and despair by adding that creating a new world is possible. While they acknowledge the overwhelming burden that comes with changing a world replete with violence that is dominated by corporate exploiters, government armies and state paramilitaries, the conclusion they have reached is not to remain silent or be bystanders, but rather, to respond with '¡Ya basta!' ('Enough is enough!'). '¡Ya basta!' was the cry that launched their uprising in 1994, and remains their ongoing response to the oppressive and dispossessive forces they continue to face. Notably, their '¡Ya basta!' is also a response to any apathy, fear or pessimism that might be holding us back from building better worlds. That a poorly equipped and outgunned liberation army composed of Indigenous peasants, farmers and landworkers would confront the Mexican State and federal military seems rather ridiculous on one level, yet they saw it as entirely reasonable and did it anyway.

In doing so, they were not only able to force the Mexican state to hear their '¡Ya basta!' and take their cause seriously, but their uprising reverberated throughout the world and inspired a multitude of other '¡Ya basta!'s. In a sense, the Zapatistas were able to mobilise international solidarity and a diverse array of support from across the globe for their dream, which served to protect the seed of resistance and an alternative world they planted. That they were able to carve out space to construct autonomy on their terms – and have been able to defend it for over 30 years – is a laudable achievement. Moreover, that they have been able to marshal and continue to build solidarity across geographies with a vast array of diverse sympathisers is testament to the energy, vitality and hope that was unleashed by their '¡Ya basta!'

In recent writings, Subcomandante Galeano has used a dialogue between two Zapatista characters, two little (albeit tenacious and strong-willed) girls to be precise, named 'Defensa Zapatista' and 'Esperanza Zapatista', to explain the Zapatista mission. In a communiqué released in late 2020, when asked by Defensa if she understands what the mission of building an alternative future in the face of colonial-capitalist modernity ('storm') entails and means for them, Esperanza, knowing what they are up against, responds: 'I know we will die miserably.' What is telling here is that Esperanza, without missing a beat, swiftly follows up with the line 'but we will make it count'.

This is radical hope. It is the type of hope engendered by those who, even though they have the odds stacked against them and are facing seemingly impossible circumstances, feel in their heart that they must neither give up nor apathetically bystand – and must make their actions count. This emerges from the faith and conviction that something else, another world, is possible. Otherwise, why struggle?

What might alternatives look like?

To the question of whether alternative futures are possible, a well-known Zapatista character named '*El Viejo Antonio*' ('Old Antonio') draws our attention to Mother Earth, that great teacher, when he explains:

> Storms respect no one; they hit both sea and land, sky and soil alike. Even the innards of the earth twist and turn with the actions of humans, plants, and animals. Neither color, size, nor ways matter. (EZLN, 2020d)

Humans, Old Antonio continues, 'shelter and wait out the raging storm to go check what is left after it'. Mother Earth, on the other hand:

> begins to prepare for what comes next, what comes after. In that process it begins to change; Mother Earth does not wait for the storm to pass in order to decide what to do, but rather begins to build long before. (EZLN, 2020d)

Old Antonio calls on us to listen to and learn from Mother Earth, which time and time again has shown us that another world is possible. More importantly, Old Antonio calls us to begin working on bringing it to fruition. This, he alludes, is a lesson the Maya have learned. The 'people of the corn', Old Antonio points out, in planting their crops:

> dream of tortillas, atole, pozole and tamales, and even though those things are not yet manifest, they know they will come and thus this is what guides their work. They see their field and its fruit before the seed has even touched the soil. (EZLN, 2020d)

This, too, is radical hope. It is the hope that motivates one to not wait around to see what will be left by the 'storm', and it is the type of hope of those armed with the conviction that something else is entirely possible and who set out to create a path. That is, as we weather the storm, we prepare. Here, Old Antonio draws our attention to the wisdom of elders:

> That is why the wisest ones say that the morning doesn't just happen, doesn't appear just like that, but that it lies in wait among the shadows and, for those who know where to look, in the cracks of the night. (EZLN, 2020d)

In sum, 'other worlds' are indeed possible; however, they do not just happen or fall out of the sky – they lie in wait for those who know where to look in the cracks and crevices of the system. The Zapatista make it clear that they struggle for humanity, for life, for all life, for dignity, for freedom, for justice. They make it clear that at the centre of what produces the opposite is capitalism, which atomises, objectifies and commoditises land and life. They point to the fact that when we are talking about alternatives, we are talking about alternatives to capitalism. Defensa Zapatista declares: '*Si queremos tamales no vamos a sembrar calabazas*' (If we want to eat tamales, we're not going to plant squash) (EZLN, 2020d).

The statement, 'a world in which many worlds can fit' ('*un mundo donde quepan muchos mundos*'), communicates the point that we are not talking about a singular future but many futures. When the Zapatistas (EZLN, 2021) talk about humanity and the world – 'In its diversity resides its likeness' – they are recognising a plurality of life, a plurality of struggles and a plurality of futures. Put differently, the equality of humanity lies in the respect for difference. The struggle of the Zapatistas, from the start, was to 'change the world without taking power' (Holloway, 2002a). The rebellion was not aimed at taking over the state and imposing their vision and ideals on Mexico; their uprising was about creating a Mexico where all Mexicans could fit, and being a 'seed to seek other seeds'.

The Zapatistas reiterate both 'hegemony' and 'homogeneity' are attacks on freedom and humanity itself. In fact, as they point out, it is only in knowing others that we can progress. In this way, the Zapatistas remind us that the struggle against capitalism is not a struggle to replace it with some other hegemonic system or homogenising force. Rather, the Zapatistas point to a struggle against colonial–capitalist modernity's 'Empire of Money', which is founded, on the one hand, on racism, sexism, ableism and other forms of intolerance, and on the other, on the exploitation, dispossession and alienation of land, labour and the planet. Here, in recognising that decolonisation is indeed 'not a metaphor' (Tuck and Yang, 2012), they propose building solidarity across difference as a way of resisting and overcoming both.

Figure 5.1: A mural on the side of a Zapatista building that depicts four arms with closed fists representing solidarity across difference and the struggle for freedom, justice, democracy and peace

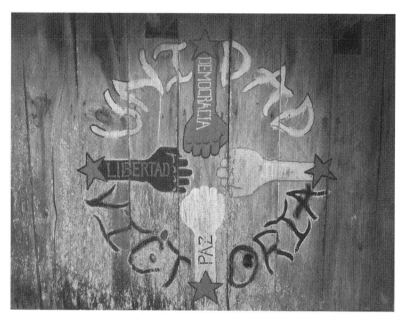

Radical hope via 'asking, we walk'

As a way of concluding, we feel it is useful to reflect on the Zapatista practice and theory of creating a new world in light of the Maya story of creation in the *Popul Vuh*, a Pre-Columbian Maya text. In the *Popul Vuh*, the creators are faced with the challenge of creating human beings, which, in effect, resonates with the challenge identified by the Zapatistas – a struggle for life and for humanity. The *Popul Vuh* narrates:

> In the beginning there was silence, before the first word there was silence, there were no animals, trees, men, or birds. There were only the creators, all were there.

The *Popul Vuh* then notes the creators came together in a council, joining their thoughts and their words. At first, the creators tried making human beings out of clay, but these beings failed to honour and give thanks to their creators. They forgot to show gratitude and so were destroyed. The creators then tried creating human beings out of wood, but these beings not only failed to honour and show gratitude to their creators, but also mistreated their implements and nature itself, and so these implements, along with nature itself, turned against them and, hence, were also destroyed. Finally, the creators sought the advice of two elders who helped them to create human beings out of corn. These human beings immediately honoured their creators and were allowed to exist.

Creation begins with a dream of what is 'not yet'. It is a dream that is the result of coming together with others, the result of dialogue, the joining of words and thought. It is a collective journey for life that seeks the elders, that seeks others. Creating life, however, is not a straightforward process. It requires 'walking by asking'. 'How shall we create human beings?' ask the creators, and they act. Their ideas and attempts did not work either the first or the second time, but the creators continued asking, dialoguing, acting and seeking others. The essence of radical hope is that they did not give up and would eventually succeed the third time around. It is with this poignant wisdom in mind that we now turn to the role that political education, critical consciousness and dialogue has played in the Zapatistas' creation of a new world/reality for their communities.

6

Critical consciousness and praxis

> Do you remember that saying about not being able to see the
> forest for the trees? Well, as Zapatistas, we see the roots.
>
> The Zapatistas

Education is at the heart of all politics, values and ethics ... or lack thereof.
Paulo Freire, author of *Pedagogy of the oppressed* (2018), in critically analysing
the malevolent relationship between colonisers and the colonised, oppressors
and the oppressed, the privileged and the underprivileged in Brazil, provides
us with an invaluable insight into how education can be put to the service
of freedom. In particular, his notion of critical consciousness (*conscientização*)
equips us with critical tools we can use to expose, dissect and abolish cultural
norms and social institutions that are both founded on and reproduce
oppression and exploitation. That is, in order to co-create a socially just and
democratic society, Freire notes we must work from the bottom up (that is,
the grassroots) to critically analyse the systems and institutions that compose
a society and make the political decision to collectively act against repressive
forces. On this point, Freire (2018: 39) writes:

> The more radical the person is, the more fully they enter into reality
> so that, knowing it better, they can transform it. This individual is not
> afraid to confront, to listen, to see the world unveiled. This person is
> not afraid to meet the people or to enter into a dialogue with them.
> This person does not consider theirself the proprietor of history or
> of all people, or the liberator of the oppressed; but they do commit
> theirself, within history, to fight at the side of the oppressed.

Most importantly, Freire is a strong proponent of not only recognising
but also taking seriously the agency, acumen and knowledges of the poor,
oppressed and communities-in-struggle.

From there, and in order to change the world, Freire endorses engaging in
praxis, which broadly is the simultaneous process of questioning authority and
institutions; being present with communities; developing ideas together; and
both acting and reflecting on how we are organising against *structural* violence,
oppression and inequality. Structural inequality is the result of systems of
power obstructing certain groups and communities from benefiting from
and enjoying the same privileges, rights, opportunities and life chances as
majority or normative groups. Structural forms of inequality are rooted in

norms, institutions, policies and organisations, all of which affect everyone in one way or another. Freire notably argues praxis is grounded *intellectual* work, and where revolutionary ideas, theories and solutions to structural inequality are born. Put differently, participatory dialogue/action with communities, social movements and the oppressed that is oriented toward emancipation is where transformative ideas come from. This, regrettably, is not always recognised by university managers or even acknowledged by academics in bourgeois institutions who are preoccupied with award cultures, self-branding and advancing their individual careers. Accordingly, we begin this chapter with an overview of the histories and legacies of colonialism and race as well as the role and tactics of the state and nation in upholding these oppressive relations, followed by praxis-oriented examples from pedagogical approaches and feminist ethics that seek to build critical consciousness.

Freire (2018) suggests conscientisation is a potent weapon to wield in the fight against injustice as he believes that oppression feeds off institutionalised ignorance, obliviousness and even purposeful bad faith. Put differently, the acquisition of information and the process of getting a degree or diploma is not enough to end mass human suffering and alienation, given most contemporary education systems are founded on liberal-Western worldviews, which are arguably colonial – meaning, we are inculcated from an early age that obedience, bystanding, individualism and nationalism, to name but a few, are natural and normal (Springer, De Souza and White, 2016). Conscientisation allows us to recognise how these are not only dangerous, but also dehumanising. Here, Freire explains that dehumanisation is not only experienced by the oppressed when they are denied their humanity, but that oppressors, as well as those who are complicit with allowing institutionalised oppression to continue, are being dehumanised themselves, given they are culpable for suffocating possibilities of freedom, peace and dignity. The battle for critical consciousness continues, and in order to get there a good starting point is taking seriously the ongoing aftermaths of colonialism and race.

Colonialism and race

> Come, then, comrades, the European game has finally ended; we must find something different. We today can do everything, so long as we do not imitate Europe, so long as we are not obsessed by the desire to catch up with Europe.
>
> Fanon (1963: 251)

Frantz Fanon, in his call to create anew in this quote, alludes to the end of imperial rule and the beginning of political independence for former colonies by referring to colonialism as a 'game' run by European occupiers. In doing so, Fanon encourages once colonised countries to embark on a different path and to breathe life into new political, social and economic systems that depart from the racist logics, compulsion to dispossess land and dominate 'Others' and ethnocentric worldviews of Western colonisers, that is, 'the European game'. Accordingly, this section will focus on the social institutions and ongoing systems of domination that have emerged from the colonial, racist imagination. We will also detail the links between imperialism, capitalism and Eurocentrism, as well as the exploitation and manipulation of working-class and negatively racialised labour forces under colonial-capitalism.

Before diving into the content, however, we begin by noting that colonial processes, practices and worldviews are all still ongoing. So, even though dispossessed and formerly enslaved populations across the 'Third World' have ostensibly gained their independence, many previously colonised countries in the Global South/Majority World still remain governed and regulated, in one way or another, by empire. Our main argument, then, is that anti-racist political education, collective action and a commitment to non-metaphorical decolonisation can emancipate minds, land and people from supremacist racial ideologies, liberal self-centrism and the capitalist state, all of which continue to prevent countless societies from actualising justice and freedom.

At various historical points, essentialist ideas of race have been used to construct taxonomies of people, cultures and societies (Narayan, 2012), with discourses in anthropology, comparative anatomy and social biology being used to justify the 'European game' mentioned in Fanon's opening quote. Founded on ostensibly racist theoretical models, racial stratification has enabled the most violent practices employed by the imperialists during colonialism. As a way of dehumanising the racial 'Other', colonial forces adopted theories of racial difference to enact genocide or justify the enslavement of people. 'Others' were marked as different and subsequently backward and inferior to the bourgeois 'White' norm.

Fanon (1963) explains how colonisers, through violence, not only stole the humanity of forcibly enslaved people while decimating Indigenous populations, but also stripped themselves of their own humanity and relinquished their own dignity. For readers familiar with West African and Caribbean lore, colonisers tried to make zombies out of humans – to capture 'Others'; sever them from their souls, consciousness and kinship; and enslave/exploit their bodies (Moreman and Rushton, 2011). Fanon rightly associated colonisers with betrayers, who, according to Dante in *Inferno* (Alighieri and Musa, 1971), would ultimately be cast into the deepest realm of Hell, because this is precisely what they were doing to humanity – betraying it. Europe (and later the US) took it upon itself to perform a so-called 'spiritual cleansing' of the civilisations that imperialists deemed profane, barbaric and wicked due to their physical appearances and ethnic differences. In reality, people were condemned for their lack of 'Whiteness'.

With similar 19th-century developments in anthropology, romanticism and racial 'sciences', the concept of the nation was defined in terms of racial or civilisational progress or decline. As witnessed in the 20th century, the European preoccupation with 'racial hygiene' became a prominent feature within Nazi Germany, with notions of the health of the Aryan nation, civilised morality and law and order becoming intimately tied together. As Paul Gilroy (2000: 39) writes: 'Where the political chemistry of nation, race, and culture came together ... the rebirth of fascist thinking and the reappearance of stern, uniformed political movements was not far away.' The promotion of 'racial cleansing' depended on the existence of subordinate racial 'Others' (Jews, Africans, Roma, Travellers) who were invariably defined as having tendencies towards criminality, disorder and mental inferiority, as well as being carriers of various diseases and pestilence (Gilroy, 2000).

Nationalism and the state

> The destructive advance of Capital, always through war, demolished the first fiefdoms and kingdoms. Upon their ruins it raised nation-states.
>
> EZLN (2017)

European colonisers proceeded to build commanding empires on racial animus, stolen resources, large-scale kidnapping, forced bondage, mass slaughter and unimaginable brutality that lasted for centuries on end – worldwide. Indeed, exploitation was, and remains, a betrayal of humanity. The liberal state subsequently became enforcer and garnered consent and loyalty via nationalism. Accordingly, Fanon (1963) correctly remains suspicious of and incisively questions 'modernity' and orthodox notions of 'development', as well as cautions us that nationalism is a trap given that racism, exploitation and repression are the foundation on which liberal-capitalist values and nation-states were built. It would be foolish to think that colonialism is a thing of the past, as numerous purportedly postcolonial societies remain stripped bare and dependent on their former imperial powers (Mbah and Igariwey, 2001). Many also remain beholden to institutions and models of social organisation and governance that were installed or heavily influenced by European occupiers (for example, Westminster), with present-day members of postcolonial ruling classes often mimicking and reproducing the very mindsets and hierarchies of colonisers who had targeted and dehumanised their ancestors. There is good reason that anti-imperialist revolutionary Amílcar Cabral (Manji and Fletcher, 2013), when diagnosing the failure of postcolonial societies to reckon with the class stratifications and anti-democratic hierarchies that remained after political independence, ascribed it to the 'problem of the nature of the state'.

By analysing the imposed economic, political and social systems of imperialists, as well as the contemporary and continued lasting consequences these systems have, it is easy to discern that the aftermaths of colonialism carry on. That is, the material, spiritual and moral violence of colonialism, as well as the 'coloniser's model' of the world writ large, remains alive and well (Blaut, 1993). 'Colonial' – alongside 'capitalist', 'heteropatriarchal' and 'ableist' – arguably wholly define countless present-day nation-states and societies, be they in the Global North or Majority World/Global South. We believe political education, which necessitates a critical intersectional understanding of race, class and gender, is part of the solution.

First and foremost, it is necessary to understand that the link between colonialism and capitalism is underpinned by hierarchical and value-laden constructions of race and nationalism. That is, over time and via the colonial imagination, some people have been negatively racialised while others have been positively racialised or seen as the 'norm' and/or part of the nation-state, for example, Whiteness, citizenship. Class, of course, mediates these racialisations and is inextricably linked to race (Rodney, 2018). Racial and national divisions, in turn, are used to legitimise the eradication or exploitation of condemnable and even 'killable' groups. The invention of race, in addition to the 'modern' nation-state, facilitated the segregation and 'compartmentalisation' (Fanon, 1963) of humans, which rearranged the world socio-spatially.

Dividing people along racial and national lines was convenient because, under capitalist (accumulation-oriented) economies, it could be used to suppress labour forces and even used as a psychological weapon to convince workers that social mobility is impossible for them to achieve due to their purported inferiority (Césaire, 2001). Numerous critical theorists further explain that race is a well-plotted scheme initiated to divert the majority without capital from the issue of class consciousness. Hence, if we are concerned with effecting better, freer and just realities and worlds, processes of negative racialisation, engineered class stratifications and prevailing notions of nationalism must be addressed and overturned hand-in-hand without one superseding the other (Walia, 2021). We would also argue that gender justice and an end to ableism is part of this emancipatory project.

The problems of racism and nationalism are more complex and dynamic than simply believing that racism is applicable merely to people's individual behaviour alone. Racism is a systemic issue. To fully grasp terms like 'race' and 'racial prejudice' one must be aware of multiple definitions and understandings, as well as understand how they operate on contrasting institutional, cultural and psychological levels (Razack et al, 2010). Grosfoguel (2016) offers a straightforward summary of racism in the world-system, noting that it involves the inclusion and exclusion of particular groups or individuals based on specious racial distinctions, which hinder them from fully benefiting from opportunities, privileges, resources and services that societies have to offer.

That is, race, in conjunction with state nationalism, are key factors wrapped up in how societies are structured (Gilmore, 2002), how their institutions operate and who is allowed to belong and/or constructed as a foreign 'Other' or criminal threat in a given state, which is why you will hear the term 'structural racism'. This, however, does not fully incorporate the entirety of race, as analysing race alone can mean other significant factors of life and identity are left out, for example, gender, class, ability (Collins and Bilge, 2020). Race intersects with other categories of identity, class and prejudice, including ethnicity, gender, income level, sexuality, disability, language, nationality, citizenship status, religion, and so on. In short, race, as it has been constructed under 'modernity' (that is, colonial-capitalist-liberal), remains tethered to Eurocentric ideals and values, which have been centred and privileged as the norm (Dei et al, 2000). Countless states were built on and maintain racialism of this nature, but often convince a populace otherwise via a manufactured sense of shared unity – nationalism, which Fanon (1963) cautioned against and warned us about. On this point, Fanon's (1963: 312) foreknowing caution seems as pertinent as ever: 'Europe now lives at such a mad, reckless pace that it has shaken off all guidance and reason and is running headlong into the abyss; we would do well to avoid it with all possible speed.'

Divide and conquer/rule/exploit

Race, as it predominantly operates today, was created via colonial worldviews by mainly European imperialists and White supremacists to justify colonial conquest and the massacre of and theft from 'Others', which, on occasion, included different groups who later became 'White' in some contexts (for example, Irish, Italian, Eastern European). Other forms of institutionalised discrimination are connected to and operate alongside race, which continue to either privilege or subordinate people on a variety of intersectional fronts (Mohanty, 2003). Racism, as it operates in contemporary times, is primarily Anti-Black/Anti-Indigenous, noting well that being Black or Indigenous is not mutually exclusive, and that racism is mutable and experienced by numerous other groups (for example, Muslims, Travellers, Asian populations).

Here, we note well that White folks have been oppressed historically and can very well be exploited and exposed to structural violence in the current moment too, particularly if they are working-class or cash-poor (for example, the opioid crisis, suicide rates). Indeed, the degree to which White people are suffering, being neglected or experiencing trauma is rarely, if ever, due to the fact of their White skin (Gahman, 2020b). With that said, we need as many White people contributing to the anti-racist cause as possible, not least of which is due to that fact that race/racism alone is not the sole source of oppression in this world, and the only way things will get better is if we are committed to multi-racial working-class solidarity across incommensurate struggles. On a host of fronts and in myriad contexts, class overdetermines the life chances, or lack thereof, of countless people. Even so, we still need to look at the rationale behind the construction of race, the creation of racists and the ways in which racism is part of neoliberalism and has become institutionalised so we can decipher just how humanity became so divided (Goldberg, 2009).

In deeming different ethnic and darker-skinned groups in 'distant' geographies (from the metropole, that is) 'barbaric' and 'wretched', everything associated with them would carry the same label. For example, the cultural practices, spiritualities, languages, customs, beliefs, lifestyles, economies, social norms, types of dress, expressions of love, hair styles, relationships with ecosystems, land use practices, types of music and styles of dance of 'Others' from 'exotic' places (typically Black, Brown and Indigenous people) were often deemed 'profane' or 'uncivilised' (Said, 2012) In turn, colonisers, in conjunction with their penchants to accumulate and dispossess, wanted to impose shame on, humiliate or just extract free labour from these invented 'Others'. The idea for Europeans to brand themselves more worthy and respectable than the rest of the world, largely due to a difference in melanin levels, stems partially from the colour symbolism used in the bible, which associates 'White' with good and 'black' with evil (that is, the 'Manichaeistic' worldview Fanon [1963] wrote about).

The role of religion (for example, patriarchal Christianity) played a major part in the establishment of racism as people of colour were often regarded as 'enemies of Christ' who must be educated on the 'proper' and 'respectable' ways of living (Dussel, 1998). We will note here that Christianity is not a monolith, and that there are also plenty of Christians in the world who are committed to anti-racist politics and emancipatory praxis. Nevertheless, European colonisers thought of themselves as intellectual, learned and benevolent. They also felt they were 'burdened' with capturing and spreading their way of viewing and ordering the world to 'Others' (Kipling, 1998 [1899]). Fanon noted this arrogant racialism was the epidermalisation of *superiority*. Opposition to European values and parochial religious dogma was punishable for newly labelled inferior races, yet resistance always remained. It is important to note that while most history books call for 'modern development', and present-day advertisements for international aid often erase the political agency and creativity of 'Third World' people, both have always been present and remain. People and communities across the Majority World/Global South and peripheral North are often still represented as poor and pitiable subjects; exotic or erotic others; noble or threatening savages;

or incapable or impediments to development. This is a product of race, nation and hierarchy, and important to be aware of and push back against.

Cheap shots and sucker punches

> Europe undertook the leadership of the world with ardour, cynicism, and violence.
>
> Fanon (1963: 311)

Now that we have an understanding as to why European colonisers thought that they were of an advanced race and that it was their duty to improve 'backward' civilisations by mass genocide and forcibly imposing European lifestyles and respectability politics on 'Others', we will now explain how imperialists (and colonial states) benefited from the forms of racism they institutionalised. As Fanon (1963), it was imperative for colonisers to spread the belief – by any means necessary – that their economic policies, spiritual beliefs, and socio-cultural norms were superior to those of darker-skinned people so that they could plant psychological seeds of doubt and self-loathing in the minds of said 'inferior' races. This is a form of mass racial gaslighting called 'internalised oppression' that can affect the psyches and self-perceptions of those who are exposed to institutionalised racism.

Under colonialism, there is always the risk that people can be targeted, inculcated and trapped into thinking they belong to an archaic civilisation, outmoded form of social organisation, or that they are less beautiful because of their skin colour, hair texture or physical attributes. One famous example of this is the Kenneth and Mamie Clarke 'Doll Test' that was used in the historic *Brown v Board of Education* (1954) case that was instrumental in desegregating US public schools. However, as Kiri Davis' short documentary *A girl like me* (2005) illustrates, the perverse effects of internalised racism continue to play out in the psyche of youth today. This is a powerful and cruel process, but was effective and useful for colonisers regarding domination. Fanon (1967: 13) termed it 'the epidermalisation of *inferiority*', and went on to note that the oppressed will often – as a result of institutionalised racism and psychosocial manipulation – 'believe the worst about themselves'.

People who see themselves as worthless are easier to exploit and control. From the coloniser's point of view, it is also easier to justify exploiting and enslaving 'Others' if they are deemed 'subhuman' or have 'empty souls'. Likewise, from a racist point of view, it follows that in order for abject subjects to improve and fit into the scope of what colonisers saw as fully human and deserving of dignity, 'Others' must be conscripted into colonial value and belief systems of self-proclaimed more 'advanced' and 'developed' civilisations (that is, White, Western, bourgeois) (Rodney, 2018). Ironically, these 'advanced' civilisations were murdering, raping and subjugating people who refused their impositions or saw the world differently. Regrettably, these behaviours on the part of self-avowed 'more developed' nations still remain.

As previously mentioned, racism plays a pivotal role in capitalist exploitation and processes of accumulation by dispossession, both in colonial-era and contemporary societies. The primary objective of European (and later US) invaders was to dispossess lands, accumulate resources and spread Eurocentrism as widely as possible in order to enshrine their own economic systems, individualistic-liberal values and colonial-capitalist worldviews (Fanon, 1963). With colonialism, then, came deeply embedded colour-class hierarchies, which, of course, favoured wealthy White people, generally men, and deemed them the elite and 'masters of mankind'. White land-, estate- and plantation-owners were thereby able to unleash colonial worldviews and racial labels upon Indigenous, Black and Brown bodies towards the end of elimination and/or enslavement. Certain humans, under colonial-capitalist social arrangements, could then be sent on death marches, yoked in chains, molested at will, overworked till death, treated as property, captured and purchased, hunted if free, cast aside and disposed of (Maldonado-Torres, 2007). Estate owners benefited from the violence of enclosure and confinement in the form of maximising profits due to having a bonded labour force, a claim to private property and the 'rule of law' (judicial system) of a liberal (militarised) state to protect their interests.

Under this colonial ordering of the world, wealth and power became concentrated among upper-class and ruling elites, which was no product of hard work, but rather, because the institutions colonisers and white supremacists built and continue to maintain are the product of globalised ego and greed, and were essentially achieved by throwing sucker punches, cheap shots and betraying humanity. While race is inextricably linked to capitalism; its exploitative penchants not only harm the negatively racialised (for example, working-class families, cash-poor groups). In brief, class stratification, too, is part of the ongoing colonial state of things (that is, capitalism), and there will be no end to the persistent coloniality of modernity if there is also not a mass commitment to class struggle, anti-classist dissent and gender justice operating in tandem with anti-racist politics. So goes the colonial status quo, which, whether most care to acknowledge it or not, continues to define much of the world today. Notably, the role of education as well as gender and power relations must not be looked over, which is where we now turn.

Banking model education

We determined that a report card or certificate of study was not necessary, and it was the same in the case of an evaluation and exam:

that a certain number of questions will be given to students and if they
answer correctly, then they pass ... we concluded this was not right.
Dorotoreo, Zapatista education promoter (*La Escuelita* 'Little
School of Freedom According to the Zapatistas' gathering)

Freire's (2018) notion of critical consciousness focuses on education that
facilitates achieving liberation through engaged pedagogies and dialectical
methods that allow students to have a voice and participate. Mainstream
neoliberal education, including most conventional (colonial) practices of
pedagogy and teaching methods, often suppress and silence the voices of
the oppressed, marginalised and people who do not hold credentials or
have authority in any given space. Hence, it is only fitting that pedagogy
be placed in the service of liberation, and that classrooms become vibrant
sites of discussion, discovery, encounter and sharing. Here, Freire criticises
orthodox education due to its overreliance on what he refers to as the
'banking' or 'transmission' model of education. This type of pedagogy does
not inspire student engagement, participation, dialectics or self-actualisation.
For students, while learning is effortful and at times uncomfortable, it should
also be equally as meaningful and enlivening.

Under banking modelled pedagogies, a teacher, lecturer or professor's role
is to 'deposit' pre-approved knowledge into students who are inculcated
to take for granted the authority of the expert in the room, sit in silent
isolation, record notes and memorise and regurgitate information. Banking
model approaches are now so ubiquitous and banal that they are not readily
recognised by universities, administrators and even some faculty members as
being fundamentally anti-democratic and stifling human development. We
would argue that banking model education is also colonial – it is a process
of domestication, a proverbial death by PowerPoint and a performance of
deferring to professional credentials all at once. And while, of course, there
are teachers and lecturers who are wonderful and knowledgeable, and that
direct instruction (for example, lectures) is generative in some instances, to
be expected to passively absorb professorial 'expertise' without being able
to participate, speak or query it is not an education at all.

Banking modelled pedagogy limits student autonomy, imagination and
analytical development as it either hinders or does not even allow learners to
work out ideas with each other and their teachers, lecturers and professors.
This has devastating consequences when it comes to developing critical
thinking, media literacy, and even social skills. Banking model education
coerces students into accepting the status quo by manufacturing consent
and suppressing political education. It signals to students, as well as lecturers
and professors, that they should be more devoted to institutional protocols and
bureaucratic convention than fighting exploitation and unsettling the
ongoing colonial order of things. Creating a sense of alienation for poor,

working-class or 'Othered' students, the banking model divorces education and pedagogy from the socio-cultural and economic realities in which people live. This is ironic given how much most universities purportedly care about 'student experience', yet not too surprising, given that most universities are upper- and middle-class spaces demarcated by bourgeois (read 'professional') decorum. Fuck that. So long as managers and lecturers are content with performative respectability politics and 'putting on a good show', institutional hierarchies, authoritarian relations and banking module education – that is, the status quo – will remain the same.

Freire proposes critical consciousness and praxis as antidotes; encouraging students (and administrators and lecturers) to identify the historical roots of current global challenges, while seeking out possible solutions to them. It is not unreasonable to argue that foregrounding critical consciousness, praxis and political education in classrooms will consequently mark the beginning of a new era, an era that attacks and challenges Eurocentric conventions, neoliberal ideas and staid exclusionary ways of doing things, as well putting an end to the suffering and plights of targeted and oppressed communities and people.

The fact of the matter remains that universities are domesticating forces and disciplinary institutions for those who harbour dissident liberatory politics. Academics, lecturers, professors and researchers – in signing contracts, performing labour and following university rules – are captured. They become complicit with and culpable for the reproduction and (re)instantiation of oppressive institutions, relations and structures. This is all despite the acts of resistance and reluctance some engage in and feel when doing so. Students deserve better. That said, figuring out how to carve out space and time within universities to pursue praxis and operate unencumbered from authority and bourgeois decorum while avoiding complicity with a neoliberal and colonial status quo remains a crux for anyone in a university who is committed to freedom.

Clearly, within neoliberal academia, there is no pure form of either emancipatory praxis or perfect place for resistance. Nevertheless, the desire to maintain revolutionary convictions, topple repressive structures and spark hope – not to mention the fact that some academics and students feel education must be defended from colonial worldviews, capitalist logics and androcentric knowledge – is what keeps so many of us signing on and showing up to struggle in universities.

Feminist ethics and dissent

bell hooks (2014a: 39), in writing about how feminist ethics can assist us in co-creating better worlds, notes: 'When women and men understand that working to eradicate patriarchal domination is a struggle rooted in the longing to make a world where everyone can live fully and freely, then we know our work to be a gesture of love. ... Let us draw upon that love to heighten our awareness, deepen our compassion, intensify our courage, and strengthen our commitment.' When we speak of feminist ethics and praxis, we note that feminism has a great deal of heterogeneity, and comes with many currents of thought and practice (Code, 2002; Collins, 2002). However, our reading of a feminist ethic does not find fertile representation in the types of 'empowerment' or grievances peddled by neoliberal, entrepreneurial, bourgeois or transphobic feminists, who are arguably not feminist at all. Such neoliberal or 'mainstream' feminisms are a rehash of heteropatriarchal norms for a modern society. As analyses of the #MeToo movement show (Phipps, 2020), the movement has developed from the Black feminisms of liberation, which originally had an explicit focus on structural inequality at the intersections of race, class and feminism, to now become a public show of punishment for individual 'bad men'. The argument being that the 'political whiteness' at play within mainstream feminism not only leaves violent structures intact (that is, the carceral system, entrepreneurial capitalism), but also invests in institutions that have violence against 'Others' at their core – the judicial system and global capitalist economy being significant examples of this. In other words, mainstream neoliberal feminism, rather than seeking to dismantle oppressive structures and build just and equitable alternatives to them, simply demands equal participation in ongoing violent and oppressive structures and exploitative institutions that continue to alienate and dominate others, as well as develops liberal award cultures within systems of exploitation and repression to ostensibly evidence and reward 'progress' made by either individuals (which does nothing for the collective) or corporations.

In considering the 'coloniality of gender', Lugones (2008) argues that the dominant binary gender system that operates today was imposed by processes of European colonisation. Extending on arguments of race and colonialism – particularly Quijano's (2000) ideas on the imposition and development of racial difference by colonisers – Lugones suggests that gender is to be included in our ongoing struggles against coloniality. Specifically, Lugones (2008: 85) notes that through the imperative of European capitalism 'the imposition of this gender system was as constitutive of the coloniality of power as the coloniality of power was constitutive of it'. It is through this multi-layered, intersectional feminist lens that Eurocentric patriarchal norms are made noticeable, that sexism and gender-based violence are exposed, and that binary views of gender and sexuality are questioned, queered and subverted.

Crass (2013) elaborates on patriarchal societies, noting that they are formed and built on the policies made by men that reinforce male supremacy, dominance and androcentrism across social institutions. Patriarchal social norms then develop, which encourage people to believe that men are the superior beings since they alone acquire the ability to 'reason', while women or 'females' are 'emotional', weaker and lack logic. Patriarchal cultural mores dictate, both overtly and subtly, how individuals 'perform' according to a rigid and dichotomous gender-sexuality system (Butler, 2011). The role of patriarchy in exploitation and capital accumulation on the global scale also cannot go overlooked (Mies, 1998). Committing to feminist ethics, in turn, means tenaciously mobilising against gender-based violence; prioritising consent; recognising that the sexualisation and exploitation of women is dehumanising; not blaming victims when they are targeted for rape, assault or harassment; and that the labour of social reproduction is for everyone (not just women), to name but a few.

However, the active and collective participation in efforts of gender justice is of vital importance for all of humanity. Developing feminist consciousness prompts the realisation that we are all limited by archaic patriarchal doctrines. For example, prevailing hegemonic definitions of what it means to 'be a man' and ideas about masculinity confine men in very small boxes (Connell and Messerschmidt, 2005). Being compelled to be 'macho', 'alpha' or a 'big man' is disputably a discursive straitjacket and comes with a host of deleterious upshots, both socially and psychologically. Crass (2013) explains that consequences of patriarchal social relations on men include emotional isolation, low self-esteem, increasing fear of failure and increased risk-taking behaviour. Furthermore, such behaviours and psychological states have the potential to lead to destructive coping mechanisms, including workaholism or drug and alcohol addiction or impulsive and violent behaviour as ways of performing masculinity (Miedzian, 2002). Notably, men, as well as women and others, can all be complicit in reproducing these gender norms. As Federici (2004) argues, the reification of the binary system of gender works to uphold the capitalist system by framing gender along teleological reproductive terms, wherein the division of labour is split into productive and reproductive, excluding women from many aspects of public life. In short, feminist ethics are for everyone.

Lugones' (2008) account of gender and coloniality is motivated by a desire to find practical alternatives to the current hegemonic system. In claiming that gender has been affected by colonial worldviews, we are not stating that gender was non-existent prior to colonialism; rather, we are acknowledging how narrow and fixed characterisations and performances of femininity and masculinity serve colonial–capitalist and heteropatriarchal agendas of domination and expansion. One practical solution is provided by Ahmed (2017), who notes that in order to make sense of and ultimately change an unjust world is to become a 'killjoy'. Feminist killjoys challenge oppressive institutions and ideologies with the ultimate goal of creating the world anew, a world in which no one is ridiculed, repressed or alienated by deeply entrenched patriarchal norms and structures. Feminist killjoys, while often derided by liberal bystanders who benefit from or are not injured by the status quo, are doing necessary and important work. It is not always easy to be 'that person' who unsettles the room or social gathering – the one who calls out the taken-for-granted and damaging convention that leads people to suffer in silence.

On this point, political revolutionary Claudia Jones (1949) identifies capitalism as one point source of exploitation and domination, particularly for women who are negatively racialised and working-class. In turn, we wonder what the development of feminist ethics and consciousness might look like, and how being a killjoy would play out in the face of neoliberal capitalism. Markedly, developing feminist politics is a key part of advancing critical consciousness and political education; where we no longer rely on passive modes of learning (that is, the banking model), but instead challenge whether colonial and masculinist institutions such as Eurocentric gender norms and liberal aspirations are indeed benefiting humanity. Notably, developing critical consciousness is a political act that ensures the social inequalities that are part of daily life are exposed and opposed. As such, the Zapatistas, who have both recognised and are acting on the various social and gender inequalities that plague the planet and threaten life, provide an example of working towards justice via political education as a means of bringing forth a world wherein we abandon the ridicule, repression and alienation of liberal-capitalist norms and heteropatriarchal structures, which we detail in the pages to come, in Chapters 7 and 8.

7

Political education and radical pedagogy

If you could go to all those corners of our moribund planet, what would you do? Well, we don't know what you'd do, but we Zapatistas, nosotros, nosotras, nosotroas would go to learn. To dance, too, of course, but we don't think the two are mutually exclusive.

EZLN (2020)

A fire in the master's house is set

The namesake of the Zapatistas and the Zapatista Army of National Liberation (*Ejército Zapatista de Liberación Nacional*, EZLN) calls back to Emiliano Zapata (Marcos and de Leon, 2002), the agrarian revolutionary who organised and led the Liberation Army of the South's peasant struggle under the rallying cry '¡*Tierra y libertad!*' ('Land and freedom!') during the Mexican Revolution (1910–20). The emergence of the contemporary Zapatista communities (comprised of rural Indigenous villages, bases of support and autonomous municipalities), and the EZLN (their army) dates back to 17 November 1983. The EZLN is an armed politico-military organisation inclusive of a hierarchy, strict rules, disciplined training and prepared insurgents. It is guided by Clandestine Revolutionary Indigenous Committees (CCRIs) – a group of appointed delegates and elders that direct the EZLN, but only after participatory consultation with Zapatista communities.

The EZLN is distinct from the more horizontalist Zapatista communities and movement-at-large, yet is comprised of freely associating volunteers, put in the service of collective self-defence, and fighting to eventually put down their weapons, that is, 'for peace'. While internally the EZLN is not democratic, its general command is. That is, the EZLN receives its 'marching orders' from Zapatista communities. In late 1983, a handful, six, as most accounts report, university-educated militants with connections to members of the *Las Fuerzas de Liberación Nacional* (FLN) journeyed into the Lacandon Jungle of Chiapas, which is Mexico's most impoverished state, to establish a guerrilla vanguard to fight for and bring about a socialist future (Ramírez and Carlsen, 2008). This is largely seen as the genesis of the EZLN.

On arriving in the jungle and 'mountains of the Mexican southeast', their efforts, which were being supported by an intricate network of sympathisers with links to dissident Marxists, liberation theologists and proletarian socialists, were subsequently transformed by the Indigenous (largely Maya) communities, culture and *cosmovisión* (worldview) they encountered. Notably, the lifeblood and driving force at the heart of Zapatismo in its current form, as well as one of the aspects of the movement that receives the least amount of attention and credit, are the Indigenous worldviews and ways of being/ organising that define Zapatista communities and democratic processes. At the time of the uprising, Indigenous communities in Chiapas were living through and continuing to withstand five centuries of ongoing colonial violence, land dispossession, *encomienda* (plantation) bondage, landowner exploitation, ruling-class arrogance and racist humiliation (Collier and Quaratiello, 2005). What ensued thenceforth was over a decade of rural clandestine organising, mutual aid, reciprocal learning and collective discernment in the face of the trauma of plantation relations and exploitation under global capitalism (Marcos, 2005b; Stahler-Sholk, 2007).

This brings us up to 1994, the year the North American Free Trade Agreement (NAFTA) was set to take effect. The ramifications of the NAFTA were so intensely visceral for peasants and subsistence farmers across Mexico that the Zapatistas, who are primarily from Indigenous Ch'ol, Tzeltal, Tzotzil, Tojolobal, Mam and Zoque communities in southern Mexico, dubbed the century's most vaunted free trade agreement a 'death certificate' for Indigenous people (Gutierrez, 1996). This is because the 'free trade' arrangement of the NAFTA would eliminate price controls for domestic products (for example, coffee), and imported surplus products, chiefly subsidised corn from the US, would inundate Mexican markets and undercut crops and food commodities being produced by Mexican *campesinas* (peasant farmers) and rural landworkers. The outcome of this 'agricultural dumping', which is the exportation of subsidised products to other markets and countries at prices well below those of the receiving nation's home-grown goods in order to destabilise local competition, was the uprooting and displacement of thousands of working-poor and subsistence farmers from their countryside communities and homes (Fanjul and Fraser, 2003). Moreover, the NAFTA was initiated in conjunction with the Mexican state's reform to Article 27 of the constitution, which opened the door to land privatisation and foreclosed possibilities for communal *ejidos* (land holding), which is part of what Emiliano Zapata and the anarchist *Magonistas*[1] were fighting for during the Mexican Revolution (Nuijten, 2003).

In turn, Mexican farmers and food producers, many Indigenous, were simultaneously losing land, being ousted from their communities and having their livelihoods stripped away. Rapid urbanisation then ensued as dispossessed landworkers sought employment in *maquiladoras* (industrial warehouses and sweatshop factories where labour conditions are highly exploitative, abusive and dangerous) that were mounting in number because of increases in foreign capital, external investment and financial speculation (Jordaan, 2012). It is key to note here that 'free trade' and the growing presence of transnational corporations represent direct threats to the livelihood strategies and ways of being for peasants and Indigenous people, which is true not only in the context of Central America, but also all over the world. Other Mexican peasants and landworkers made vulnerable by the NAFTA were left with no other choice than to attempt to cross the border and to try to socially reproduce themselves in family-splitting foreign worker programmes or risk exposure, border enforcement antagonism, police hostility, indeterminate confinement, internment and dehydration in the desert by journeying to the US as undocumented workers and migrant labour (Green, 2011; Otero, 2011).

In the face of this global political-economic deck-stacking by an international consortium of the neoliberal technocrats and 'First-World'-aspiring Mexican state officials, the Zapatistas armed themselves and readied for battle – 'Against neoliberalism, for humanity', Then, on the eve of New Year's Day 1994, the day the NAFTA was set to take effect, insurgents from the EZLN threw down the gauntlet against both global capitalism and its ruling-class administrators (Clarke and Ross, 1994). Under the cover of mask and fog, organised regiments and equipped Zapatista guerrillas stormed out of the shadows to declare '¡Ya basta!' ('Enough is enough!') to the malevolence and deprivation that had been historically, and was continuing to be, foisted on them (Marcos and de Leon, 2002). During the insurrection,

Figure 7.1: An assembly building where Zapatistas practice participatory democracy. Images include an insurgent woman from the EZLN, Emiliano Zapata, Maya people in customary attire, corn and a woman with a paliacate (bandana) representing their (the Zapatistas') collective heart

the EZLN stormed cities, occupied government buildings, freed political prisoners, burned plantation land deeds, set fire to the trumped-up arrest records of Indigenous political organisers who were unduly criminalised, announced Zapatista 'Women's Revolutionary Law', expelled *hacienda*-owners, ousted plantation overseers and exchanged bullets with the Mexican army (Khasnabish, 2013). To put it succinctly, the Zapatistas set fire to the 'master's house' (Lorde, 2018).

Who must ask for pardon?

The fighting lasted for a total of only 12 days and garnered a prominent amount of international media attention and empathy for the Zapatistas. It was a political opportunity they took advantage of via a poetic public relations campaign that made use of news reports and a nascent internet (Cleaver, 1998). As the skirmishes came to a halt, attempts to broker a peace agreement, the San Andrés Accords, ensued. The San Andrés Accords mandated that the Mexican government must concretely recognise the dignity, rights, culture and lands of Indigenous people. The negotiations, however, eventually stalled, and after years of government equivocation ultimately failed due to the deceit, betrayal and duplicity of the state and its acolytes (Speed and Reyes, 2002; Rus et al, 2003).

Of note, is that immediately following the uprising in January 1994, the President of Mexico, Carlos Salinas de Gortari, offered absolution to Zapatista insurgents who would put down their arms and disaffiliate from the movement. While doing so, President Salinas continued to militarise the region and christened Subcomandante Marcos (the spokesperson [not the leader] of the movement) a 'traitor', 'usurper' and 'professional of violence'. At this time, the state also began promising any Indigenous Zapatista that they would be 'pardoned' if they paid heed to his words to surrender, submit and acquiesce to the government's demands. The Zapatistas, through a communiqué penned by Subcomandante Marcos entitled '*Amnistía*' ('Amnesty') (Henck, 2007: 213), responded with a potent combination of militant irony and tactical query that has come to characterise the movement (Katzenberger, 1995; Martín, 2004; Di Piramo, 2011). Their impassioned, irreverent and creatively disrespectful reply to the state's offer of 'forgiving them' for their uprising and rebellion, worth reading in its entirety, but only shared in part here, reads as follows (Marcos and de Leon, 2002):

> Why do we need to be pardoned?
> What are we to be pardoned for? For not dying of hunger? For not accepting misery in silence? For not accepting humbly the historic burden of disdain and abandonment? For having risen up in arms after we found all other paths closed? For not heeding the Chiapas Penal

Code, one of the most absurd and repressive in history? For showing the rest of the country and the whole world that human dignity still exists even among the world's poorest peoples?

For having been carefully prepared before we began our uprising? For carrying guns into battle rather than bows and arrows? For being Mexicans? For being mainly Indigenous people? For calling on the people of Mexico to fight by whatever means necessary for that which belongs to them? For fighting for freedom, democracy and justice? For not following the example of previous guerrilla armies?

For refusing to surrender? For not giving up? For not selling out? For not betraying our cause?

Who must ask for pardon – and who can grant it?

Since that time, and despite an ongoing counterinsurgency being spearheaded by the Mexican government and the paramilitaries it finances (Marcos, 2018), the Zapatistas have concentrated their efforts on establishing a peaceful existence that centres their Indigenous notion of *sts'ikel vokol* (from the Tzotzil). *Sts'ikel vokol* is a polysemic term that roughly translates as 'resistance', but when thoroughly explained is better understood as 'withstanding suffering' (Brown, 2013). More precisely, as elaborated on by a Zapatista *votán* (guardian of the heart of the people) during *la Escuelita*, the term signifies a withstanding of the suffering generated by the injurious products of capitalist social relations, state power, colonial hierarchies, racist and misogynistic mentalities and xenophobia, to name but a few.

Markedly, when speaking of 'resistance', one must tread cautiously because it is at once a capacious and contested term (Baaz et al, 2016). Moreover, its myriad roots run deep and its countless rhizomes span far (Zibechi, 2012). However, when resistance is defined in the manner the Zapatistas express it, that is, withstanding suffering, possibilities blossom, possibilities that resistance can mean convivial empathy and emotional labour, as well as compassion and mutual aid, regardless of one's background and standing or time and place. Resistance, hence, can be as generative of a forward action as it is a militant response of defence.

In addition to engendering decolonial praxis via fortifying their communities and culture against the existential threats posed by capitalism, colonialism and heteropatriarchy (Harvey, 2016), the Zapatistas are pursuing *lekil kuxlejal*, roughly meaning 'living well in reciprocal dignity and collective harmony'. Broadly speaking, the Zapatista solution to the problems of alienation and annihilation that have been marshalled in by colonial-capitalist modernity, as well as escalated by heteropatriarchal relations, has been constructing autonomy through building that 'world where many worlds fit' detailed earlier. It is with a focus on the Zapatista creation of an inclusive and dignified 'pluriverse' (Escobar, 2018) that we address some of the key pillars of their resistance, autonomy and destabilisation of colonial-capitalist modernity, all of which have political education at their heart.

Autonomous (rebel) education

> In our dream, children are children, and their work is to be children. ... I do not dream of the agrarian redistribution, of big mobilisations, of the fall of the government and elections, and the victory of a left-wing party, or whatever.
> I dream of the children, and I see them being children.
>
> Subcomandante Marcos

Collectively, we have been able to learn several valuable and transformative lessons about what education can be based on learning about the Zapatista struggle. Some of us have been able to spend time in Zapatista territory, while others continue to learn about what their communities are co-creating from afar. What has resonated with us most powerfully is the humble, hospitable and heart-filled disposition the Zapatistas engender while simultaneously embodying defiance and unwavering courage in the face of violent incursions into their lands. The violence they experience, which is both discursive and material, and, we would suggest, is rooted in colonialism, manifests itself through capitalism, institutionalised racism, state power, neoliberal policies, paramilitary aggression and extractivist-driven damage to the environment.

Despite the violence, critical consciousness and steadfast liberatory convictions – coupled with caring and compassionate politics – define the Zapatista resistance. These aspects of their rebellion are reflected in the principles of Zapatismo and are made evident every day in how they approach grassroots education. And because Zapatista education is an ongoing process of community-based praxis that centres the infamous cry for '*Tierra y libertad!*' ('Land and freedom!') mentioned earlier, it means their pedagogy is holistic, engaged and land-based.

Zapatista education is rooted in political struggle, an awareness of injustice and a commitment to social transformation. Paralleling concepts similar to those touched on in Paulo Freire's (2018) *Pedagogy of the oppressed*, the Zapatistas focus on how the poor and dispossessed have been and continue to be targeted for subjugation and domination, as well as ways in which they can collectively work towards liberation when placed under the shadow of power. This entails shedding light on the injurious contradictions, hypocrisies and paradoxes that arise from the capitalist economy, colonial institutions and heteropatriarchal norms.

For the Zapatistas, education involves learning, organising and speaking 'from below and the left', a phrase with multiple meanings, signifying both 'from the heart' and working non-hierarchically from the grassroots without seeking prestige or accolades. The Zapatista approach can thereby be thought of as a form of popular emancipatory education which recognises that education is never politically 'neutral', particularly in conflict-affected contexts in which poverty and oppression are created by capitalist exploitation, racialism and concentrated state power. The rebel autonomous schools they have constructed thereby means the Zapatistas are embodying the spirit of revolt, systemically engaging in the practice of freedom, and that each lesson they teach is one more insubordinate step away from the state, as well as an outright rejection of capitalist profit logics and neoliberal ideals.

The topics of education taken into consideration when developing the curriculum for each Zapatista community consist of core subjects related to reading, writing, maths and science. In addition, there is a heavy focus on the revolutionary history of Mexico; each region's respective Indigenous language(s)/customs; anti-consumerist perspectives regarding land and nature; gender equity through Zapatista 'Women's Revolutionary Law'; and the historical and geopolitical context of the Zapatista struggle. Because the Zapatistas often refer to capitalism as the caustic 'hydra' mentioned at the outset (one of their many definitions for it), their schools do not glorify profit-seeking or teach entrepreneurialism, individualism or competition. Rather, Zapatista lessons see students engaging in collective work, mutual aid, critical thought, self-reflexivity and planting food. Other key themes in Zapatista education include community health/hygiene, arts and crafts, as well as singing, dancing, storytelling and physical education/play.

At the Zapatista communities we were able to visit, there were weekly lessons that took place via film screenings (enthusiastically referred to as '*Cine Pirate*' ['Pirate Cinema']), which involved an amiable and good-natured education promoter theatrically explaining the often-unseen power relations, politics and systems present in the film. This same education promoter later held numerous conversations on the topics of subjectification, Maya *cosmovisión* and languages, decolonisation, discourse analysis, communal relationality, accumulation by dispossession, gender justice, polysemy/semiotics, anti-power, modernity's view of time versus alternative perspectives on time, NGO'ification, critical geopolitics, critical pedagogy and Freirean conscientisation, among many others. We mention this not to suggest these topics are representative of the entire Zapatista curriculum, but rather to highlight the ingenuity and eclecticism of the Zapatistas, as well as to provide a small glimpse of what type of 'teachers' and content Zapatista students engage and spend time with.

This type of education ultimately prepares learners for community roles that they might later take up as they advance through the system, grow older and develop their own interests. Democratic process and community decision-making skills thereby constitute lessons that are learned via Zapatista education. Notably, an unapologetic critique of power, exploitation, individualism, imperial history, capitalist logics and colonial institutions – in conjunction with an emphasis on the value of land and freedom – are part of the curriculum. The strong sense of togetherness and political consciousness that are encouraged within Zapatista autonomous schools consequently attenuate alienation and allow the communities to safeguard their Indigenous worldview and values of collectivity, relationality and radical ('from the roots') democracy.

Organising political education

As stated, Zapatista autonomous education system seeks to develop and protect the movement's Indigenous *cosmovisión*, languages and practice of self-determination, including their shared political, social and cultural autonomy (Baronnet, 2008, 2012). After their 1994 uprising, the Zapatistas desired an education system that was more in line with their Indigenous approach to communal land relationships, cooperative work, participatory democracy, agroecological practices and production and sharing of knowledge. More readily, they wanted education to be put at the service of their communities, rural livelihood strategies, solidarity economy, political consciousness, spiritual wellbeing and collective memory. They also aspired to have an education system that would be ran by and for their communities, encourage and allow for local sustainable development, and maintain and foster intergenerational ties on an everyday basis. Moreover, they wanted to build relationships that were to be imbued with values that departed from the top-down 'aid' focus of liberal NGOs and the orthodoxy of conventional (capitalist) 'development' agendas.

In short, the Zapatistas see themselves as Indigenous people and communities-in-struggle who are a part of Mexico but want to be free from neoliberal models of education that are being pushed by the state (Shenker, 2012). While the state of Chiapas is rich in biodiversity and 'natural resources', it is 'poor' in financial terms, conventional development indicators and per capita income. Although these metrics are all limited, partial and problematic, they are nevertheless instructive apropos what communities are abandoned by and experience deprivation under colonial-capitalism. This all meant that schools, medical centres and employment opportunities for Indigenous and peasant communities in Chiapas were substandard and lacking for generations on end. When it came to economic development and education, countless Indigenous people across southern Mexico were cornered, often having to accept the charity and cultural values of missionaries, bourgeois, purportedly 'non-political' NGOs and state teachers – who, despite being well-intentioned at times – often promoted worldviews and held ideals that were not defined by Indigenous communities themselves.

Prior to the 1994 uprising and even the formation of the EZLN in the jungles of rural Chiapas in 1983, inaccessible education and institutionalised racism and classism posed a serious problem for an untold number of peasant and Indigenous families. The political manifestation of the Zapatista movement, alongside its grassroots character and Indigenous heart, thereby went a long way towards ensuring that the educational needs of Indigenous villages throughout the countryside could be fulfilled. In addition to constructing an independent system of organic political education within their rebel territories, the Zapatistas began organising an autonomous system of healthcare in rural Chiapas. The Zapatistas were dissatisfied with the education and language programmes that were being imposed by government institutions, as well as growing weary of facing neglect, racism and disdain on account of being Indigenous when they entered public institutions – so they built their own schools and hospitals.

It is important to note that the Zapatistas maintained that the government education system in Chiapas was of poor quality vis-à-vis *political* education; neglectful of provisions that would accommodate Indigenous worldviews and languages; and was generally inaccessible for remote villages. Put differently, state schools were neither culturally safe nor even reachable for the rural peasant farmers and Maya communities. The failure to properly fund an educational system responsive to the cultural needs of the Indigenous people left Zapatista communities with an insatiable appetite for the development of a new, alternative education system.

Given the state was either unwilling or incapable of accommodating the rural Indigenous villages, local Maya communities united together to create a viable alternative that took a community-centred approach to education. Notably, the schools were set up where local Indigenous people could access them, and were sometimes constructed in the former estate houses of plantation owners. The creation of Zapatista autonomous education was established and has since transformed education across their rebel territories. The Zapatistas, of course, often note that their education system is a mutable work in progress. Accordingly, their lesson plans and curriculum make use of Indigenous linguistic traditions, celebrate local cultural heritage, teach political history and include collective work and organising 'from below' (Fitzwater, 2019).

According to the Zapatista communities, their rebel autonomous education system has several objectives. From a cultural perspective and due to their Maya roots, even though there are distinct Maya groups in different zones, they incorporate Indigenous traditions, celebrations, cuisine, spiritual practices and beliefs, medicinal practices and agroecological techniques, to name but a few, into their schools. Thus, Zapatista youth learn about identity, culture, politics, gender and power relations, and history from their own community members. From this, the role of education takes on a new form; it protects Indigenous cultures, values difference and diversity, and prioritises collectivity and mutual aid. Engaged participation and equality of opportunity across all individuals is encouraged, and the notion of unity and struggle across difference is often built into day-to-day learning.

Bending discourse, being 'otherly'

The Zapatistas foreground inclusion and foster an appreciation and respect for diversity in their education system. Through our experience in their territories and engagements with Zapatismo, we have come across numerous intersectional discussions surrounding race, class, gender, sexuality, ability, difference and 'othering', some specifically relating to queer struggle. While in the *caracol* (administrative centre) of Oventik, we heard the phrase that Zapatista territory was 'a home to all who struggle'. Relative to the politics of belonging and inclusion, it is arguable that the Zapatistas are on the leading edge of anti-oppressionist practice. This is perhaps most noticeable in the efforts they have made to queer their discourse, solidarity and praxis. And while it has been reported that gender-variant, queer and transgender people are uncommon among the rural communities, the Zapatistas have also stressed on numerous occasions that queerness and non-conformity – be it in the realm of gender norms, desire or otherwise – is to be neither scolded nor persecuted. This commitment to queer inclusion is reflected when looking at the discourse of the Zapatistas and their frequent explicit use of the word *compañeroas*, sometimes seen as *compañer@s*. *Compañeras*, for context, is the Spanish term of affinity, camaraderie and solidarity used by Zapatistas – *compa* for short. There is no precise translation because it is a polysemic signifier that roughly means 'companion-comrade-coworker-accomplice-friend'. Given the gendered nature of Spanish, it is conventionally expressed as *compañero* (masculine) or *compañera* (feminine). More recently, the Zapatistas have been using *compañer@* or *compañeroa* as a political move to hold space and include people of all genders and identities.

Akin to this, there are several international Zapatista communiqués addressing the issue of queerness through references to *otras amores*, which translates as 'other loves' and acknowledges LGBTQI+ community members. In many respects, the Zapatistas have reclaimed and transformed the word 'other', which has typically been used to negatively racialise different groups. That is, given the Zapatistas understand all too well how being socially 'othered' (negatively racialised, stigmatised and stereotyped) leads to repression, exclusion and violence against marginalised groups, they subversively have taken up the word 'other', transformed it into the adjective 'otherly', and have begun using it as a political yet playful compliment and mark of respect. We should all be so lucky as to be very '*otherly*'. Thus, the prospect of being the 'other' (*otroa* or *otr@*) is now a signifier of positive regard in the discourse of Zapatismo. This recuperation of the word 'other' stems in part from the recognition that queer and transgender people have been 'othered', that the Zapatistas themselves have been 'othered', and, as a result, they can relate to people who are persecuted because of who they are through a shared experience of being cast as very '*otherly*'.

These whimsical yet solidaristic shifts in language have made the topic of 'difference' visible in Zapatista communities, but they have not done so in a way that positions difference as abject, derogatory or something to be ashamed of. In this way, Zapatismo, when shared in the political terrain of education, and, more precisely, in the classroom, destabilises oppressive binaries in regard to discourses related to gender, sexuality and ways of being. It also inhibits heteronormativity by stifling the shame-inducing rhetoric and acts of abuse and intolerance that being 'different', 'other' or 'queer' so often comes with. Consequently, the queering of discourse the Zapatistas practice brings forth more recognition, regard and respect for non-conformity, while at the same time unsettling rigid dualisms and reductionist categories.

Although the Zapatistas have overcome countless obstacles to reach where they are in the current moment, they still face provocations and differing forms of violence that stem from government counterinsurgency, paramilitary groups, vandalism and harassment, military surveillance and bigotry – not least of which is connected directly to heteropatriarchal norms and gender-based violence. Despite this, one of the key objectives of the Zapatistas is to remain free from dependency on external aid, private capital and ostensibly benevolent philanthropists. They consequently see their rebel autonomous educational system as a key pillar of their self-determination, not to mention a point source of learning to respect and value diversity. In turn, the political education and respect for 'others' attained by Zapatista students throughout their autonomous municipalities as a result of building a rebel school system grows along with each new generation of children who are born into the movement, as well as remains something they both hold precious and continue to defend.

Applying the principles of Zapatismo to pedagogy suggests that differences of identity/ability, cultural exclusions and social hierarchies be explicitly addressed and dealt with in order to achieve widespread social transformation. Zapatismo as an approach to education thereby frames classrooms (in whatever form they may take) as 'spaces of encounter' where 'that which is repressive, is not tolerated'. Put another way, when informed by Zapatismo, the settings where teaching and learning occur become meeting places (figuratively and literally) where people can experience, get to know and listen to 'others'. In this way, practising Zapatismo entails acknowledging 'difference' and power, and making concerted efforts to defy the exclusions and non-belongings that arise as a result of contrasting social axes of identification (race, class, gender, sexuality, ability, age, nationality, belief system, citizenship, and so on). Committing to Zapatismo also involves challenging, contesting and undermining the oppressive, peripherilising and subordinating tendencies surrounding socio-spatially constructed notions of difference, and becoming disobedient in those instances when we are required to be complicit with them or are tacitly expected to be liberal bystanders.

Non-hierarchical decolonial learning

As Tuck and Yang (2012: 1) have so succinctly put it, 'decolonisation is not a metaphor'. Meaning, land is at the heart of decolonisation. And because tending to crops, children, food production/distribution, collective self-determination and a life of rebellion are inherently learning experiences, the Zapatistas have constructed an independent education system that emerges from the bioregional assemblages and cultural-environmental settings within which their communities exist. In a phrase, Zapatistas learn from the land. This is evident in the 'from below' focus they take in their approach to teaching and learning, as well as how they consider everyday life and their ecological surroundings a classroom.

Praxis-based education is fundamental to the Zapatistas. The Zapatista method of engaged education emerges from the unique yet interconnected relational assemblages, shared histories and environmental systems (that is, *places*) that compose their rebel territories. Local knowledge and Indigenous worldviews are so central among their communities that many of the *promotores de educación* (education promoters), *promotores de agroecología* (agroecology promoters) and *promotores de salud* (health promoters) in each school often come from the same *places* (figuratively and literally) as their students and speak the same Indigenous language. The Zapatistas refer to their teachers as 'education promoters' in order to soften the hard boundaries between 'those who know, and those who do not know'. This discursive practice allows them to decentre authority, contravene institutionalised hierarchies of 'expertise' and unsettle any false claims to 'rock star' academic status that could potentially fragment their horizontal system of education.

In day-to-day practice, identifying as education promoters is a step towards subverting the hierarchies and self-centrism that arise in 'modern' institutions that are preoccupied with fallacious notions of meritocracy, professional titles and liberal award cultures. There is little to no tiered distinction or rank-pulling among teachers – everyone is simply and unpretentiously an 'education promoter'. If transferred into university settings, this would be the equivalent of abolishing high paid managers outright, as well as eliminating professionalised bourgeois designations (for example, distinguished, full, senior, associate, assistant, adjunct, sessional) and careerist titles (for example, dean, vice chancellor, president, reader, professor, lecturer, champion) in favour of recognising everyone as an 'education promoter'. It is also a step towards undermining the notion that knowledge can be privatised (mirroring their viewpoints on land and food) and subverting the vertical relationships that arise from the regimes of credentialisation and 'excellence' that govern Western institutions and corporate entities.

Given Zapatista autonomous schools embrace Indigenous cultural traditions and heritage, another aim is to protect the various Maya languages of the region. Indigenous languages are spoken within the households of numerous remote villages scattered across Chiapas' countryside, mountains and forests. Thus, in order to animate and signify the value of their languages, Zapatista schools have created learning materials, books and songs in Indigenous languages. This is a product of the collective work of local education promoters and villagers who teach in the schools. The materials often contain drawings, objects and stories that encourage children to learn the language, letter by letter, day by day. As a result, youth within communities are no longer ashamed and are more enthused about speaking their Indigenous languages. This is not only occurring within their home life, but also for various other daily activities. Although Indigenous languages could be found in some public schools, it was being slowly erased due to the hegemony of Spanish and because the 'language of business' (for example, capitalism, commercials, advertisements) is not spoken in an Indigenous tongue.

This dedication to non-hierarchical practice highlights how the Zapatistas are not tethered to the disciplinary mechanisms of league tables, global rankings, publication lists, 'prestigious' grant monies, CV lengths, high citation counts (which are heavily facilitated by self-promotion, privileged networking or individual ambition), and even email signatures. Rather, Zapatista educators (and researchers, for that matter) are focused on questioning, curiosity, co-learning, practice and dialogue. Such a prospect is made possible through autonomy, humility and centring Indigenous epistemologies, all of which emerge from resisting colonial governance, capitalist social relations, neoliberal mentalities and the trappings of individualism and careerism. Relatedly, each Zapatista school develops its own schedule of lessons through popular assemblies composed of horizontal democratic decision-making that address the needs, concerns and desires of respective communities. This process takes into consideration the ecologies and local environments in which communities are living, and after going through a process of communal discussion, Zapatistas develop a curriculum accordingly.

Further bringing to life decolonial theories that attenuate rigid divisions typically found within capitalist education, the Zapatista schools do not employ hierarchical scales of evaluation. Children are not seen as static empty vessels that need to be filled with information. Rather, they are active agents of creativity, imagination and knowledge in-and-of themselves, who

Figure 7.2: A rebel Zapatista primary school with a mural and inscription that reads: 'Autonomous education builds different worlds where many truthful worlds and their truths fit'

are capable of learning and sharing knowledge with the community, as well as pursuing their own interests. The role of the education promoters is to share experience, provide context and information, offer guidance and direction, and foster a non-punitive environment as children ask questions and follow wonder. This means that there are no strict divisions or reprimands among those who 'know more' and those who 'know less', and that as students go through the learning process, they are not punished for getting things 'wrong'.

Land- and place-based education

The Zapatista autonomous school system is tailored to rural life, agrarian change, solidaristic production and distribution, and the realities faced by Indigenous people. In turn, to further incorporate the practical application of political education in their curriculum, Zapatista students are frequently educated outside the physical classroom. This is so they can sharpen their planting and harvesting skills through the use of organic, sustainable and agroecological farming techniques, as well as learn Indigenous customs and revolutionary history while being connected to their ancestral territories and local ecosystems. For students, this form of education, one in which relationship with land is foregrounded, underscores the importance of learning skills that will support the Zapatistas' efforts in achieving food sovereignty for future generations. It also provides an incisive overview of how transgenic modifications and privatisations of seeds and crops are deemed to be overt threats and blatant attacks on the Zapatistas and their

Maya culture as they are the 'people of the corn', a reality passed down from their Indigenous origin stories (Ross, 2006).

Ecological knowledge, as well as the emphasis the Zapatistas place on agroforestry and food sovereignty, means that the curriculum is saturated with hands-on experiential learning (JBG, 2013d). The schools' teaching methods allow students to discuss and practice an array of differing farming approaches and techniques given that the school year is oriented around planting, harvesting, rainy and dry seasons. Students learn how to cultivate assorted medicinal plants to alleviate ailments, prevent disease and even care for livestock. Moreover, natural sciences, environmental management and the physical sciences are taught in conjunction with practical agroecological lessons, which all serve the community's agricultural activities, cooperative endeavours, pursuit of food sovereignty and alternative solidarity economy. Lessons focus on how students can adapt to and use their surroundings without exploiting nature via low impact chemical-free techniques that can contribute to both their immediate family's livelihood and overall community wellbeing (JBG, 2013b). The communal process of learning encourages students to interact with and help each other. Consequently, 'going to school' for Zapatista children consists of engaging their bioregional surroundings, ancestral knowledge and history of rebellion. This all may very well take the form of and coincide with gardening, tilling, composting, feeding animals and performing a skit about the life of Emiliano Zapata – all of which nurture both the fertility of their local soils – and rebel spirits.

With respect to agroecology, the Zapatistas have made a political and planetary health-focused decision to eliminate the use of genetically modified organisms, chemical insecticides, herbicides and pesticides in favour of biological deterrents and organic fertilisers (Vergara-Camus, 2007). This area of agricultural and land management education stresses the importance of attaining the necessary applied skills to achieve food sovereignty for future generations. It also means the Zapatistas' land-based pedagogy corresponds with efforts they make in sustaining and fortifying their Indigenous epistemologies and forms of knowledge production (for example, centring ancestral wisdom, companion planting, communal work, celebrating Maya customs). Collective, land-based education prompts students to discuss, problem-solve and talk about their rural lives and Indigenous farming practices without embarrassment, which subverts the scorn agrarian peasant communities can experience in the face of the notions of entrepreneurial 'success' promoted by liberal-capitalist institutions that are governed by bourgeois respectability politics and classism.

In addition, children of different ages learn the same subjects together, in the same classrooms, and are taught how to teach each other while doing so. Similarly, there are no final marks distributed that signify a terminal end to the learning process, and there are no grades used to compare students to each other. In this way, Zapatista pedagogy underscores that learning is neither a competition nor something to be 'completed'. Consequently, by steadfastly refusing to relinquish their indigeneity, as well as weaving their ancestral worldviews and Woman's Revolutionary Law (covered more in the following chapter) into their day-to-day teaching and struggle (Eber and Kovic, 2003), the Zapatistas are decolonising their rebel education system by eliminating shame from the process of learning. As their education system is unimpeded by the state, and because it is rooted in defending, protecting and safeguarding their local Indigenous traditions, customs and socio-territorial identities, the Zapatistas effectively engender decolonial praxis in every aspect of their teaching and learning (Barbosa and Sollano, 2014). Ultimately, what they are revealing through their advances in autonomous education, sustainable farming and food sovereignty is that Indigenous worldviews and land-based education offer viable alternatives to our alienating and arguably destructive status quo.

Given these aspects of the Zapatista approach to pedagogy, it is evident that learning under the principles of Zapatismo becomes a decolonial and situated learning experience that is intimately tied to the *places* (that is, land, ecological settings, socio-spatial relationships, oral histories, kinships, customs) their communities are part of. Their education system is a product of Indigenous autonomy and the advancements they have made in non-metaphorically recuperating land and disciplined organising against an exploitative economy and neocolonial state (Silva Montes, 2019). Accordingly, their dedication to collective resistance and mutuality has enabled them to autonomously create a revolutionary process of learning comprised of the continual practice of critical thought, community introspection, collective action and reciprocity. Learning is deeply rooted in intergenerational kinship, questioning convention, being engaged in local physical environments and revitalising the languages, stories and wisdom of ancestors. Hence, what Zapatismo represents for sympathisers, including us, is an invigorating and inspirational possibility with respect to what exists in the way of actually decolonising a curriculum, nurturing critical thought and putting education in the service of freedom.

A capacity for discernment

The Zapatistas have noted that state-sanctioned schools and government legitimated universities have the tendency to become 'corrals of thought domestication'. This is due to the increasing emphasis corporatised higher learning is placing on transforming students and faculty into citizen-consumers and ambitious entrepreneurs. Put differently, the tenets that capitalist education is pushing on students and faculty is that their creative abilities must be reigned-in, packaged and advertised as economically productive skills that can yield profits for respective buyers. In doing so, people in neoliberal universities are suffering, while simultaneously being individualised into oblivion.

The Zapatistas have responded to these debilitating abuses of capitalist education by revolting against them. In successfully doing so, they have attained autonomy and now exercise it unreservedly in their grassroots system of rebel learning. Since liberating themselves from state power, the education they promote has taken a decolonial, anti-patriarchal, radically inclusive, participatory and cooperative form. Their 'curriculum' covers a host of revolutionary topics and geographically situated applications. And despite the depth, breadth and expanse of what the Zapatistas are imparting within their communities, the goal of their process of education can be summed up as trying to instil one thing – a capacity for discernment.

In addition to learning about their Indigenous cultures, values and languages, in order to flourish as communities and foster political consciousness, Zapatista schools incorporate critical discussions about human and land rights and *relationships* that go beyond Western-liberal interpretations and definitions of rights. Time and time again, it has been and continues to be noted that Indigenous people's rights have persistently been ignored and trampled on. The autonomous schools create an atmosphere to equip students on topics of collective resistance, alternative economics and political history 'from below', which are not taught in the state education system run by the Mexican government. Students in the autonomous schools also learn critical lessons about neoliberalism, privatisation, exploitation, commodification and individualism, which is generative regarding political education because these things run counter to the communal land rights, low-impact agroecology, interdependency and collective-cooperative forms of work Zapatistas learn as part of daily life in their villages. Their rebel education system thereby instils students with an understanding of responsibility to community, the importance of democratic participation and the value of individual uniqueness and creativity that contributes to the diversity and vibrance of a larger collective whole.

To raise awareness of gender justice and to make an intervention into patriarchal social relations that still remain in the region, young girls are encouraged, from an early age, to start school and learn about and participate in their local traditions, heritage and systems of governance. Introducing gender justice early in the curriculum has encouraged more women to take up community leadership and organising positions within their autonomous municipalities. It has also resulted in an increase in confidence, bodily autonomy and speaking out on the part of women, many of whom are taking on governance responsibilities so that women are more involved in shaping communities and cultural norms (Gahman, 2020a). Via the autonomous education system and their focus on land and building a solidarity economy,

Zapatista women are creating new jobs, collectively starting cooperatives and sharing their handicraft and weaving products, which at once showcase their artisanal skills to the wider public and provide an income for their cooperatives, villages and families. Notably, older women in the communities have been instrumental in encouraging younger girls to pursue education, to become literate and to not shy away from taking on leadership roles in community governance and Zapatista alternative economic projects, political organising and the international solidarity gatherings that are now being hosted in their rebel territories.

Providing the opportunity for students and teachers to participate in discernment through a relational and communal sense of work, organisation and support is what comprises Zapatista education. That being said, there is, of course, no universal model or standardised manual. The Zapatista way is neither a doctrine to be imposed and nor is it a product to be bought or sold. Rather, Zapatista pedagogy means planting seeds of resistance and harvesting the subsequent hope that emerges by allowing democracy and justice to surface organically, without imposition. It encourages imagination and participation among all members of a community without ridicule.

For example, an education promoter we spoke with noted one definition of 'community' is 'an ensemble of diversity'. In doing so, she stressed the importance their communities place on being able to identify how capitalist

Figure 7.3: A mural on the side of a Zapatista cooperative representing their history; connection to land, corn and community; and shared sense of collective identity (that is, as rebel seeds)

actions and neoliberal subjectivities debilitate communities as a means to head off at the pass the trappings of self-centric thinking and capitalist social relations. She then discussed how the recognition of a collective subject and priority of instilling youth with a capacity for discernment were ways in which communities nurtured critical consciousness, invigorated Indigenous knowledges and rejuvenated their communities. She concluded by stating that Zapatismo is 'a bridge that makes things possible'. From this standpoint, when reflecting on what many of us experience in neoliberal universities, Zapatismo offers us possibilities for resistance, insurrection and insurgency, as well as for creativity, mutual care and a resuscitation of our own 'ensembles of diversity'.

'Asking, we walk' (and resist)

Undeniably, the story of the Zapatistas is one of dignity, courage and revolution. Moreover, it is an enduring chronicle of over five hundred years of resistance to the attempted conquest of the land and lives of Indigenous communities. More precisely, the ongoing tales of the Zapatista insurrection – as well as their commitment to political education – provide a dramatic account of how people working together can shield themselves from, defy and throw a wrench in the gears of the machinations of state violence, oppressive gender roles and capitalist plunder (Klein, 2015).

In standing up to the aggression of the driving forces of capital accumulation and concentrated power of the state, which is often called *el mal gobierno* (the bad/evil government) within their communities, the Zapatistas now practice education on their own terms – free from colonial-capitalist modernity's narrow-minded logics and myopic rationalities (Quijano, 2000). Zapatista teachers and students are not beholden to the parochial oversight and disciplinary apparatuses of managerialist bureaucracies like many of us in neoliberal universities are. On the contrary, as we have explored throughout this chapter, Zapatista education comes 'from below' and is anchored in relationships with land, grassroots struggle and Indigenous worldviews (Klein, 2015). Their praxis-driven approach is best illustrated by the earlier referenced duelling axiom *'preguntando caminamos'* ('asking, we walk'), which sees Zapatista communities generate their curriculum through reflective popular assembly, participatory democracy and communal decision-making (Zibechi, 2013). This grounded and horizontalist process advances by focusing on the histories, ecologies and needs and desires of their communities and autonomous municipalities.

On the whole, the repertoire of emancipatory perspectives that Zapatista education promoters draw from when teaching are as diverse as they are dialectical. Overall, however, the principles, practices, core values and aims that define Zapatista education are typically bound by a few common threads, which we propose students demand from their own universities:

1. Prioritising critical consciousness and collectivity. The Zapatistas recognise that political education is, as did Fanon (1963), 'a historical necessity'. In turn, they also understand that nurturing a capacity for discernment, critical consciousness and a sense of mutuality while working together cooperatively is, arguably, the lifeblood of revolutionary change.
2. Engaging in prefiguration and interdependency. The Zapatistas are *imagining* a world free from domination, oppression and abusive exercises of power, control and authority. In doing so, they are building an education system that teaches students to understand that histories, geographies, generations, communities and memories are interconnected and never exist in isolation.
3. Centring praxis, relationality and reciprocity. The Zapatistas value critical analysis, collective action and reflective introspection– iteratively and concurrently – with respect to their efforts and engagement in struggling for social change. In doing so, they also foreground the practice of care, recognising the dignity of others and figuring out how to cultivate meaning, purpose and a sense of self-efficacy and worth for all involved.
4. Attending to power relations and positionality. Zapatista education promotes critical self- and collective reflection with respect to how differential social identities, statuses, credentials, securities and privileges (or lack thereof) mediate life chances, choices, opportunities and day-to-day interactions. While recognising and valuing the lived experiences and truths of individuals, they prioritise a structural analysis that explicitly foregrounds and wrestles with the social, political, economic and historical forces that have generated the conditions and realities in which people are living.
5. Focusing on the particular, place-based and peripherialised. The Zapatistas are deeply sceptical of, in not rejecting outright, grand theories, totalising narratives, assertions of neutrality and claims of 'objectivity' that have come with 'modernity' and Western-liberal 'Enlightenment'. Their movement recognises the unique, situated and idiographic differences of varying communities, contexts, people and places. It also, in many respects, advances with a preferential option for the poor, oppressed and dispossessed. For example, what would your education look like if it respected, valued and made use of Indigenous and peasant knowledges 'from below'?

In sum, Zapatista rebel education is marked by its tendency, penchant and passion for challenging convention, unsettling orthodoxy, mending wounds and constructing alternatives. Animating pathways out of structural violence and mass alienation while seeking peace and harmony are also part and parcel of the Zapatista curriculum. For us, the spirit of Zapatista education is defined by its affinity for dissent, disruption, care, compassion and revolutionary change. And while neither strict doctrine nor policed dogma, for the most part, Zapatista processes of education, as best we have seen and learned about them, entail getting organised, doing homework, listening closely, practising empathy, showing up, being prepared, attending to power relations, engaging in active self-reflection and not only earning but also sustaining trust. This teaches students to exist in the world (collectively), not merely in themselves (self-centredness). Moreover, in assessing what type of education Zapatista communities are promoting, the adjectives 'politically conscious', 'theoretically driven', 'empirically rich' and 'evidence-based' all come to mind. Zapatista pedagogy, as heterogeneous and variegating as it is across their communities, is as grassroots and revolutionary as it gets.

Given the geopolitical context of their movement, Zapatista community-anchored and land-based teaching methods, which have at their heart Maya *cosmovisión*, languages and subjectivities, constitute acts of decolonisation in and of themselves. This leaves one to wonder if neoliberal universities might learn a thing or two from the Zapatistas with respect to endorsing political education, Indigenous worldviews and land-based education as essential to any programme of study. And despite the depth and breadth of the Zapatista education system we have covered up to this point, the overarching aspiration of their rogue pedagogy can be summed up as trying to instil a capacity for discernment through moving forward ('walking') while being critically reflective ('asking').

Get free, whatever your calendar or geography

> I dream I am jumping, swimming, running, and climbing. I dream I burst out laughing, I am leaping across a river and chased by a pack of cars – that never catches up with me.
>
> Fanon (1963: 15)

All revolutionaries, as Fanon expresses in the preceding quote, are concerned with and committed to the essence of what it means to be fully human: freedom. In concluding our overview of what we feel the Zapatistas have to offer us in the way of political education, emancipatory politics and co-creating pathways towards better worlds, and getting free, we must explicitly confess that we have little to no faith that the neoliberal academic status quo will ever be reformed. Audre Lorde (2018: 16) rightly told us 'the master's tools will never dismantle the master's house', just as Emma Goldman (1910) argued that 'the most violent element in society is ignorance'. Most conventional universities, regrettably, have been assembled using an ignorant master's racist and patriarchal logics (Bhambra et al, 2018). Put differently, the Western academy was broken to begin with, and remains that way.

Hence, when it comes to the existence of any 'modern' entity or institution that emerges out of the coloniser's playbook (for example, the neoliberal university), we agree with Frantz Fanon (1963: 235) who states, 'we must shake off the heavy darkness in which we were plunged, and leave it behind'. Neoliberal ideology – the world's current 'heavy darkness' – must be cast out, and the institutions in which it is being taught must be pummelled into ruin. Despite the fact that such a comment may seemingly be replete with cynicism and despair, we feel it is actually deeply rooted in yearning, desire and hope. Indeed, even if living under the shadow of colonial-capitalist modernity and an alienating and exploitative neoliberal status quo, we do not have to submit to a racist, sexist and ableist order of things. We can both resist and organise (EZLN, 2016a).

In turn, let us all 'be Zapatistas' and collectively change our realities and worlds, whatever they may be. Let us all look each other in the eyes, take each other by the hand and 'set fire to the master's house'. Let us find one another, get together and go plant a garden, read *The wretched of the earth* (Fanon, 1963), tell stories, sing songs, paint pictures, play games, cook meals, share food and learn a new (sign) language with one another. Break bread, raise a barn, storm the bastille, burn a plantation, turn a flag into ashes, and act like a kid again. Smash patriarchy, bend gender, put on a costume, mask up, create a carnival, get queer, and dance a dance (in whatever way you 'dance'). Have someone's back, give thanks, burst out laughing, fall in love, find joy, and go breathe life into and build 'another world' (Roy, 2003) – and share it far and wide. Keep looking – and struggling – to the stars. Finally, take care of yourselves and take care of each other, because neither the state nor capitalism give a damn, and nor are they even capable of doing so (Dirik, 2016).

If ever there was a time to earnestly commit to and act in the interest of 'building a world where many worlds fit', it is now. The Zapatistas (EZLN, 2015b) are right – just as are so many others out there like yourselves – 'we really are going to begin building the world we need and deserve' (Zapatista Women, 2018). Down with neoliberalism, down with capitalist modernity, down with liberal bystanding – and to hell with the colonial worldviews and racist war machines they rode in on. 'Be a Zapatista', whatever your 'calendar and geography', because we must, as the Zapatistas have done, make the colossus, the hydra and the dehumanising 'condition of this fucking capitalist system' – to quote the *compañeras* (Zapatista women) – tremble.

8

Gender justice and social reproduction

> Or we can agree to struggle together, as different as we are, against
> the patriarchal capitalist system that is assaulting and murdering us.
>
> Zapatista Women (2018)

The (ongoing) colonial state of things

Colonialism penetrates. Land and lives, territories and cultures, as well
as bodies and psyches are the target. With the dual end of domination
and accumulation as motive, the preferred means of colonisers have been
dehumanisation, dispossession, enslavement, exploitation, humiliation,
disappearance and death, to name just a few. To be as forthright as possible,
the colonial-capitalist order of things has been defined by alienation and
annihilation. For over five hundred years, the fanatical contempt, rapacious
greed and unadulterated violence of colonialism has been codified and
globalised to such a magnitude there is virtually no geography it has not
shattered or (dis)ordered. Indeed, the world and modernity as we have come
to know and exist in each have been (re)arranged and compartmentalised
via colonial worldviews, along with their arbitrary hierarchies and attendant
exercises of illegitimate authority and control.

Correspondingly, to speak with accuracy about colonialism is to recognise
its inseparability from capitalism and heteropatriarchy, not to mention to
distinguish the racist character that defines them as inextricably entangled
social structures, cultural institutions and systems of power. Gender and
melanin levels taken in vain, patriarchal colonial-capitalism has constructed
its 'Others' and has set about condemning them as it pleases. It is paramount,
here, to recognise that these condemnations and desolations of lives, cultures
and histories occur in places. That is, while global in scale and resonance,
the machinations and aftermaths of colonialism are unquestionably situated,
unique and particular, albeit interconnected. Hence, historicised and
geopolitically contextualised analyses are necessary towards confronting,
preventing and finding solutions to the ongoing structural violence of
colonial, capitalist and patriarchal social orders. And when it comes to
seeking and discussing solutions to the global inequalities, human suffering
and ecological destruction wrought by colonial-capitalism, a focus on
resistance and alternatives, as well as interdependence and relationality,
is vital.

History shows us there is nothing tender or humble or playful or joyous about the institutions, discourses, states and economies (that is, relationships) that have been imposed by colonisers, capitalists and the cultural mores established by heteropatriarchy. This simply means it is urgent to start centring these humanising aspects of life in the alternatives and solutions we pursue. Meaning, if we, humanity, are to advance towards freedom (hooks, 2014b), redemption (Marley, 1980) and social harmony (Escobar, 2018) in the here and now, might it not prove instructive for us to look and listen to movements like the Zapatistas who are actively building 'cultures of dissent' and 're-envisioning and reshaping communities' (Mohanty, 2003: 215) while caring for one another and having each other's backs? Similarly, what could we learn if we pay close attention to those places where 'a politics of collective action ... is cultivating new forms of sociability, happiness, and economic capacity ... through a mixture of creative disrespect and protective caution' (Gibson-Graham, 2006: xxxv) And finally, if we take seriously Federici's (2012: 3) assertion that

> it is through the day-to-day activities by means of which we produce our existence, that we can develop our capacity to cooperate and not only resist our dehumanisation, but learn to reconstruct the world as a space of nurturing, creativity, and care ...

might we then recognise that the terrain of social reproduction, inclusive of our everyday interactions and concern (or lack thereof) for others, is a key site of political struggle for radical ('from the roots') transformation?

In finding merit in all of the preceding queries apropos escaping the maelstrom of capitalist-misogyny into which humanity has been plunged, our concentration for this chapter focuses on the power relations operating at the nexus of gender and social reproduction. Specifically, the oppressive and exploitative colonial realities and concurrent intensifications of patriarchal domination that were inflicted on Indigenous women in what is now Chiapas, Mexico, over five hundred years ago (Olivera, 2005; Gahman, 2020b). By extension, we are also aiming to cast critical light on what the rest of the world has to learn from the socially reproductive labour and socio-territorial struggles for liberation the Zapatista were respectively tasked with and took up. It is with the hope of finding answers to these questions, then, that the thrust of this chapter advances by placing at the centre the emancipatory politics, collective mobilisations and everyday practices of the Zapatista *compañeras*.

Social reproduction as 'point zero'

That's why we say that the capitalist system is patriarchal.
The patriarchy rules, even if the overseer is a woman.

> So we think that in order to fight for our rights – the right to
> live, for example
> We have to fight against the capitalist system. They go together.
> Comandanta Amada (Zapatista Women, 2019)

Our first major aim with this chapter is to raise awareness about, while contributing to, the body of literature primarily being spearheaded by autonomist, anti-racist and socialist feminists that takes seriously and responsively grapples with the day-to-day power relations and gendered politics of social reproduction (Jones, 1949; hooks, 1990; Gibson-Graham, 1996; Collins, 2002; Roy, 2003; Luxton and Bezanson, 2006). More expressly, we propose that social reproduction be more intentionally foregrounded as a strategic site of anti-capitalist, anti-colonial and anti-heteropatriarchal struggle for structural (politico-economic and socio-cultural) transformation. In defining social reproduction, we are in accord with anti-neoliberal feminist scholars (Federici, 2012; Bhattacharya, 2017; Fraser and Pettifor, 2018). The Kilombo Women's Delegation (2018), contextualising it within our prevailing (neo)colonial, capitalocentric and heteropatriarchal status quo, suggest social reproduction is all of the activities, both inside and outside the home (for example, kitchens, bedrooms, schools, hospitals, community centres, parks, streets, fields, *milpas* (cornfields), and so on), that (re)produce both daily life and, unavoidably, labour-power and exploitable workers.

In situating our political-intellectual stance on social reproduction as a matter of praxis, we further draw from Federici (2012: 2–3), who, in identifying it as a critical terrain on which to fight for revolutionary change, explains:

> Reproductive work is undoubtedly not the only form of labour where the question of what we give to capital and "what we give to our own" is posed. But certainly, it is the work in which the contradictions inherent in "alienated labour" are most explosive, which is why it is the *point zero* for revolutionary practice, even if it is not the only point zero.

With this notion of social reproduction as our conceptual anchor, another objective we have is to demonstrate that the efforts of the Zapatista women, in particular their mobilisation of a 'politics of collective action' (Gibson-Graham, 2006) and struggle at 'point zero' (Federici, 2012) via their commitment to *lekil kuxlejal*, are transforming their culture, social relations and reality at large by (re)valuing social reproduction. That is, they are co-creating, and collectively organising, the dignified life-giving world they want to be a part of 'from below'. As a refresher from the last chapter, *lekil kuxlejal* is the Tzeltal term meaning living a dignified life, communally and reciprocally, through a recognition of interdependence and the interconnectedness of the spiritual and physical – as well as natural and supernatural – worlds (Mora, 2017). For a more nuanced overview of the term's dynamic meaning, practice and depth, we recommend Mora's (2017) *Kuxlejal politics*.

In discussing social reproduction and the political agency of Zapatista women, we offer an analytical narrative not only as a means to induce optimism and incite action, but also, so that readers might be inspired to find merit in and make more concerted efforts to legitimise the acuity and insights of non-state-captured, non-credentialed organisers and anti-systemic organic intellectuals like the Zapatistas. That is, to recognise rural peasants who are labouring and living at 'point zero', á la Fanon (1963), and other scholars engaged with grassroots social movements (Speed and Forbis, 2005; Altieri and Toledo, 2011; Rosset and Martínez-Torres, 2012; Mora, 2015; Marcos, 2018), as valid and citable sources of knowing and knowledge production. We disclose here that our motivations are critical of liberal 'good intentions', as well as repudiating both careerism and classist canon-building (Morrison, 1988; Cusicanqui, 2012; de Leeuw et al, 2013).[1] Antithetically, the convictions underpinning this chapter emanate from the inspiration, imagination, creative vision, (Indigenous) resurgence (Simpson, 2008) – and, quite simply, hope – that we feel the Zapatistas, in particular the *compas*, offer the world.

Given there are no Zapatistas from Chiapas in the academy, we consider it paramount and a historical-political necessity to traffic as much *Zapatismo* into orthodox knowledge production and mainstream Westernised education as possible in as responsible and conscientiousness, and cautious of a manner as possible. That is, from our vantage point, mindfully amplifying the ethics, principles, practices and story arcs of the Zapatistas is urgent because of the concrete alternatives and real prospects they offer us with respect to changing and making the world more compassionate and rebellious. Finally, in centring social reproduction as central to emancipatory struggles for gender justice and cultural transformation, we hold firm that the topic should neither be approached as an apolitical term that gets catalogued as a passing academic fad, nor treated as an immaterial or fringe concept that is dismissed as something to be 'dealt with later'. Because, undeniably, labouring at 'point zero' has existed since time immemorial, as well as coming with both material consequences and lived ramifications. More pointedly, as we detail in the next section, it is often as thankless as it is exhausting – especially for rural peasant woman in the agrarian Global South. Social reproduction, then, in addition to the ways in which it is dismissed and devalued, is one of the most crucial things we can learn about and take seriously with respect to transforming the world and making it a more just place.

Figure 8.1: A women's cooperative in Oventik with a mural of a rebel Zapatista woman with a flower, gun and baby that reads: 'Office of the Women of Dignity'

Peasant woman's burden: reproducing everyday life

Over the past half-century, rural peasant women have been subjected to unprecedented levels of corporate-driven, state-sanctioned, global capitalist policies of economic liberalisation, free trade, privatisation and austerity (Rosset et al, 2006; Altamirano-Jiménez, 2013; Chattopadhyay, 2014). For them, the yields entail escalating experiences of displacement, dispossession, indebtedness, poverty, precarity (low-waged seasonal, temporary, contracted work) and hazardous working conditions (Akram-Lodhi and Kay, 2012; Benería et al, 2015). Neoliberal knock-on effects such as these are also coinciding with state rollbacks in social spending, as well as sweeping cuts to government subsidies and regulations that safeguard and conserve the environment (Heynen et al, 2007; Peluso and Lund, 2011).

As a result, rural women engaged in informal or subsistence living are confronted with seemingly insurmountable structural barriers regarding their prospects of straightforwardly accessing essential and indispensable social services (for example, healthcare, counselling, shelters/safehouses, educational training, childcare, legal aid) (Benería et al, 2015). The costs of systemic obstacles generate detrimental public health issues that disproportionately affect women. These include high vulnerability rates of malnutrition, injury, exhaustion, disease, infection and chronic pain, in addition to increased chances of infant mortality and maternal death

(Kuhlmann and Annandale, 2012; Kwan, 2016). Rarely considered, too, are the spikes in and prolonged experiences of emotional despair and deteriorations in psychological wellbeing (for example, undue stress, anxiety, despair, angst) these barriers induce (Saxena et al, 2007).

Disaggregated gender analysis on the agrarian Global South reveals that rural women are far less likely to find jobs in formal (agricultural and non-agricultural) employment than both men and urban women (Rockenbauch and Sakdapolrak, 2017). Peasant women thus assume a higher risk of working without labour protections, adherence to workers' rights, and even (officially recognised) support from trade unions (Deere and De Leal, 2014). Furthermore, while women across the board continue to be underrepresented in politics, governance and decision-making at every level of society, when compared to urban women as well men in general, rural women face inordinately higher degrees of exclusion (Benería et al, 2015). Tellingly, as the Inter-Agency Task Force on Rural Women reported within the last decade, 'With only a few exceptions, rural women fare worse than rural men and urban women and men for *every* Millennium Development Goal indicator for which data are available' (WomenWatch, 2012; emphasis added).

Time poverty, the amount of time spent per day undertaking socially reproductive work without having any other choice other than to do so, is another indicator of structural inequality rural women experience. Gender-focused labour studies inclusive of countries in the periphery specify that when both waged and unwaged work are taken into consideration, rural women work an average of 16 hours per day, roughly two hours more than men, which, over the course of a week, means they are labouring a total of 12 hours more in aggregate (IFAD, 2016). In the midst of accruing all these overtime hours, yet being compensated nothing for them, rural peasant women must also navigate, daily, infrastructure problems, mobility constraints, limited social networking opportunities and exposure to the elements (Grassi et al, 2015). In many (post)colonial rural settings, it is not uncommon for the often distant infrastructure to be of relatively poor quality or low standard (Lyon et al, 2017). This means the (free) domestic labour peasant women are performing (inclusive of household chores, caretaking, food preparation, fetching water/wood/fuel/supplies, and so on) is typically being carried out either in the absence of, or with only marginal access to, adequate equipment, information, technology, transportation, training and even camaraderie.

Further vulnerabilising rural peasant women are the perils they inherit with respect to the ecological aftermaths, and requisite political fallouts, of human-induced climate change (Lambrou and Nelson, 2010; Carr and Thompson, 2014). These consist of environmental degradation, deforestation, sea level rise, crop failure, soil erosion/acidification, resource conflict, water shortages, famine, ecosystem disruptions, species dislocation/extinction and disasters that result from extreme weather events (flooding, drought, mudslides, cyclone/hurricane damage, water shortages, contamination, famine, and so on) (Nixon, 2011; Klein, 2014). Correspondingly, the wellbeing, livelihoods, knowledge, thoughts and ideas of peasant women in the periphery remain some of the most neglected, if not ignored outright, areas of foci that exist in terms of state support, international aid, development agendas, policy consultations and even university outreach programmes (Tuck and Yang, 2012).

A final interlocking set of indicators illustrating the co-constitutive products generated by the machinations of neoliberal logic and neocolonial policy is that if analysed carefully, one can discern that the vast majority of all this robust, yet damning, data typifies the life circumstances of only certain kinds of women. That is, those who are rural; working class or poor; racialised (of colour) or Indigenous; neither formally 'educated' nor professionally credentialed; and living in the Global South or peripheral North. Indeed, the capitalist patriarchy that is our global economy appears to have a premeditated pattern, as well as preferred target. Not coincidentally and in parallel, all of the listed empirical evidence profiling the yoke of drudgery that a rural peasant woman has foisted upon her, as we will see in the sections to come, was directly applicable to Zapatista women.

Prelude to an uprising

> That is what we Zapatistas want, and it's what we want for the whole world: that there be no rulers, that there be no exploiters, that we as Indigenous people not be exploited.
> Compañera Selena (EZLN, 2015a: 104)

Prior to the EZLN's uprising that took the international media by storm on New Year's Day in 1994 (the day the NAFTA was ratified), Indigenous people in Chiapas lived during what is referred to as the *acasillamiento* (EZLN, 2015). This era, which saw numerous differing iterations over multiple generations, dates back to the invasion of conquistadors and the imposition of the *encomienda* (commissioned plantation) system (Olivera, 2005). It is defined by the capture and enslavement of otherwise free people as indeterminately indentured peons who are subjected to the authority of rural *caciques* or *hacendados* (landowning bosses/ruling-class overseers) and tethered to *fincas* (commercial plantation estates) or *ranchos* (market-oriented livestock operations) (Rus, 2010). While the *acasillamiento* started gradually disbanding during the 1940s up through the early 1980s, a time during which only a few sequestered *fincas* still operated under the system, the impacts it had on the minds and bodies of Indigenous people remained. Miriam (EZLN, 2015a: 89), a Zapatista *comandanta* (commander), provides a general depiction of what life for women was like during the *acasillamiento*:

> They [colonisers] stole our land and took our language – our culture. This is how the domination of *caciquismo* [local despotism] and landowners came into being, along with our triple exploitation of humiliation, discrimination, marginalisation.

While Miriam's words capture how stifling life under patriarchal-colonialism and the plantation for Indigenous women was on the whole, to get a more detailed sense of the travails and protracted misery to which they were exposed, the devil is in the details (of the everyday).

For the five centuries preceding the implementation of Zapatista Women's Revolutionary Law (WRL) in 1993, it was not uncommon for an Indigenous woman's day to begin at 4 in the morning and to end around 10 at night (JBG, 2013c).[2] What occurred during that roughly 18-hour stretch was what many of us would consider unremitting and underappreciated – both physical and emotional – hard labour. Labour rendered unseen and devalued because it was women performing it, and because it was being completed in-and-around and for the home/family. As Federici (2012: 45) notes, 'behind the sudden interest for housework lies the old truth that this work *remains invisible* only as long as it is done' (emphasis added). Correspondingly, the only attention paid to the domestic work women were doing was if it were *not* completed, which, if this were the case, often resulted in punitive repercussions.

Sweeping the floor, tidying the house, fetching water, gathering wood, starting a fire, preparing coffee, mixing *pozol* (a fermented corn drink) and cooking breakfast were among the first tasks. After the men had had their fill and set off for the fields, the morning work continued. Feeding children, grinding corn, kneading, pounding and flattening *masa* (dough) to make tortillas, washing dishes, hand-laundering clothes, hanging them to dry, and trekking to the forest to find, cut and lug back more firewood followed. Sowing, weeding, picking, reaping, threshing, shucking, sorting or winnowing varying grains, fruits and vegetables ensued thereafter, as did weaving, mending, sewing, embroidering and hemming clothes. Shelling coffee beans and grinding salt occupied long stretches of the day, and a mere handful of one or the other was what hacienda bosses 'paid' the women (JBGc, 2013c).

Miriam (EZLN, 2015a: 89) offers a glimpse of their abandonment:

> The fucking bosses had us as if they were our owners; they sent us to do all the work on the haciendas, without caring if we had

children, husbands or if we were sick. They never asked if we were sick; if we didn't make it to work, they sent their servant or slave to leave the corn in front of the kitchen so that we would make tortillas for them.

This process was repeated over the course of the day, oftentimes with an infant wrapped tightly in a sash and slung snuggly against their back. Interruptions to the day's monotonous toil[3] took the form of caring for, cleaning up after, fielding questions from, and perhaps reining in one of the many curious and wandering children who were (solely) under their mother's keep.

Zapatista women's realities

A woman nursing, teaching, washing and having anywhere from six to ten children over the course of a generation had become a familiar scene in the rural Chiapan countryside. Marriages were arranged and compulsory regardless of what a woman desired and felt in her heart. Psychological abuse and physical violence were also not uncommon, even normalised, to a certain degree (JBG, 2013c). Women rarely left the home, and if they did, they were subject to ridicule and reprimand. Miriam (EZLN, 2015a: 90) describes the demeaning mockery:

> Years passed and women suffered like this. And when our babies cried and we nursed them, we were yelled at, made fun of, insulted physically; they said that we didn't know anything, that we were useless, that we were a bother to them. They didn't respect us and they used us as if we were objects.

Although recognising that women were oppressed, men in their communities rarely contributed to reproductive labour.[4] This stemmed from the imposition of colonial-patriarchal gender regimes, coupled with the pervasive *machismo* that was fusing with the capitalist impulse to deem economically (re)productive/waged labour, individual ownership and work outside domestic spaces more substantive and valuable than socially reproductive work. Guadeloupe (JBG, 2013c: 18), an education promoter, details the progressive incursion and confluence of liberal notions of property/possession with male domination:

> Women, upon the arrival of private property, were given as gifts. It passed to another level and what is now call patriarchy arrived, with the plunder of women's rights, with the plunder of the earth – *it was with the arrival of private property that men began to command*. We know that with this arrival of private property three great evils took place,

which are the exploitation of men, the exploitation of women, and the exploitation of all, but of women more. As women we are exploited by this neoliberal system. (Emphasis added)

In further explaining the complex dynamics regarding how colonial gender regimes were internalised within Indigenous communities, Miriam (EZLN, 2015a: 92) describes how the men, although opposed to the denigrating and abusive ways that plantation overseers treated Indigenous women, mimicked similar patriarchal behaviours, habits and modes of thinking:

[O]nce they [Indigenous men] were living in the communities, those ideas that came from the boss or the *acasillado* were brought in. It's as if the men drug [sic] these bad ideas along with them and applied them inside the house. They acted like the little boss of the house. It's not true that the women were liberated then, because the men became the "little bosses" of the house ... the women stayed at home *as if it was a prison*. (Emphasis added)

That is, the men refused to do 'women's work', and wilfully defended not having to via essentialised sexist rationalisations. The taken-for-granted patriarchal tradition of men not lowering themselves to the level of a woman thereby served as a convenient justification to deride and confine women to the private sphere. The captive isolation women experienced, as well as the absolution from domestic work men granted themselves, was chalked up as 'natural' due to purported, albeit erroneous, 'biological differences'.[5]

Furthermore, women did not venture far from the house, unless to sow seeds or reap crops in the fields. They worked seven days a week, held no tenure, and were not allowed to organise or get an education. 'There were no Sundays (that is, rest), and there was no land', as one *compa* expressed.[6] Community decision-making, public undertakings and civil affairs were off-limits. Their experiences of state institutions, if allowed in, were characterised by epithet, neglect or threat, even of non-consensual sterilisation (Olivera, 2007). Women's voices were deliberately silenced, their ideas unheard. They were taught to cast their eyes to the ground and to keep their heads down, that they should not exist (JBG, 2013c). Oppression, worthlessness and misogyny were overtly imposed, and more subtly, internalised. Being an Indigenous peasant woman was a life sentence of parochial oversight, obligatory deference and hard labour. It meant subservience and discipline, which were expected and administered within the confines of the domestic spaces to which they were consigned. Indeed, the rhythms, routines and repressions of an Indigenous peasant woman's daily life mirrored those of both a plantation and a prison.

Women's Revolutionary Law

> Those women who are no longer here. But who are with us nonetheless.
>
> We do not forget them. We do not forgive those who took them from us.
>
> We struggle for those women, and with them.
>
> Indigenous Zapatista Women's Address, International
> Women's Day (Zapatista Women, 2021)

In addition to the reverence the Zapatistas[7] have earned in the eyes of the anti-capitalist left, one can also contend that their communities serve as a paragon of intersectional feminist analyses, politics and praxis, despite the fact that they do not necessarily identify as 'feminist' in all instances.[8] Intersectionality is reflected in the words of Comandanta Esther (2001), one of the early stalwart commanders of the EZLN, who encapsulates the interlocking oppressions of Indigenous women when she asserts: 'We have to fight more because as Indigenous we are triply looked down upon: as Indigenous, as women, and as poor.' And fight against these manifold subordinations is exactly what the Zapatista women did.

Markedly, in March 1993, a decade after the EZLN was covertly founded, and nine months prior to their declaration of war against the Mexican state and global capitalism, both the EZLN and their civilian bases of support implemented 'Women's Revolutionary Law' (WRL). This was a landmark moment in the battle being waged by women against the abuse, non-participation and reproductive unfreedoms they were experiencing (Marcos, 2018). In principle, the edicts of WRL are the direct result of dissident peasant women gone rogue, collectively. In practice, the revolutionary laws function as mechanisms of both empowerment (for women) and accountability (for men).

The account of what unfolded when the laws were announced reports that Comandanta Susana, an EZLN commander, carried with her into a community assembly the cumulative sentiments of thousands of Indigenous Zapatista women. On reciting the demands of the women to a hushed and attentive crowd, the men in the room started getting restless and worried. The women, on the other hand, growing with enthusiasm and confidence, began applauding (Marcos, 1993). Subcomandante Marcos (now Galeano) writes that when Susana concluded reading the proclamations aloud, the men were left 'scratching their heads' while the women 'were singing' (Marcos and de Leon, 2002: 69). Marcos (1993) finishes matter-of-factly with: 'The EZLN's first uprising was March 1993 and was led by Zapatista women. There were no causalities, and they won.'

While the writings of Subcomandante Marcos should be taken with a grain of salt and always cross-referenced with realties on the ground, the fact remains that the Zapatista WRL became decree – and it was done so via the political agency, collective action and dedicated organising of the Zapatista women. That is, the *compas* had thrown down the proverbial gauntlet against both the normalised violence that was imperilling them and the long-standing devaluation of their labour and lives as women. Remarkably, in the midst of clandestinely strategising for the armed revolt that would eventually come to fruition on 1 January 1994, tactical discussions of guerrilla warfare and military manoeuvres took a backseat to those of women's realities, social reproduction and bodily autonomy. And even though not initially well received by many men, the laws were eventually taken up, with the substance of the decrees asserting women's rights to equal participation, individual agency and, quite simply, dignity (Newdick, 2005). Issues surrounding representation, recognition, safety, reproductive work and sexual autonomy feature prominently too.

Broadly speaking, the WRL codifies and concretises a woman's right to involvement and self-determination (Altamirano-Jiménez, 2013). More specifically, the laws mandate that women hold key positions in the guerrilla army (the EZLN), are equitably represented in the *Juntas de Buen Gobierno* (Council of Good Government), take part in agroecological projects/work outside of domestic labour, are freely able to enter/exit relationships, can choose when and how many children they will have, are supported in speaking out against/seeking justice for domestic abuse, and have the latitude to develop their own alternative economic cooperatives (for example, weaving, handcrafts) (Klein, 2015). Additionally, one of the more pathbreaking generative upshots of the WRL is how it exposed the inextricable links that androcentrism and patriarchal modes of thought have with capitalist rationale and derisions of social reproduction. That is, under marketised profit logics, because 'women's work' in domestic spaces (for example, household chores, nurturing, teaching, community-building) is typically neither attached to a wage nor understood as revenue-generating, its misplaced depreciation is inevitable (Federici, 2012). It is fundamental to state here that domestic labour's first belittling stems from the sexist belief that because it is generally being performed by women, it is not of as much value. Meaning, patriarchy is a system of domination that can exist unto itself, although it rarely does, and when operating alongside racial capitalism it is further entrenched, metastasises and can even become internalised.

Along these lines, the WRL, too, was an intervention made by the Zapatista women against structural forces and cultural norms that were alienating them while debilitating their respective senses of self-worth and emotional wellbeing. Valentina (JBG, 2013c), an education promoter, succinctly attests to the psychological ramifications women endured, when she states: 'The capitalists had us believing their ideas; their story that women are not worth anything.' Relatedly, on International Women's Day 2018, at their 'First International Gathering of Politics, Art, Sport, and Culture for Women in Struggle', a Zapatista organiser explains:

> We saw that whereas before we women only had our houses and fields, now we have schools, clinics and collective work projects where we women operate equipment and guide the struggle. We make mistakes, of course, but we're moving forward, with no one telling us what to do but ourselves. And now we see that we have indeed advanced – even if only a little bit, we always manage to advance somehow. Don't think it was easy. It was very hard, and it continues to be very hard. Not just because the fucking capitalist system wants to destroy us; it's also because we have to fight against the system that makes men believe that we women are less than, and good for nothing. (EZLN, 2018)

These testimonies illustrate how the symbiotic relationship of patriarchal authoritarianism and capitalist modes of thinking not only foreclosed women's life chances and took physical tolls, but also that the effects were equally harmful to their individual psyches, personal mental health and the social psychology of the communities (Watkins and Shulman, 2008). The

Figure 8.2: A mural of a woman's eyes amidst corn, which symbolises the connection they have to both the crop and the Earth as Indigenous people. The artwork is on the side of an Office of Council Advice building in Zapatista territory used for community outreach and cohesion

statements also indicate that the sites of social reproduction (for example, houses, fields, schools, health clinics) serve as 'point zero' (Federici, 2012) of where the Zapatista women would collectively struggle for dignity and change. And as was witnessed at the beginning of this section, the *compas* response to the untenable patriarchal capitalist realities they had levied against them, was a '¡*Ya basta!*' ('Enough is enough!') and uprising of their own.

Outcomes and critiques of Women's Revolutionary Law

> To women everywhere, we are saying, "Let us fight together" … we are inviting all women to fight, so that we (all women) will not continue to suffer.
>
> Comandanta Esther (2001)

Prior to the WRL, the consequences wrought by heteropatriarchal social relations were relegating the lives of women to isolation and discipline, in matters of both work and love. The fallouts were commensurately *discursive* (for example, sexist stereotypes framing women as weak, incapable, histrionic, irrational) and *material* (for example, socio-spatial boundaries confining women to the household, private sphere, kitchen/laundry, child-rearing/ reproducing). On a day-to-day level, the biopolitical corollaries dually manifested themselves in two ways: (1) violence being perpetrated against women, which had become accepted as commonplace; and (2) the banal entrenchment of male entitlement(s) (for example, to land, marriage, bodies, sex, *not* performing domestic labour). With the implementation of the WRL, then, the Zapatista women were directly and unapologetically confronting both culturally embedded expectations and structurally entrenched practices of (hetero)male supremacy. The revolutionary laws thus functioned as a political tool the women could brandish to disrupt inflexible gendered conventions that were limiting their movements and ability to participate (Sierra, 2001). Likewise, the laws served as a moral appeal and policy check they could use to confront misogynistic behaviours that were unduly regulating their lives and encroaching on their freedoms.

While sometimes criticised for appearing to draw from Western ideals, liberal human rights discourse and (misguidedly presumed) static/archaic Indigenous traditions, at its core, the WRL and its empowering upshots are confronting both unequal gendered power relations and the structural repression of women (Marcos, 2005b; The Kilombo Women's Delegation, 2018). Indirectly, and perhaps more subtly, the WRL is championing a dynamic and evolving Indigenous ontology that promotes reflexively engaging in mutuality and reciprocity, as well as identifying with a collective subject (Speed and Fordis, 2005). These contrast with liberal worldviews imposed by colonisers (for example, those of modernity, the Enlightenment, classical liberalism) that reify people as disparate and atomised actors whose individuated notions of 'self/identity' are thought to be definable independent of the social and ecological relationships they exist within.

This is of tremendous consequence given the primacy that is afforded to the Zapatistas' (Indigenous-rooted) relational interpretations of *Kuxlejal* 'collective life existence' (Mora, 2017). Coercively restricting a person's ability to participate in or contribute to the community would be dehumanising. That is, given their *cosmovisión* privileges (1) relationality and accountability to the community/collective and (2) socio-territorial intersubjectivity (the interdependency, interconnectedness and 'subjecthood' of all people, animals, land, nature, ecosystems), the WRL protects Zapatista women from being severed from either. Hence, it is safeguarding their dignity and ability to be fully human.

In light of this, the WRL was not only a declaration of individual rights, but more fundamentally, a transformative instrument of socio-cultural change that has radically reconfigured gender relations. Put differently, in the hands of the *compas*, the laws are a protective shield they can raise to defend themselves from the physical and psychological violence women disproportionately absorb under patriarchal norms. More proactively, the WRL is a weapon they can wield as women against chauvinistic standards and behaviours that prevent them from embracing the pursuits, relationships and emotions of their desire (Klein, 2015).

In transparently addressing the politics surrounding issues of bodily autonomy and reproductive freedom, Sofia, a health promoter, explains:[9]

> [C]ompañeras decide who they marry, they are no longer forced. Youth are now involved in every area so they talk and meet each other and spend time together. Who they love is up to them. There is family planning and birth control. This depends on the community and family, but is not common everywhere. Some things are an uphill battle. There are "bad" customs and "good" customs. We try to change the bad ones and learn as we go. This is the situation and our struggle.
>
> We can say that women do now choose their partner and how many children they will have. This is a success.

Comandanta Rosalinda (EZLN, 2015a: 95) also discusses the groundswell of confidence women were being imbued with around the time the WRL was being marshalled through the communities:

> We were poorly treated, humiliated and unappreciated because we never knew that yes, we did have the right to organise, to participate, to do all types of work. No one gave us an explanation of how we could organise to get out of exploitation. ...

Little by little we came to understand and in this way moved forward until 1994 when we came into the public light – when we could no longer stand the mistreatment of those capitalist fuckers. There we saw that it was true that we [women] did have courage and strength, just like the men, because we could face the enemy without fear. This is why we are ready for anything this evil capitalist system tries to throw at us.

... we lost our fear and timidity, because we now understood that we [women] had the right to participate in all areas of work.

As Rosalinda indicates, under the dark clouds of a protracted, estranging and bleak patriarchal-capitalist reality bereft of colour and joy, the WRL was nothing less than an emancipatory 'politics of collective action' (Gibson-Graham, 1996) through which rural peasant women could organise together, empower themselves and reinvigorate their lives. Moreover, it was a project and process that enabled and emboldened them to build a 'culture of dissent' (Mohanty, 2003), leverage their common voice and shed much-needed light on as well as begin severing at the roots the maltreatments and subjugations they were enduring. In short, what the Zapatista WRL shows us is that the collective political agency of women 'from below' is a righteous force to be reckoned with.

Together and side by side

We must act as if it is possible to build a revolution and radically transform the world.

And we have to do it all the time.

Angela Davis (2014)

Women are rarely offered fair and equal recognition for the foundational roles and crucial work they take on in social movements and liberation fronts (Marcos, 2005b). Despite this they, as Angela Davis (2014) alludes to, have historically been, and will continue to be, the backbone of struggles against extractivism and systemic repression and for structural change. As the women of *La Via Campesina* (International Peasants' Movement) articulate:

Women have had a key role in pushing forward the political and organisational strategies for the future ... against the looting, the devastation, the death and the oppression caused by entrepreneurial and colonial capitalism. (2013)

Identifying with this conviction and recognising this fact prior to even *La Via Campesina* stating it, with the installation of the WRL the Zapatista women were able to trigger discussions in their communities about the gendered imbalances and inequities of social reproduction, as well as spur efforts forwards related to securing more autonomy, involvement and self-efficacy for themselves as women (Speed et al, 2006). Up to that point, women in the bases of support had historically been devoting an exceptionally unequal and unrecognised amount of time, effort, energy and emotional labour to the day-to-day upkeep and nourishment of their rural villages, not to mention the insurgency at large. Given this, the *compas* felt it necessary to rethink and transform the way reproductive work was being performed and valued (JBG, 2013c).

Notably, despite the fact that many of the men were (and sometimes still are) reluctant to accept the WRL, on being reminded that resistance for Zapatistas advances *juntos y a la par* (together and side by side), they ultimately agreed to adopt and abide by the statutes. This is due to a shared recognition that any struggle against colonialism and capitalism is necessarily a struggle against patriarchy. The fact that the Zapatista women were implacably relentless and indefatigably steadfast in animating the merits of the WRL was also a driving force. This dynamic is accentuated by Alejandra, a health promoter-in-training, who, when disclosing what tactic was most effective in convincing men to get on board with the WRL, explains: 'We weren't going to put up with their shit anymore.'[10]

And while *machismo*, gendered divisions of labour and double standards have not been wholly eradicated from Zapatista communities (Klein, 2015), the imposition of the WRL did unsettle pervasive sexist notions of what work women 'naturally must do' (that is, socially reproductive labour), as well as the retrograde and regressive ideals about what was assumed women were 'incapable' of doing (for example, governing, generating ideas, solving problems, offering opinions, working outside of the home/domestic sphere). Speaking candidly about the gender relations operating within Zapatista communities, as well as even giving a bit of credit to Zapatista men for eventually coming around on the WRL, Comandanta Dalia offers her frank assessment of the current situation:

> Even though our men were bastards before, we knew how to get them to understand. There are a few that still act like little assholes sometimes, but at least now it's not all of them. The majority now understand. (Quoted in EZLN, 2015a: 98)

It is not uncommon to now hear Zapatista men speak to the value of, as well as see them engage in, reproductive work, emotional labour, and even the forgoing of indulgences. That is, one significant offshoot of the women's collective organising has been unified agreement to refrain from using alcohol and drugs, a community policy that is now supported and enforced by the

Juntas de Buen Gobierno (Council of Good Government). This sacrificial pledge was not made out of sanctimonious piety, but because alcohol has historically been used as a weapon of colonisation against Indigenous communities. It also has the tendency to, as María a health promoter notes, 'put people to "sleep" and led to abuse'.[11] Since its inception, the decision to abstain from alcohol has resulted in less violence against women, less emotional abuse, less debt to landowners and an overall improvement in the health and security of Zapatista communities, individuals and even the environment (Klein, 2015).

Zapatista women are now more involved than ever in positions of responsibility and decision-making, in addition to taking the lead on projects related to independent media/political communication (*Los Tercios Compas*, 2014), food sovereignty/agroforestry, education, medicine, healthcare, reproductive justice/birth control, land 'recuperation' (land recovered from *hacendados* [ruling class estate-owners]), weaving/artisan cooperatives, and even public relations (Speed, 2006; EZLN, 2018).[12] In attesting to the new reality the Zapatistas are constructing, Peter Rosset, a food sovereignty specialist with *La Via Campesina* who has extensive experience in southern Mexico, indicates the impact of the WRL by stating:

> Yesterday a Zapatista agroecology promoter was in my office and he was talking about how the young Indigenous women in Zapatista territory are different from before … he said they no longer look at the floor when you talk to them – they look you directly in the eye. (Rosset, 2014)

Compañera Lisbeth (EZLN, 2015a: 101) elaborates on the advances the Zapatista women have made in expanding their contributions to – as well as (re)valuations of – reproductive work within the movement:

> We women are already participating in all types of work, such as in the area of health, doing ultrasounds, laboratory work, pap smears, colposcopies, dentistry and nursing; and the three areas of midwifery, bone-setting and medicinal plants.
>
> We are also working in education as *formadoras* (teacher trainers) and coordinators, and education *promotoras* (education promoter/teacher). We have women broadcasters and members of the *Tercios Compas* [Zapatista media team]. We participate in *compañera* collectives, in women's gatherings and youth gatherings. We are also participating as municipal authorities, which includes many different kinds of work, and we women do these tasks. We are also working in the *Juntas de Buen Gobierno* as local authorities, and as board members for the *compañeras'* businesses.

[W]e can tell you clearly that this work is hard, it is not easy ... but these tasks are how the people rule and the government obeys. We now see this as our culture.

In effect, the *compas* have reconstructed the daily rhythms of both their villages and the insurgent body politic. This is made evident given that women are now regularly involved in all aspects of community life, political organising and autonomous governance. More broadly, by placing social reproduction, gender justice, communal intergenerational activities and collective work/reflection at the forefront of their resistance, the Zapatista women have arguably, in a span of only three decades, turned centuries of seemingly intractable patriarchal oppression on its head.

In claiming this, we should offer a caveat, noting that the form and function of the WRL is complex, heterogeneous and adhered to unevenly across differing communities and zones. Meaning, patriarchy has not been totally eliminated, and not all of the 'bad customs', as a *compa* describes them, related to gender relations, have been entirely eradicated. However, what has emerged as a result of the Zapatista women's collective dissent and action in the domain of social reproduction is their ability to question, to speak, to make choices about family life, to claim respect, to live free from abuse and scorn, to demand their partners be co-responsible for domestic tasks and childcare, to work and receive fair pay, and to participate in

Figure 8.3: Young Zapatista women look at various works of art while visiting international sympathisers at the 'Comparte por la Humanidad' ('Sharing Art for Humanity') festival

governance regarding decisions being taken about political organising, community matters and public events (Sierra, 2001; EZLN, 2018). And while the *compas* modestly admit to still having a 'long way to go' in terms of wholly toppling androcentrism, male-dominated decision-making and *machismo*, it is conceivable to say that the gains they have made in the face of the capitalist hydra towards (re)valuing reproductive work and effecting gender-just structural change, as well as advancing both women's collective empowerment and emancipation, are not only among the world's most evolved, but also the most effective.

Other (life-giving) worlds

> [W]e would make another world, a bigger, better one where all the possible worlds fit, for the ones that already exist, and the ones that we haven't yet imagined.
>
> The Zapatistas

In this chapter we have attempted to demonstrate that the everyday sites and spaces of social reproduction are fertile ground, as well as a crucial political terrain on which to struggle, for revolutionary change. The place-based evidence we laid out to do so draws from personal attendance at a host of differing Zapatista events and encounters – content offered by decolonial feminist writers approved by Zapatista communities to conduct research in their territories, as well as, most importantly, taking seriously the voices and collective organising of Zapatista women. On account of the evidence at hand, we propose that the Zapatistas can be seen as inspiration par excellence of an autonomous social movement that is co-creating the gender-just social relations and inclusive politically educated culture its members desire. In addition, we have illustrated how anti-capitalist/anti-colonial resistance, the practice of mutuality and Indigenous worldviews that promote interdependence and interconnectedness can galvanise a diverse and heterogeneous critical mass, animate pathways out of structural violence and transform realities/worlds.

To end, for over 30 years now, the Zapatistas have been forging ahead via '*preguntando caminamos*' ('asking, while walking') on three revolutionary fronts where countless other left activist, academic and advocacy organisations have faltered for decades, if not generations. From our vantage point, these three fronts can be summarised and explained by pointing to a trifecta of the most ubiquitous axioms found in rebel Zapatista territories and communiqués:

✪ '*Un mundo donde quepan muchos mundos*' ('A world where many worlds fit'): The Zapatistas are breathing life into an aspirational alternative pathway out of structural violence and mass alienation that hinges on pluralistic inclusion, the construction of autonomy and rejuvenates an Indigenous worldview that focuses on dignity, interdependence and intergenerational connection.

✪ '*Para todos todo, para nosotros nada*' ('Everything for everyone, nothing for us'): The Zapatistas practice and privilege mutual aid, humility and compassion for others while simultaneously cultivating a collective subject, culture of dissent and critical consciousness in day-to-day life.

✪ '*Cuando una mujer avanza, no hay hombre que retrocede*' ('When a woman advances, no man is left behind'): The Zapatistas, as a result of the political agency of women 'from below', have placed gender justice at the centre of their movement and have revalued social reproduction due to the recognition that colonial-capitalist modernity has not only disproportionately targeted women, but has also dismissed and devalued work that reproduces society, which women are typically tasked with.

Markedly, these principled adages, a veritable prefigurative rebel poetics of autonomous socialist-feminist struggle and selflessness, are given substance through the organised daily praxis of the Indigenous Maya who take up the mantle of becoming 'zapatista'. In light of what has been unfolding across the autonomous municipalities of the Chiapan countryside for the past three decades, the Zapatistas have confirmed that alternatives rooted in 'mutualism, reciprocity, moral economy, sovereignty, and solidarity' (Scoones et al, 2017: 11) not only exist, but can also provide viable pathways out of patriarchal darkness, colonial ruin and capitalist oblivion. Put differently, Babylon can be burnt down.

Bearing in mind the Zapatistas, as Indigenous Ch'ol, Tzeltal, Tzotzil, Tojolobal, Mam and Zoque people, have been one of the primary targets of over half a millennium of the unrelenting infiltrations and provocations of colonial power and racial capitalism, as well as a repressive and negligent state – in addition to the paramilitary shock troops it funds – the strides they are making with respect to building 'another world' and women's collective empowerment are nothing short of miraculous (Comandanta Ramona, 1997; EZLN, 2005). This is neither coincidence nor accident because on becoming familiar with the clandestine genealogy of the Zapatistas (Ramírez and Carlsen, 2008), their stunning underdog upset seems like a foregone conclusion. They are, after all, the renascent embodiment of Zapata's rallying cry for 'Land and freedom!' ('Tierra y libertad') and, contrariwise, the abhorrently labelled yet grossly underestimated 'dirty barefoot Indians' who declared war on neoliberal capitalism and a belligerent racist government (EZLN, 2015a: 94).

Equally impressive is that in the midst of sustaining their ongoing insurrection, the Zapatistas – who have been dispossessed, reviled, persecuted, 'shit on', abandoned, forgotten and quite literally made into the 'poorest of the poor' at the time of their resurgence in 1983 – have shielded their self-determination and independent systems of education, healthcare, participatory democracy, food sovereignty and solidarity economics from dependency on any state, corporate, philanthropic or supranational entity (Speed et al, 2006; Vergara-Camus, 2014). Now, nearly a quarter of a century after the armed uprising of the EZLN, the Zapatistas continue to carry out their construction of autonomous and non-metaphorical decolonisation, collectively, with a healthy dose of militant yet whimsical irony (Olesen, 2007; Di Piramo, 2011; Tuck and Yang, 2012). Notably, rebel Indigenous women, and the socially reproductive labour and care work they do each day, are at the heart of both the movement's emancipatory politics and life-giving world they are building.

9

Health, food sovereignty, solidarity economies

Another world is not only possible, She is on her way.
On a quiet day, I can hear her breathing.

Arundhati Roy

And it is clear that in the colonial countries the peasants alone
are revolutionary, for they have nothing to lose and everything
to gain.

Frantz Fanon

We need not turn any further than the words of Arundhati Roy (2003) and Frantz Fanon (1963) to gain insight into what most threatens life and dignity on this planet, as well as where the ground is most fertile for decolonisation and widespread transformative change. Whether it be mutually recognising the inherent worth of others, decentralising governance, fostering communities of care, co-creating cultures of dissent, actualising emancipatory politics, decommoditising nature, degrowing the economy, effecting food sovereignty or securing material and psychological wellbeing for all, both Roy (2003) and Fanon (1963) rightfully suggest that we just might have something to learn from peasants in identifying what lies at the roots of structural social problems and global inequalities, as well as how to wisely confront and solve them.

As detailed earlier in the book, one of the greatest threats the world currently faces is neoliberalism. As a refresher, the logic of neoliberalism, which endorses responsibilising (blaming) people for the structural conditions they face, entrepreneurial capitalism and free trade agreements that are, paradoxically, heavily regulated by state officials with corporate conflicts of interest, is made manifest through economic policies that promote privatisation, deregulation and cuts to public spending (Mohanty, 2013). Despite rarely being criticised or even mentioned by state officials and mainstream media, neoliberal programmes, practices and rhetoric continue to give rise to unprecedented levels of poverty, anxiety and anguish. This is true not only for the global economy, but also for the global food system and global health.

In light of increased calls to consider neoliberal capitalism as a significant determinant of human and planetary health (Mair, 2020; Sell and Williams,

2020; Flynn, 2021), our focus in this chapter offers an analysis of the entanglements between the social, political and economic factors that shape health and wellbeing. Drawing from examples in EZLN communiqués, as well as on-the-ground food systems and economic practices, we show how the Zapatista struggles offer viable solutions to the devastation caused by global capitalist modernity. Through centring values of care, solidarity and pluralism, the Zapatistas illustrate the realities of thwarting (as much as possible) the devastating and deadly effects of capitalism. It is within these alternative systems and economies that we hear Fanon's (1963: 254) reminder that 'Humanity is waiting for something other from us.' Rather than playing the imitation game of catching up with modernity, the Zapatistas are providing that crucial 'other' that humanity has, for so long, been waiting for.

Autonomous health, care and wellbeing

> We are Zapatistas, carriers of the virus of resistance and rebellion.
>
> EZLN (2020a)

With an announcement that various Zapatista delegates were going to travel to Europe in the summer of 2021, the EZLN published a series of six communiqués between October 2020 and January 2021.[1] Unsurprisingly, given the timing of their release, these writings addressed the COVID-19 pandemic, the subsequent social and economic fallout, and how our community-wide health and wellbeing is circumvented by governments motivated by capitalist logics and economic growth. Specifically, the murder of activist and radio broadcaster, Samir Flores Soberanes, is highlighted here. After months of opposing the Proyecto Integral Morelos, an energy mega-project involving a thermoelectric plant in Huexca and a gas pipeline that would cut through the community of Amilcingo, Samir was shot dead outside his home in February 2019, sparking nationwide protests (Lopez y Rivas, 2019; Wattenbarger, 2020; Oropeza, 2021). Despite continued resistance to the project, as of March 2021, plans for the construction of the plant remain (Alabab-Moser, 2021). The EZLN describe Samir's death as a manifestation of 'the hidden genocides behind the megaprojects, conceived and carried out to please the most powerful player – capitalism – which wreaks punishment on all corners of the world' (EZLN, 2020a).

These communiqués come at a time when social inequalities and injustices have become painfully more evident. The racial and economic disparity in COVID-19-related deaths has been widely documented, with racial minorities across the Global North and South more likely to contract the virus (Mackey et al, 2021; Razai et al, 2021). Subsequent fallout saw social and political institutions being met with rage as people worldwide took to the streets in movements for Black lives, workers' rights, police abolition and climate justice, to name but a few (Press and Carothers, 2020). Therefore, these communiqués arrived at a historic juncture when political decisions were acutely determining the life chances of billions of people across the globe (El-Khatib et al, 2020).

Such a tumultuous year has led to deep questions of the values at the heart of our not too distinct global communities, with the EZLN claiming that 'Despite paramilitaries, pandemics, mega-projects, lies, slander, and oblivion, we live. And by that we mean, we struggle' (EZLN, 2020a). Reflected in these communiqués is the global struggle for healthful lives, pointing to the necessity of opposing systems, institutions and ideologies that cause more harm than good but yet on which our daily lives are continually organised around. Encouraged by these communiqués, we now turn to consider the intersections of global health and capitalism. Focusing on specific themes of politics, medical knowledge and care, we argue for a reconceptualisation of health that restores the notion of dignity to our understanding of health. Notably, although these communiqués document how the Zapatistas are grappling with ideas of 'living well' in light of our global and local realities, they can also be seen as an invitation for the rest of the world to think about what living well and healthful lives looks like, wherever we are.

Figure 9.1: Young Zapatista health promoters gather and greet others at a commemoration for Galeano, a Zapatista education promoter who was murdered by paramilitaries in 2014

Being well outside of colonial-capitalist logics

> Living is not just about not dying, about surviving:
> living as human beings means living with freedom.
> Living is about art, science, joy, dance and struggle.

The Zapatistas

For the purpose of envisioning a better, more equitable picture of global health, the recent communiqués open up questions of living well, healthful lives from Indigenous perspectives. In particular, *Part Five: The gaze and the distance to the door* invites us to consider the doorway as a metaphor for death that can be near or far, depending on the circumstances into which we are born, live or work:

> Among the ordinary peoples that today are Zapatistas, before, death was a door introduced early, almost as of birth. Children often reached that door before five years of age, crossing over with fever and diarrhea. What we tried to do on January 1, 1994, was push that door into the distance. We did, of course, have to be ready to go through the door in our effort to achieve that goal, although that wasn't what we wanted. Since then, our determination has been and continues to be to push that door as far into the distance as possible, to "extend life expectancy" as the experts say. Dignified life, we would add. (EZLN, 2020b)

The act of pushing the doorway further into the distance provides a reflection not only of the state of health in Chiapas, but also on global health and wellbeing writ large. Here death and ill health are directly correlated to social and political contexts within which we live. Prior to 1994, the health of the Indigenous population in Chiapas was poor, with high rates of morbidity and mortality largely attributed to poverty and lack of access to healthcare facilities (Cuevas, 2007). Still today, state-sponsored healthcare in Mexico remains a contentious issue for Indigenous, rural or welfare-dependant and precariously employed citizens (Padilla-Altamira, 2017). Entitlements to healthcare in Mexico are administered via a complex social welfare system, contingent on labour market position and distributed across a hybridised system of care (Kierans, 2019). This means that adequate healthcare is frequently dependent on one's socio-economic status, insurance arrangements and proximity to hospitals and clinics. Bringing attention to frequent instances of childhood mortality shows that for the Zapatistas life – prior to the 1994 rebellion – was worth risking for a better future.

However, simply extending the years that we are alive is not nearly enough. The Zapatistas' life – whether short or long – must be lived with dignity at its heart. The Zapatistas' 'revolution of dignity' (Holloway and Peláez, 1998) goes beyond traditional revolutionary concerns with class, exploitation and power. Putting dignity at the centre of revolutionary projects holds wider political implications, as it takes seriously the values of self-determination, liberation and care. Achieving dignity through autonomy has radically altered not only areas of governance but also public health within Chiapas (Cuevas, 2007; Gallegos and Quinn, 2017).

> We try to distance that door to the point that it can be pushed off to the side, very far ahead of us. That's why we said from the beginning of the uprising that "we would die in order to live." After all, if we do not hand down life – that is, a path – to the next generations, then what did we live for? (EZLN, 2020b)

For those of us who live and work within neoliberal societies, these reflections must be turned back onto ourselves. The Zapatista response to global capitalism and transnational corporate interests in their lands provides the rest of the world with an opportunity to ask themselves the following questions: What is it within our political and social environments that puts us closer to death and keeps us in states of distress or ill health and, more importantly, what can we do about it? In this world of fast-paced global capitalism – where everybody must grasp 'opportunities' for wealth fulfilment, and where a rising precarious 'hustle culture' is chipping away at our mental and physical health (Thieme, 2018) – what values and what futures are we handing down to the next generation?

That said, while many critical scholars, policymakers and health practitioners seek to critique the often-imperfect health systems that they are accustomed to, it is worth bearing in mind that critique only goes so far. And yet, envisioning alternative ways of practising healthcare or sustaining healthy lives for ourselves and our communities may seem like an impossible task. However, Ferrell reminds us that, 'Our inability to imagine alternatives, or to imagine that alternatives can work, may tell us more about the power of the present system than about the alternatives themselves' (1998: 106). Given the relative success of the Zapatista healthcare system, although not perfect, their example of autonomous governance seems like a good place to start when searching for sustainable alternatives. Echoing well-known anarchist perspectives of dismantling the state, we would do well to remember that 'it is not enough to destroy', wrote Kropotkin (1975); 'we must also know how to build.' In other words, how can we engage with Zapatismo in order to build a different way of doing politics, health and care in our respective contexts?

Building a politics of health

Since the publication of the influential Commission on Social Determinants of Health report (WHO, 2008), the effects of non-medical factors that shape health – such as economic stability, the physical environments and education – are increasingly recognised (Collins et al, 2011). Moreover, this report (WHO, 2008) concluded with a sufficiently political message stating that ultimately health is shaped by 'the distribution of money, power, and resources at global, national, and local levels'. However, the political determinants of health – including systems of governance, development agendas, sociocultural norms and political ideologies – are yet to gain a similar level of attention (Kickbusch, 2015; Dawes, 2020). Nevertheless, examining health through the lens of politics is indispensably important since social determinants are more often than not dependent on political action (Bambra et al, 2005). Examining the socio-political determinants of health requires attending to the multiple and varied networks of power (including institutions and ideologies) that impact wellbeing across and within various socio-political contexts. In other words, we must question the environments in which we are born, grow, work and live, as well as the structural and systemic forces that shape the conditions of daily life.

In particular, when we consider the determinants of health for Indigenous communities, we see that focusing on 'social' factors is not enough. As Greenwood, de Leeuw and Lindsay (2018) point out, we need to move beyond the social in order to incorporate the political and historical determinants of health. Extending our conceptualisations of health means recognising factors such as 'spirituality, relationship to the land, geography, history, culture, language, and knowledge systems' (Greenwood et al, 2018: xxiii). Crucially, the historic and ongoing social inequality facing negatively racialised and Indigenous people has meant that racism and active colonialism feed into contemporary manifestations of health and wellbeing. Legacies of genocide, slavery and forced migration continue to play out in the physical and psychological health of descendants whose ancestors were directly affected by the colonial global forces that shaped the 'modern' world (Fanon, 1963; Mignolo, 2011; The Fanon Project, 2010).

In this regard, political education is paramount, enabling us to see how these legacies play out today. Raising critical consciousness (Freire, 2018) is important for health as we begin to awaken to, and eventually tackle, the social issues that are causing harm. From the Zapatistas, we learn of one such action in countering the harm that is wrought by neoliberal ideals of hyper-individualism, which is to centre collectivity in their praxis. Speaking of their response to the pandemic, the EZLN uphold the importance of collective efforts, and that 'facing the threat as a community, not as an individual issue' has allowed them to continue their work of 'resisting, living and struggling' (EZLN, 2020a).

Whether it is through their response to COVID-19 or the NAFTA, the value of collective organisation is reiterated throughout Zapatismo. In the nearly 30 years since the Zapatistas collectively rebelled against the Mexican state, they have managed to build health systems and clinics by cooperatively responding to the needs of local communities. While economic realities remain, the struggle and resistance that the Zapatistas embody has not been foreclosed by the global pandemic. On the contrary, it is the very foundation of community, rather valorising individual people, states or nations, that has seen them through:

> We do need to get back on the streets, yes, but to struggle. As we've said before, life, and the struggle for life, is not an individual issue, but a collective one. Now we see that it's not a national issue either, but a global one. (EZLN, 2020a)

The message is clear — the struggle for life is a collective global struggle. Life and its various components — education, relationships, employment, the natural world — while discrete phenomena are not isolated from each other. Instead, they operate together in a state of interdependence. Once we recognise this, we can take steps toward not only fostering healthy people, but also building healthful and sustainable communities, environments and futures. The increasing trends within Western healthcare to responsibilise individuals for their own healthcare needs is dangerous and even deadly (Sakellariou and Rotarou, 2017). When we fail to put health into its historical, sociocultural or political context, then we fail to see health as a collective concern that requires coordinated action on multiple levels of governance.

Collective resistance for the purpose of health requires us to recognise what is keeping us sick. Whether this be increased work hours, no access to sustainable, healthy food, or toxic natural environments, we can no longer remain ignorant to the fact that the status quo of neoliberal modernity destroys physical and psychological wellbeing while greatly serving a small few (Flynn, 2021). Collective resistance requires courage, and yet it is when we are working in cooperation that we become more steadfast in our resistance. Knowing that we have the support of others around us makes it easier to tackle the socio-political determinants of health that are facing us today.

Integrated health knowledges

Generally speaking, the biomedical model of disease dominates the study and practice of Western health. Founded on Enlightenment principles of empiricism, progress and scientific rationality, biomedicine distinguishes itself from other forms of healing through its reliance on highly technoscientific explanations of health, and the elaboration of risk and surveillance as a means to wellness (Clarke, 2014). Furthermore, as a theoretical framework, biomedicine locates disease in the corporeal body, asserting that organisms function as a collection of discrete parts that are influenced by changes in biochemical processes or structural arrangements (Good et al, 2010), resulting in a narrow and overly deterministic view of health. Additionally, over the past four decades we have witnessed a profound transformation wherein the medical sciences have become increasingly incorporated into global market logics, with medicine becoming an entrepreneurial space that explicitly encourages the commercialisation of its research and 'products' (Sunder Rajan, 2006, 2012; Cooper, 2008). Sunder Rajan (2012) suggests that a variety of legislature and policy changes in the US in the 1980s has resulted in the capitalisation of the life and medical sciences, including a supportive legal climate for the patenting of life forms and the openness of financial markets to bet on biotechnologies, while promoting a culture and ideology of innovation.

Furthermore, recent trends in medical travel exemplify this commercialisation of medical knowledge. For example, the so-called 'psychedelic renaissance' has ushered in clinical and corporate interests in traditional plant substances, rituals and practices (Sessa, 2012). The boom of medical travel sees health clinics (and even holiday-style resorts) in countries across Latin America attract overseas visitors seeking health or psychologically transformative experiences (Harris, 2020). While the growing evidence for psilocybin, ayahuasca, ibogaine and dimethyltryptamine as mental health interventions are indeed promising, there are potential problems with such enterprises. First, once classified as a 'medicine', substances that grow freely in nature (for example, psilocybin or ayahuasca) come under the purview of biomedical-legal frameworks (Pilecki et al, 2021). Consequently, questions arise as to how these substances are to be 'controlled' without circumventing any spiritual or traditional applications that these experiences were once rooted in (Tupper and Labate, 2014). Second, such enterprise potentially enables the appropriation of Indigenous knowledges while romanticising 'neo-shamanic' imagery for the purpose of marketing and capital gain (Dei et al, 2000). The following quote reiterates these concerns of greed and exploitation that capital interests bring to the natural world, and the destruction and harm it causes to those who 'worked and lived off of the land':

The mother Earth, the first mother of all, will rise up and reclaim her house and her place with fire. Upon the arrogant edifices of Power, trees, plants and animals will grow, and in their hearts Votán Zapata will live again. The jaguar will again walk its ancestral paths, reigning once again where money and its lackeys sought to reign. (EZLN, 2020c)

In light of this, we want to draw attention to the health system that operates in Chiapas that blends both traditional and Western biomedical approaches (Berlin and Berlin, 1996; Cuevas, 2007; Gallegos and Quinn, 2017). Curanderism (coming from the Spanish word to heal) is a varied system of healing that can be traced back to the folk practices of pre-Columbian cultures and is influenced by African spirituality and liberatory Catholicism (Kelly and Griffin, 2010). While biomedicine adopts a materialistic and atomised view of the body, curanderism includes the human soul or spirit in processes of healing, attending to both the material and immaterial aspects of health and wellbeing (Torres and Sawyer, 2005). However, biomedical frameworks disregard such practices as cultural relativism or pseudo-science operating on the level of placebo effect (Moerman, 1983; Bala and Gheverghese, 2007). In Chiapas, the most common forms of curanderism are practiced by *yerberos* (herbalists) and *parteras* (midwives), showing that traditional healing practices retain value for the communities (Gallegos and Quinn, 2017).

However, the acceptance of traditional medicine does not preclude the practice of biomedicine. Writing on the death of 12 *compañer@s* due to COVID-19, the EZLN stated that they are focusing on disease prevention measures 'with the support of nongovernmental organizations and scientists who, individually or as a collective, are helping us orient our approach in order to be in a stronger position for any potential new outbreak' (EZLN, 2020a). Following the guidance from scientific advisers, the communities in Chiapas took preventative measures, including: distributing tens of thousands of reusable masks to decrease transmission rates; advising a two-week quarantine for those who were potentially infected; as well as endorsing health promotion messages of hand washing, keeping safe distances and avoiding busy cities (EZLN, 2020a).

Zapatismo opted for prevention and health safety measures based on the advice of scientists who offered their counsel without hesitation. The Zapatista communities want to show their appreciation for this assistance. (EZLN, 2020a)

The Zapatista approach to healthcare provision does not place traditional and biomedical methods in opposition to each other. Writing about the significance of curandersim in Chiapas, Aloisio (2009) states that contemporary Zapatista medicine can be seen as a synthesis of four healing cultural practices, including: traditional Indigenous Maya heritage; contemporary Mexican culture (with its Spanish influence and predominantly Catholic faith); modern Western technological culture; and the Zapatismo ethos of autonomy. This combination of these four elements shows an attempt at reconciling the advantages of both biomedicine and traditional medicine with spiritual and cultural heritage in order to suit the needs of an autonomous social movement. Such a pluralistic form of medicine cannot be viewed outside of its historical and colonial context, which is a necessity when we consider that, outside of Chiapas, adequate public health for rural, cash-poor or Indigenous people in Mexico are still limited (Padilla-Altamira, 2017).

> The conviction that there are many worlds that live and fight within the world. And that any pretence of homogeneity and hegemony threatens the essence of the human being: freedom. The equality of humanity lies in the respect for difference. In its diversity resides its likeness.
>
> The understanding that what allows us to move forward is not the intention to impose our gaze, our steps, companies, paths, and destinations. What allows us to move forward is the listening to and the observation of the Other that, distinct and different, has the same vocation of freedom and justice. (EZLN, 2021)

Too often 'modern' global health, and the biomedical model that it is predicated on, neglect the person as a whole entity. The Zapatistas are striking an intricate balance by providing a holistic approach that attends to the physical, psychological and spiritual elements of the human experience as well as being cognisant of any social and political contexts wherein they

Figure 9.2: A hospital in Zapatista territory with a mural of Maya spirituality and the revolutionaries Che Guevara, Emiliano Zapata and Comandanta Ramona, a revered Zapatista leader

are situated. At the heart of this hybridised health system is a demand for the autonomy to choose – to be provided with up-to-date information and guidance from the medical community, but to ultimately to decide on health practices that suit individual and collective needs.

Centring dignity and care

To hand down life.

EZLN (2020a)

As we emerge into a post-COVID-19 world, how can we use the rage – which saw striking moves against capitalist greed, racism and ecological terrorism – to ensure that we do not return to the 'deadly normal' (Haiven, 2020)? We need only to examine the case of global mental health to see the 'deadly normal' at play. The so-named 'deaths and diseases of despair' (for example, drug and alcohol addiction, suicide) have swamped working- and middle-class citizens in the US with reasons such as long-term labour market decline and lack of material welfare cited as major contributors (Case and Deaton, 2020). It has now become a cultural norm that contemporary participation in colonial-capitalist modernity comes with particular health risks – largely those that are physically and psychologically chronic in nature (Friedman, 2019; Flynn, 2021). As these problems continue to rise, radical change is needed.

In this regard, practices that put care at the centre are crucial. As global life expectancy increases, we are facing a future with a significant ageing population and subsequent higher rates of burden of disease (living with illness/injury or dying prematurely) (Global Burden of Disease Study, 2019). This, in addition to the dual crises of environmental breakdown and social inequality, means that care needs to be central to not only healthcare systems but also all areas of social living (Lawrence and Laybourne-Langton, 2021). COVID-19 has shown us the importance of building caring communities, as evidenced by the rise in mutual aid cooperatives and community-based efforts to distribute food and resources (Care Collective, 2020). Additionally, the struggles and protests against underfunded health services, workplace exploitation, toxic environments and a racist criminal justice system are all fundamentally struggles for life – to live with dignity and care. In searching for ways to enact practices of care, the work of liberation theory and its application to not only individual psychological health but also to community psychology, provides key principles for building caring communities.

The life and work of psychologist Ignacio Martín-Baró (1991, 1996), who championed the liberation movement across Latin America, is of significance here. Working within the context of the El Salvadoran civil war,[2] Martín-Baró, developed a model of liberation psychology that drew on liberation theology and the critical pedagogy of Paulo Freire (2018). Liberation psychology calls on all psychological disciplines (including health, counselling and education) to centre the experiences of the oppressed when analysing human behaviour. For Martín-Baró, taking a view from the margins and joining the oppressed in the fight for social justice was the only way towards liberation. In particular, he called out the colonial defenders of North American/European psychology for its liberal focus on individualism, positivism, hedonism and its lack of perspective on how historical injustices play out to further subjugate and oppress people today. In effect, liberation psychology is a prototype of what a politics of health could look like.

The primary goal of liberation theory and practice is the awakening of critical consciousness within the person or the group (Tate et al, 2013). Martín-Baró (1991: 227) states that critical consciousness is not simply becoming 'aware of a certain fact, but rather it is a process of change'. Thus, if we know that colonial-capitalist modernity and neoliberal governance are increasingly the cause of physical and mental distress, how can we act on it? Liberation theory and praxis forces us to question whether the work that we currently do is the work that is needed for the purpose of human liberation and freedom. By answering the simple question – does this work make yourself and others free or does it maintain the status quo? – liberation theory interrogates the social and political contexts that impact health and wellness.

Crucially, if we consider the work of medicine, we know that the purpose of such work is to ameliorate disease. Despite this, health has moved beyond the bounds of curative or healing principles to reach a market mindset wherein 'health' can be bought and sold at any giving price. Furthermore, the Commonwealth Fund (2019) suggests that 72 million working-age Americans are struggling to pay medical debt, with medical costs becoming one of the main reasons for personal bankruptcy. In this way, we see that the work of medicine has moved beyond ameliorating disease to now becoming a means of creating profit. In these instances, we must ask, where is the care and dignity in financially incentivised healthcare provision?

For any of us, at any given moment, there is no state of complete health or illness. Health is not static; instead it is a fluctuating phenomenon that is achieved through the absence of disease, bodily and mental equilibrium, and the presence of wellbeing. To maintain this state of balance, or health, requires care. However, care cannot be limited to ourselves but must also encompass the communities and environments that we share.

> We see and hear a socially sick world, fragmented into millions of people estranged from each other, doubled down in their efforts for individual survival but united under the oppression of a system that will do anything to satisfy its thirst for profit, even when its path is in direct contradiction to the existence of planet Earth. (EZLN, 2020a)

Notably, care is not simply about the present moment, but requires consideration and action for our present and future selves. To build systems, concepts and principles of health that are grounded in liberation and care, we first need to become aware of the multiple and complex determinants of health, while actively building worlds that enable us to live in healthful, and caring, communities. Within this spirit of care, the convergence of theory transformed into action implies 'an infinite cycle of practicing-knowing-transforming' (Flores Osorio, 2009: 15). Building unity between knowing and doing does not mean that our actions will always be perfect. Nonetheless, it means working to enact what we know is an ongoing, iterative and reciprocal process that can and must be worked through, cooperatively between ourselves and our communities.

> These are resistances and rebellions that teach us Zapatistas that the solutions may be found below, in the basements and corners of the world, not in the halls of government or the offices of large corporations. (EZLN, 2020a)

While the global capitalist economy has unparalleled productive capacity, it fails to harness this capacity for the purpose of creating global conditions that sustain dignified and healthful lives. As such, we now turn to consider two examples of practical solutions that demonstrate how we can effect change in our everyday life. Notably, these practices of agroecology and economies built around solidarity show that the fabled 'realism' of capitalism can indeed be overturned to build communities and societies that prioritise human and planetary health.

The corporate food regime

The current globalised food system, often critically referred to as the 'corporate food regime' (McMichael, 2005), fails to consider the everyday needs and rights of people. This neglect has resulted in persistent world hunger, poverty, malnutrition and injustice. The organisation Food First (2012) noted that the quantity of food produced on a global level is sufficient to feed approximately 10 billion people. Despite this, the neoliberal production, distribution and management of the current corporate food regime has left over one billion people malnourished and in acute hunger. Influenced by capitalist thinking and transnational corporations, food justice is a matter of global health.

The contrast between what actually existing food security would look like and the world's current state of food insecurity is quite severe. Here, we should point out the frequent misconception and confusion between the terms 'food sovereignty' and 'food security'. Food security is achieved when individuals have access to basic food at all times in order to maintain and support life (Stephens et al, 2018). It alludes to the sufficient availability of world food supplies that can withstand a steady rise in food consumption, as well as fluctuations in food production and prices. Even if food security is prioritised, food can be unhealthy, poorly distributed and not a good fit for a healthful life. Currently, mainstream discussions of food security often still take global capitalism and state power for granted, focusing on entrepreneurialism, profitable commodities and processed, imported and/or GMO (genetically modified organisms) food commodities. This focus comes at the expense of prioritising land access for communities-in-struggle; the practice of organic agroecology; the wellbeing of ecosystems food system workers; and the equitable distribution of healthful and culturally appropriate food (Giraldo and Rosset, 2018).

Broadly speaking, the needs and desires of communities, farmers or the planet more widely are not catered for in corporate discussions of food security (Morvaridi, 2012). The impacts of environmental degradation and the privatisation of seeds and transgenic crops are not necessarily centred either. Similarly, international trade agreements are frequently not approached critically, despite contributing to the drastic impoverishment and suffering of billions of farmers and rural workers worldwide (Mishra, 2020). Instead, rights are reserved for large corporations, with the global 'market', industrial agriculture and international financial institutions ultimately deciding what food is produced, how it is produced and to whom it is (or is not) distributed (Matsushita et al, 2015). In short, under our present-day neoliberal global economy (and its taken-for-granted free trade agreements), import dependency endures, nature remains commoditised, plantations persist, land grabbing continues and food distribution is based on who has sufficient capital to purchase it.

To link this to the Zapatista struggle, in North America, the socio-spatial fallout from the agricultural dumping that ensued as a result of the NAFTA displaced millions of working-class and peasant food producers from their homes in rural Mexico, pushing them into *maquiladoras* (sweatshops) that mark the industrial urban landscape of border cities (Jordaan, 2012). Notably, agricultural dumping exposes Indigenous people and peasants from agrarian communities to more intense degrees of vulnerability than others in Mexico and beyond, largely because Indigenous people and peasants are typically less socio-economically and geographically mobile given they: (1) experience higher rates of systemic oppression, racist exclusion and classist discrimination; and (2) are less likely to leave their ancestral lands given their kinship ties, origin stories and living histories are situated within the territories where they reside (Gutierrez, 1996). Moreover, rural Indigenous landworkers in Mexico who were uprooted from their homes by the NAFTA were less likely to be hired for the exploitative toil that was available in the *maquiladoras* (Otero, 2011; Altamirano-Jiménez, 2013). Here, we need to be cognisant of what political officials and corporations actually mean when they say they are 'creating more jobs' when marketing and sponsoring free trade agreements and setting up export processing zones.

In light of these realities, the Zapatistas responded to the impossible circumstances that had been levied against them by neoliberalism 'with fire and blood' (EZLN, 2012), via their armed uprising in 1994. And, while the ratification of the NAFTA appeared to be the direct cause of their rebellion, it is important to reiterate that the roots of their revolt actually stem from being subjected to over five hundred years of colonial persecution and capitalist exploitation. Their insurrection in 1994 was thereby only one part of a historical and ongoing reply to the prejudiced subjugation Indigenous people were facing as a result of accumulation by dispossession, cultural ignorance and state repression. Moreover, it was a collective response to neoliberal incursions that were further privatising their *ejidos* (communally held lands), disrupting their efforts to build an alternative solidarity economy, while stifling their practice of agroecology and efforts of achieving food sovereignty (Rosset et al, 2006).

Food sovereignty and agroecology

In defining food sovereignty, members of *La Via Campesina* (The Way of the Peasant) (2007), a transcontinental peasant syndicate, and one of the largest and most diverse social movements in history, claimed that it was 'the right of peoples to healthy and culturally appropriate food produced through ecologically sound and sustainable methods, and their right to define their own food and agriculture systems'. *La Via Campesina* is strengthened by the involvement of over 200 million peasants with different skills and expertise from over 70 countries. The movement, which ranges from farmers and fisherfolk to agrarian artisans and Indigenous people, has a worldwide presence but is particularly strong across the Majority World/ Global South. Under food sovereignty, food is produced and distributed via non-exploitative relationships and environmentally sustainable methods, with all decision-making powers and rights handed over to grassroots people and workers (Martínez-Torres and Rosset, 2010).

Food sovereignty provides grassroots communities with the power to shape and define food systems according to their needs, identifying which farming practices and food distribution measures are most appropriate for them. It also advocates for the equal delegation of rights for the use of land, aquatic resources and pastoral and fishery systems by farmers, landworkers and fisherfolk (Patel, 2009). This arrangement not only facilitates peasant empowerment, but also family farm-driven agroecology, community self-reliance and the domestic production and trade of organic crops and produce. Food sovereignty means that land, seeds, water and the means of production are neither privately owned nor individually patented; rather, they are held and shared in common. That is, the production, distribution and consumption of organic crops and food is determined by local communities themselves – not neoliberal market forces, transnational corporations or ruling-class political elites. In emphasising the needs and desires of local communities, food sovereignty circumvents institutional exploitation and systemic inequity, giving rise to more ethical and socio-economically just relations between food producers and consumers.

Moving beyond food security, food sovereignty is an alternative method, emancipatory practice and *political* way of thinking about global and local food networks. In other words, it is a means of achieving food security alongside empowering marginalised communities, safeguarding the environment and protecting the commons. Furthermore, there is growing evidence that rural social movements that are applying the principles of food sovereignty offer us insight vis-à-vis viable and sustainable solutions to the growing and complex problems of world hunger, the unequal distribution of food and the unnecessary production and consumption of unhealthy food items (Rosset and Martínez-Torres, 2012). Put differently, while proponents of food security are not necessarily committed to ending exploitation, ecological damage, institutionalised hierarchies, unregulated GMOs, seed patents or wealth hoarding, advocates of food sovereignty are.

An important element for achieving food sovereignty is agroecology. The methods and practices of agroecology date back to traditional organic farming, companion planting and intercropping, all of which depend principally on respecting the environment and maintaining sustainable relationships with natural ecosystems and local environments (Sevilla Guzmán and Woodgate, 2013). Such a framework significantly departs from viewing land as a source of capital from which commodities are to be extracted. Implementing practices of agroecology can improve the resiliency of food systems as they ensure a respectful relationship and symbiotic collaboration between farmers and local ecosystems. Here, consider the ancestral food systems, land management practices and socio-ecological relations that various Indigenous communities have had with their ecosystems and territories (Hammelman et al, 2020). Agroecology emphasises the rooted knowledges and sustainable practices that peasant farmers have employed for generations. Instead of centring the preferred practices of multinational corporations like Monsanto or relying on 'modern' technologies like fossil-fuelled mechanisation, industrial engineering and patented seeds/transgenic crops to increase the speed and production of large-scale monoculture (Shiva, 2001), agroecology prioritises small-scale farmers and low-impact organic farming techniques.

Today, the global food system faces countless challenges, including worldwide social inequality and the degradation of environments generated by ongoing colonial relationships and extractivist neoliberal thinking (Acosta, 2013), a phenomenon that, as we have highlighted earlier, has only been further exacerbated by the COVID-19 pandemic. However, agroecology, put in the service of achieving food sovereignty, can aid in the conservation of biodiversity and preservation of life, both human and non-human. For the peasants and rural landworkers around the world, food sovereignty and agroecology provide revolutionary solutions to these challenges. Seeking to end the power imbalances of the corporate food regime (maintained by global capitalist logics), food sovereignty provides an alternative solution wherein the means of production and distribution of food is wrestled away from multinational corporations and consolidated state power, and held in common by everyday people (Claeys, 2015). In other words, food sovereignty is practised by those who are committed to the democratic process and securing the health and wellbeing of both people and planet Earth.

Collective work, decommoditising nature

In material terms, the Zapatista food system provides landworkers with an opportunity to abandon capitalist logics and accumulation motives in order to position collective work and Indigenous notions of territory and nature as essential in maintaining the cultural, spiritual and environmental health and welfare of their communities (Lorenzano, 1998). This has come to fruition through the Zapatistas' recuperation of colonially expropriated lands, which they reclaimed from wealthy *hacienda* owners during their 1994 uprising (Barmeyer, 2003). One way in which these sentiments, as well as resistance, manifest in the Zapatistas' pursuit of seed and food sovereignty is through the application of organic agroecology practices (Hernández et al, 2020). From our time and experience in Zapatista territory, the following explains how agroecology is used in the pursuit of healthful and sustainable food systems in Chiapas.

We participated in agroecological practice via a rural *milpa* (cornfield) in a highland cloud forest of Chiapas. Here, dozens of Zapatistas from the countryside, donning dry mud-splattered shoes and rubber boots, and wielding worn steel-headed hoes and tenured machetes, gathered in an open area surrounded by steep rolling hills and low-hanging fog to plant vegetables. In fielding our many queries, an agroecology promoter explained:

> Collective work like this did not exist when the landowners were in control. We were servants. We were beaten, scolded, and alone. There was much suffering. Now we organise to grow and share vegetables. That is why we are all here [working together at the community garden]: adults, children and elders. Everyone can contribute something. Everyone has value.

Further illustrating this dynamic, a Zapatista education promoter later noted:

> We were not in control of our food, which meant they [landowning capitalists and the 'bad' government] were controlling us. Now, we have our own projects. We started to plant and sow and work the land collectively, like before. You can see the results. We are planting beans and corn together, and eating radishes, cabbages, carrots and cilantro. It is our work and we are happy. This is autonomy. You can see it in our garden.

Imagination, intergenerational relationships and critical thought are fundamental aspects of everyday life and daily work in Zapatista territory (Holloway, 2010). What the Zapatistas demonstrate is that envisioning new social relations and fostering critical consciousness are not abstracted ideals. Rather, the intellectual labour that goes into questioning the status quo, discussing ideas, seeking solutions and learning new things is recognised as a necessary and material component of their struggle against exploitation, repression and domination. All of these things are recognised as active, applied and practical exercises of crafting a world/reality that mends the 'colonial wound' (Mignolo, 2011). In other words, the Zapatistas are countering the harms and inequalities that are inflicted by neoliberalism through their

Figure 9.3: A Zapatista harvest of non-GMO corn stored at an estate house and on lands they recuperated during the uprising in 1994

agroecological practices while promoting a mutual recognition of dignity among people.

An education promoter in Zapatista territory elaborated on this critique by underscoring the links that capitalist economics, the financialisation of everyday life and (neo)liberal social relations have with each other in the following statement:

> Ideas and work that produce profit for corporations and capitalists are elevated over those that contribute to community health and the overall wellbeing of our people, of all people ... we are not going to live our lives on these terms.

Indeed, the Zapatistas took up arms against such terms, choosing instead to focus on Indigenous worldviews and the products of anti-capitalist collective work over the fickle ego-boosts of individualism and fleeting comforts of consumerism (Harvey, 2005). Not coincidentally, solidarity and mutual aid now permeate their communities, day-to-day exchanges and social interactions. This is especially true regarding their production and distribution of food – a marked effort in food sovereignty, which takes myriad forms (Hernández et al, 2020). Some of these include seed saving, collectivising harvests, refusing to use chemical products, maintaining Indigenous cultural ties with land and water, equitably distributing and sharing work, and even incorporating the tending of *milpas* (small fields of fertile land used in subsistence farming) into their autonomous education system.

Accordingly, food sovereignty for the Zapatistas, particularly when coupled with their perspectives on capitalism, means rejecting personal entitlements to wealth accumulation, eschewing state-legitimated notions of private property and severing themselves from dependency on corporate agribusiness (Bobrow-Strain, 2007). More simply, it means that reciprocated respect, selflessness and teamwork drive the Zapatista economy, rather than the exploitation, alienation and advantage-taking of capitalist economies.

Considering these descriptions, one might ask what this looks like in practice. In addressing this, the same Zapatista education promoter summed up their economy by noting that it is 'decentralised', wherein 'everyone participates'. This economy is generated and modified by community assemblies through basic questions like: 'Is everyone okay?' 'Is anyone going hungry?' 'Is the community healthy?' and 'Is the soil nourished?' to name but a few. Such questioning is in stark contrast to the fetishes and fixations that characterise capitalist economies, which are preoccupied with questions such as 'How can I gain an advantage over others?' and 'What can I do to get more?' The economy constructed by the Zapatistas is one that works for the people (rather than vice versa) and is rooted in planting 'seeds of resistance', literally and figuratively (Aguila-Way, 2014). It foregrounds ethics, empathy and collective wellbeing, which was made clear by an education promoter who stated:

> We are not preoccupied with self-interest, individual gain, or power like those 'from above'. Our economy, or whatever you want to call it, asserts the value of life. It recognises the dignity in each, no matter how *otroa* ['other', meaning different] they are.

Due to their refusal to become complicit with entrepreneurial capitalism, the commodification of nature or the privatisation of land, the Zapatistas have built a sustainable food system that functions as a moral economy that maintains and revitalises their Indigenous ancestral knowledge, land use techniques and even spiritual practices (Barbosa, 2021). It is an economy defined by participatory governance and collective ethics, and takes into consideration the health and wellbeing of individuals and communities, as well as local ecosystems, via the practice of agroecology (Morales, 2021). To put it cogently, it is a rebel solidarity economy that the Zapatistas are breathing life into with each new seed that they sow. With this in mind, it is worthwhile elaborating on the notion of the solidarity economy as it prompts us to imagine what an alternative system might look like wherever we are.

Solidarity economies: from degrowth to pluralism

Consideration of the solidarity economy is particularly important given the colonial-capitalist realities that many of us face. Indeed, Fredric Jameson's (2003: 76) often-repeated reflection that 'it is easier to imagine an end to the world than an end to capitalism' has become an unfortunate truism. Fortunately, movements like the Zapatistas offer us concrete examples of what an end to capitalism and viable alternatives could look like.

For centuries, the global economy has used the language of 'development' and 'growth' to mask exploitation, alienation and extraction. More recently, it has experienced multiple economic declines, with the Great Depression, stagflation in the 1970s, the 2008 recession and pandemic-related shocks being only a few examples. Undoubtedly, capitalism is a common denominator. Here, it is important to reiterate that capitalism's growth fetish is a colonising process and force, not to mention the ongoing product of the colonial enterprise. Capitalist growth has led to the inequitable distribution of both wealth and power, which end up being held by a minority. Moreover, poverty, alienation and environmental destruction are all direct products of capitalist economies, extraction and growth, despite the fact that these are often framed as 'externalities'. In turn, countless communities across the world have proposed and began working on alternative solidarity economies oriented towards 'degrowing' the economy (Kallis, 2011).

Emily Kawano (2013), writing as a member of the Intercontinental Network for the Promotion of Social Solidarity Economy (RIPESS [*Red Intercontinental de Promoción de la Economía Social Solidaria*]), describes the development of solidarity economies as a global movement that focuses on the wellbeing and health of the people and the planet. She further emphasises that just and sustainable economies will comprise of old, new and emergent practices. The main transformation solidarity economies provide is a departure from extractive logics, capitalist growth imperatives and authoritative state-dominated systems, such as neoliberalism. In further detailing what defines solidarity economies and degrowth, Kawano (2013: 3) writes:

> We understand transformation to include our economic as well as social and political systems, all of which are inextricably intertwined. The economy is a social construction, not a natural phenomenon, and is shaped by the interplay with other dynamics in culture, politics, history, the ecosystem, and technology. Solidarity economy requires a shift in our economic paradigm from one that prioritizes profit and growth to one that prioritizes living in harmony with each other and nature.

In elaborating, Kawano draws directly from the Zapatista notion of building 'a world where many worlds fit' (*un mundo donde quepan muchos mundos*), as this principle allows and welcomes difference and diversity with respect to socio-political ideologies and pluralistic cultures that undermine and counteract capitalism. As the Zapatistas, Kawano and others committed to 'degrowth' note (Nirmal and Rocheleau, 2019), there is an urgent need for societies and communities to prioritise the physical and psychosocial health of people, as well as that of ecosystems and environments, over commercial profits, industrial production and excess conspicuous consumption.

In order to get a better sense of what solidarity economies look like, Kawano (2013) offers the following five principles, which, in addition to Indigenous worldviews, we feel reflect what the Zapatistas have incorporated into their diverse economic practices: solidarity, pluralism, equity, participatory democracy and sustainability. Markedly, Kawano notes that implementing only one or a few of these principles individually or disjointedly will not result in a solidarity economy; rather, they must be integrated collectively and reiteratively.

Solidarity, in its name, is the practice of mutual respect, unity and collectivism across difference. Kawano (2013: 5) explains that solidarity encourages and nurtures 'cooperation, mutualism, sharing, reciprocity, altruism, love, caring, and gifting' as opposed to the teachings of capitalism that endorse competitiveness, individualism, discrimination and segregation. Solidarity emphasises the importance of socially reproductive labour and the non-monetised sector, recognising each as part of the 'real economy'. Social reproduction and non-monetised activities, as noted in Chapter 7, primarily entail care work and community building, all of which foster social bonds and collective wellbeing, and afford people a sense of connection, purpose and meaning. These activities include volunteer work, community events, helping a neighbour, eldercare, child-rearing, cooking and cleaning, to name but a few (Bhattacharya, 2017). Without this type of work, societies will not function, which raises questions as to why it has been so grossly devalued and undercompensated under capitalism social relations.

Another key principle Kawano (2013) offers is pluralism, which opposes capitalism and its promotion of a universalising 'one-size-fits-all model'. Pluralism welcomes different ways of being, worldviews, approaches and practices, as well as considers all in order to decipher what constellation of shared values and actions is best suitable for any given community's current socio-political and economic realities. Solidarity economies respect and encourage a multitude of interpretations and a variety of possibilities that are oriented towards the goal of harmonious sustainability. Sustainability, which recognises the rights of the Earth, focuses on human and non-human health and strives to safeguard the planet from destruction and exploitation, means allowing a sense of care for the future to guide what we do now. Notably, pluralism accepts that the idea of building a solidarity economy has variation within it and is not prescriptive. Different communities in different contexts will construct different economies. There is neither a perfect blueprint nor rigid model, which echoes the sentiments of the Zapatistas when they talk about their shared principles, resistance, construction of autonomy and economy.

10

A battle for the soul of education

The problems, challenges and individualism at hand

> What's ridiculous about all that is that those who oppress us today
> pretend to play the role of our 'liberators'.
>
> Zapatista Squadron 421 (2021)

When viewed in its historical and contemporary geopolitical context, the Zapatista struggle has opened up possibilities for a broad array of emancipatory ways of reorganising social relations, economies, education, governance, food systems, day-to-day activities, interpersonal interactions and even thought. As not only the Zapatistas but also many readers will know, it takes an inordinate amount of courage, fortitude and heart to stand up to and declare '¡Ya basta!' ('Enough is enough!') in the face of an oppressive authority figure, institution or status quo. The consequences and retribution can be devastating, as we are sure many of you are also all too familiar with.

In reiterating that the purpose of their resistance is 'to hand down life', the latest Zapatista communiqués related to their 'Declaration for Life' make it clear what it is we fight for – life. The purpose of our respective struggles against the pressures of capitalist-modernity is to be able to hand down life (a dignified life, you might add) to the next generation. Amidst a global pandemic, examining the political determinants of health, as well as understanding the many forms that healing can take – whether this be through gender justice, food systems or alternative economies – is one way to enact care. Creating a society of mutual care, solidarity and resilience will require deep reimagining of our 'common sense' and taken-for-granted institutions and infrastructures, to consider whether we need to reform or rebuild from scratch. The Zapatistas, and their recognition that community, health and ecosystems are interdependent, politically determined and multiple, is such one example. Despite the economic realities that remain, the struggle and resistance that the Zapatistas embody has not been foreclosed by the global crises we all are contending with, albeit differentially. On the contrary, it is the very foundations of community rather than the individual that has seen them through. The message is clear that the struggle for life is a *collective* global struggle. If not now, when?

Given their resoluteness in foregrounding care, resistance, Indigenous knowledge, mutual aid, political education and praxis as pillars of their social movement – as well as their concurrent refusal to be bystanders and to reject, absolutely, the logics of neoliberalism and the norms of a heteropatriarchal status quo – the Zapatistas can arguably be viewed as one of the most radical and progressive movements vis-à-vis decolonisation, democracy, justice – and hope – in history. That said, while the world has much to learn from various Indigenous and peasant communities regarding sustaining life and the planet, it is unethical – not to mention epistemic violence – to poach, plagiarise and expropriate Indigenous concepts. With that caution in mind, it is paramount that we learn to listen to and perhaps even take to heart Indigenous knowledges and concepts related to sustainability, health and our place within the world. Our point here is that there is undoubtedly much to be learned regarding alternatives and theories of change from the political agency, collective organising and intellectual work of communities-in-struggle. We would encourage everyone to explore, discover and cite these pluralistic knowledges 'from below' more consistently and intentionally, particularly those of us who find ourselves in universities.

On the matter of universities, it is patently obvious that neoliberalism has hijacked higher education and is holding it hostage. Managers and overseers are demanding a ransom in the form of tuition payments, housing fees and deference from students, as well as obedience, conformity and docility from administrators, faculty members and workers. The fast-paced pursuit of rank, prestige, clout, careerist attention and neoliberal 'impact', as well as subsequent award cultures, self-aggrandising behaviour, self-promoting tendencies and liberal bystanding that pervades academia and forecloses possibilities for engaged dialectics, praxis and political education, is not only disappointing, but also dangerous – both socially and psychologically, as noted earlier. There is no shortage of evidence, and we can collectively testify that this is happening across the Global North and Majority World/Global South.

Consequently, a collective struggle against neoliberal universities is exigent. A unified front is especially crucial in the given moment considering that universities are driving students, faculty and workers into states of acute anxiety, chronic depression, financial duress and pathological self-centrism. A struggle in the arena of further education is also urgent because life in neoliberal universities is replete with atomisation, hyper-competitive comparison and institutionalised evaluations that ascribe rank and worth to people based on specious bourgeois notions of excellence and merit. For example, we all know colleagues who think of themselves as brilliant and bold 'field-setting' scholars yet 'pull links' and rely on institutional pedigree, industry connections and elitist peer networks (that others have no access to) to capture grants, have their work (in)formally reviewed/published and build their careers. These privileges, conflicts of interest, acts of malpractice and corruptions, along with the public boast-posting and self-promotions that accompany them, disparately occur in the

Global North – even among scholars who are supposedly committed to critical/radical research on coloniality, race, borders, gender, development and justice. The professional is indeed the political, and anyone who argues otherwise is guilty of the most shameful type of liberal disaffiliation, absolution, and obliviousness.

Regrettably, universities are now predominantly composed of good neoliberal subjects who are either ignorant of or conveniently omit the degree to which their careers and successes are owed to acquiesce, complicity and self-centrism. People are stealing livings, brazenly, and reaping rewards for being either sycophants to or simply compliant with the status quo (and corporate journals) while duplicitous institutions and managers devote more time to collecting rent and chasing contrived metrics than nurturing critical consciousness, meaningful experiences and the hearts and minds of students and workers. It is perfectly reasonable to state that neoliberal universities either need to be stormed, set on fire and torn asunder or just walked out of and left behind altogether for something new because they are corrupting and punishing the curiosity, creativity, collectivity, imagination, integrity, joy and humanity out of us.

To unsettle the fragmenting and injurious processes and alienation that is occurring across higher education, we must be able to leverage the collective pain and rage people are feeling in ways that confront and undermine conventions and administrative decrees that are aimed at domesticating students and workers. We can disrupt the repressive norms of neoliberal universities by collectively reshaping our discourses, habits and behaviours into actions that are more inclusive, anti-racist, feminist, queer and anti-classist. The practice of care, relationality, accountability and solidarity – in addition to queering and 'killing the joy' and comfort of upper/middle-class, male-dominated, and ableist spaces – are essential in throwing a proverbial wrench in the gears of any (neocolonial) institution that is trying to compel and coerce people into becoming docile (exploitable) subjects. More pointedly, we should be promoting political education and collective action rather than self-centred entrepreneurialism and uncritical notions of 'global citizenship'. If the practice of freedom, pursuit of justice and fruition of democracy are not at the heart and soul of (y)our education, then it is not an education worth having at all.

The solution: building better worlds, realities and relations

> Everyone fits within Zapatismo, there are no universal recipes, lines, strategies, tactics, laws, rules, or slogans. There is only a desire – to build a better world, that is, a new world.
>
> The Zapatistas

We have written this book in a time of extreme conflict, intense suffering and acute crisis. Climate chaos, environmental ruin and the fallout of COVID-19 have all shown us that our response requires a *collective* global effort to rebuild economies, social institutions and sociocultural values that are fit for human flourishing and planetary revival. Rather than reproducing the same fatal inequalities in a post-pandemic era, should it ever arrive, we have the opportunity to think deeply about the political and economic forces that continue to exacerbate social inequalities and the destruction of ecosystems. Neither political officials nor ruling-class philanthropists have the solutions. They are, in fact, part of the problem. And while many have used the pandemic as an opportunity to critically appraise what is not working, we also need to provide or look for alternative visions of what can work. On this point, we note that the Zapatistas, while arguably one of the world's foremost examples of resistance, have also spent as much time, if not more, constructing autonomy and building a 'world where many worlds fit', which is characterised by shared ethics, principled action, responsible behaviour, a respect for boundaries, and maintaining healthy relationships with each other and the environment. On this point, we believe we can all learn a tremendous amount from the movement – but fostering political education where we respectively are should be the priority.

Avoiding the social destruction and spiritual death being wrought by neoliberal education, in turn, means being creative, curious, humble and in dialogue with each other (in particular, with students); engaging with communities and those who lack access; and refusing to both bystand with indifference and put any faith in middle-class moderates and wealthy managers. Put differently, the fact of the matter remains that answers to the problems of structural inequality and institutionalised oppression and solutions to the global challenges and myriad local crises we face today will be sourced from grassroots movements and communities-in-struggle, not 'prestigious' institutions and credentialed individuals. The former (prestigious institutions) are inessential if not useless and at the heart of the problem, while the latter (the credentialed class) may have a small role to play, perhaps.

Our attention must be focused on the knowledges produced by community work and the day-to-day praxis of movements 'from below' (Choudry et al, 2013). Markedly, if grounded and engaged activist work does not sound 'academic' enough or constitute 'intellectual labour' in anyone's eyes, then we would suggest they seriously reflect on their own capacity for discernment, not to mention bourgeois proclivities, classist tendencies and predilections for elitism. To put it bluntly, we need to radically rethink the types of relations we are reproducing (ourselves as authors included). This will require listening and sacrifice on the part of those with stability, security, seniority and privilege. To genuinely transform the reality of the neoliberal university, we must slow down, spend time with each other (as well as students), take seriously each other's burdens and everyday struggles, and be far more generous with solidarity. Looking out for ourselves and 'playing the game', so to speak, as individuals, while perhaps somewhat understandable, will not get us there, and is no longer an acceptable excuse or reason.

The Zapatistas, in following the aforementioned collective ethics and rebel poetics of '*mandar obedeciendo*' ('to lead by obeying') and '*para todos todo, para nosotros nada*' ('everything for everyone, nothing for us'), offer us an example of how to jettison and transcend ego, individual ambition, anti-democratic conventions and authoritarian relations by putting both others and the collective first. Moreover, adhering to the principles offered by Zapatismo within any given education system would breathe life into inclusive and liberatory pedagogies that are defined by constant and continual processes of introspection, collective action and relational care. If we are to confront the incursion of neoliberal discourses and liberal–colonial worldviews in the classrooms, workplaces, offices and hallways in which we find ourselves, it is essential we offer support, compassion and empathy to one another, as well as respond en masse when power is being abused or others are being exploited, devalued or neglected. Employing the practice of Zapatismo means putting time and effort into affective labour, building community, respecting boundaries and acknowledging the inherent dignity of others, which will safeguard us all from the estrangement and neuroses that neoliberalism is increasingly giving rise to.

The principles associated with Zapatismo sanction mutuality, liberation and freedom. Embracing them encourages us to be trustworthy and convivial with one another yet indignant with abusive institutions, administrations and authority figures. The principles also afford us the opportunity to rebuke individualism, abandon capitalist social relations and work together to transform the status quo via inclusion and imagination, as well as through acts of mutual validation and belonging. The principles of Zapatismo can inspire us to envision alternatives and move forward with creativity and conviction to realise those alternatives. To put it simply, Zapatismo nourishes hope. Not hope in an abstract sense of the word (Zournazi, 2002), but the type of radical hope that, when sown through everyday acts of respect, care and patience, and nourished by collective resistance and mutual rage, is lived and felt. It gives rise to the kind of hope that tends to wounds, comforts affliction, wakes up history and enlarges hearts. The kind of hope that causes chests to swell, jaws to clench and arms to lock when others are being belittled, humiliated or hurt regardless of whether it be by individual, institution, system, structure, apparatus or discourse.

In sum, Zapatismo suggests the affliction and estrangement of neoliberalism can be overcome, because, truth be told, neoliberalism is neither an invincible colossus nor an unassailable master – it is merely a reality, albeit one that is unrelenting and hostile to both the human spirit and life of the planet.

Nevertheless, realities can be changed, just as hydras can be slayed. We need not look any further than the Zapatistas for proof of this. What the Zapatistas have confirmed through their emancipatory praxis and commitment to political education is that Indigenous worldviews, in conjunction with anti-capitalist resistance, inclusive democratic process and commitments to gender justice, can unquestionably provide viable alternatives to the world's current neoliberal and ongoing colonial (dis)order of things. More revealingly, what the Zapatistas are illustrating for us via their collective action is that hope should not be lost, and that the practice of liberatory struggle, convivial solidarity and revolutionary humanism can certainly create pathways out of structural violence, mass alienation, institutionalised oppression, oblivion and Babylon.

To end, we call back to the Zapatista poetics offered at the outset of the book to propose that building '*un mundo donde quepan muchos mundo*' ('a world where many worlds fit') is the answer (and antidote) to the suffering, anguish and malevolence produced by colonial modernity and neoliberalism. Indeed, another world is not only possible, but is being constructed as we speak. Perhaps most encouragingly, what other possible realities and 'worlds' are imagined and eventually emerge is up to us. Let us be ruthless in our devotion towards this end—and to each other—and let us begin.

Notes

Introduction

[1] This is also the case with the photographs and images that appear throughout the text, which we collected as contributors to the *Medios Libres: Autonomos, Alternativos o Como Se Llamen* ('Free, Alternative, Autonomous Media or Whatever They're Called').

[2] We have deliberately opted to use the term 'knowledges' throughout the text to illustrate the point that 'Indigenous knowledge' is neither uniform nor fixed, but rather, are heterogeneous, dynamic, ever-evolving, and pluralistic, not to mention uniquely situated in different territories and contexts.

[3] Partial and/or updated content for different chapters throughout this book draw from the following sources: Gahman, 2016; Gahman, 2017; Gahman et al, 2019; Gahman, 2020a.

Chapter 2

[1] PRI stands for *Partido Revolucionario Institucional* (Institutional Revolutionary Party), one of the major ruling parties in Mexico. Throughout the country, those who support the party are often referred to as *PRI'istas*.

[2] Importantly, we do not speak for the Zapatistas, and nor do we speak on behalf of the Zapatistas. We are simply writing about some of our differential experiences with the Zapatistas and Zapatismo. Our interpretation and account of Zapatismo and the Zapatistas is admittedly limited and partial with any mistakes, misrepresentations or errors here being our own.

Chapter 3

[1] We use the identity-first and heterogeneous collective/community term 'disabled people' throughout the book to illustrate how some people are disabled because of the environments, institutions, cultural norms and contexts they find themselves in, which frequently are neither structured nor equipped to allow disabled people to fully participate and thrive in the societies within which they are living. In doing so, we are not suggesting 'disabled people' is the 'correct' term and also note that the person-first language of 'people with disabilities' will be the most appropriate vocabulary to use in certain contexts. While complex, the respectful thing to do is listen to and adapt to the preferences of what disabled people or people with disabilities prefer in any given interaction or situation.

[2] Women in Global Health (WGH) is an organisation dedicated to achieving gender equity in global health leadership. Further information can be found at: www.womeningh.org

Chapter 4

[1] 'Bread and circuses' is an expression denoting how any given society is pacified via indulgence and entertainment. The term refers to the ways in which the general public are appeased and placated by authority figures and the ruling class not because of substantive action, meaningful policies, or significant changes to the status quo, but through amusement, distraction, and satiating the immediate desires or most minimal needs of a populace.

Chapter 7

[1] Notably, one of the Zapatista Rebel Autonomous Municipalities (*Municipios Autónomos Rebeldes Zapatistas*, MAREZ) is named after anarcho-communist revolutionary Ricardo Flores Magón.

Chapter 8

[1] We concur with Morrison that 'canon-building is empire building' (whatever the discipline) and Cusicanqui (2012), who demonstrates that academic knowledge production is politically loaded, systemically exclusionary, often supremacist and disproportionally privileges scholars in the Global North, those who are in close proximity to journal editors/conference circuits and those who have access to prestigious, elite institutions or professional networks.

[2] This remains the case for countless Indigenous and peasant women across the world. Even given the implementation of the WRL, Zapatista women also still perform many of the tasks mentioned. The overall context, sharing of workloads and devaluation of women's efforts has changed considerably.

[3] We are not arguing here that reproductive labour is inherently 'monotonous toil' in-and-of itself. To do so would be reductive and insulting, given any and all of it can be quite meaningful and rewarding. However, we would suggest that a scenario in which it is devalued/dismissed, coerced, performed under threat and coupled with an essentialist and hierarchical gender regime, that it then does become 'monotonous toil'.

[4] Our aim here is not to vilify or stereotype Indigenous *campesino* men as a static monolith. We are also not suggesting that all Zapatista men were averse to social reproduction. Rather, the analysis of men's oppressive attitudes/behaviours appears because it is a central aspect of the women's stories that indicates just how much influence colonialism has on gender relations. It is also evidence of the dueling patriarchies faced by Zapatista women (that is, Euro-coloniser plantation patriarchs and the authoritative/*machismo* attitudes that Indigenous men from their own communities picked up or had escalated). We also mention the entitled behaviors of men so that male readers of this piece might pause for reflection. Of significance is just how self-reflexive some Zapatista men have been in identifying patriarchy as present, real, in need of overturning and something they are complicit with. There is perhaps an important lesson to learn here for men on the radical left, especially in academia, about not only recognising male privilege, but also performing emotional labour and sacrificing time (often tacit expectations of women).

[5] This logic is by no means unique to the Zapatista context.

[6] *La Escuelita*, August 2013.

[7] The Zapatistas admit to being neither a blueprint nor a model to follow. Our recognition of the *compas* is antagonistic towards fetishising the work they, as Indigenous women, are doing on behalf of life and the planet. Equally important is our stance that their struggle be neither romanticized nor glamorised as it is just that, a struggle, which has, in part, been marked by pain, loss, grief and suffering.

[8] We are by no means pinning the term 'feminist' onto the Zapatistas; rather, we are drawing a comparison given that aspects of their resistance appear similar to certain currents of feminist praxis. The Zapatistas refuse labels largely because they consider those categorical options offered by modernity to be 'traps'. Static ideological brandings are limited, and when imposed, colonial. For their orientation towards feminism, consider Marcos' (2005, 81) statement: 'Feminisms in Mexico are often submerged in practices that follow quite mimetically international feminist theories and priorities. We are inserted into the dominant global international feminist discourse, and a certain sort of feminist movement in Mexico is derivative of the US movement. ... Often, they have little to do with the context of indigenous women's feminist practices.'

[9] *La Escuelita*, August 2013.

[10] *Comparte por la Humanidad*, July 2016.

[11] *La Escuelita*, August 2013.

[12] For example, *Los Tercios Compas* (the Third Compa or the Odd Ones Out), the independent media of the Zapatistas: www.masde131.com/wp-content/uploads/2014/08/Compas7.jpg

Chapter 9

[1] These were titled: *Sixth Part: A mountain on the high seas; Fifth Part: The gaze and the distance to the door; Fourth Part: A memory of what is to come; Third Part: The mission; Second Part: The tavern; First Part: A declaration … for life*. Authors attributed to these writings are Subcomandante Insurgentes Galeano and Moisés and Comandante Don Pablo Contreras.

[2] Which ended 75,000 lives, including his own. His last words before he was assassinated were 'this is an injustice'. His supposed crime was aligning himself with the El Salvadorian people in their fight for freedom and justice (Martín-Baró, 1996).

References

Acosta, A. (2013) 'Extractivism and neoextractivism: Two sides of the same curse', in M. Lang and D. Mokrani (eds) *Beyond development: Alternative visions from Latin America*, Quito and Amsterdam: Rosa Luxemburg Foundation and Transnational Institute, pp 61–86.

Aguila-Way, T. (2014) 'The Zapatista "Mother Seeds in Resistance" project: The Indigenous community seed bank as a living, self-organizing archive', *Social Text*, 32(1): 67–92.

Ahmed, S. (2017) *Living a feminist life*, Durham, NC and London: Duke University Press.

Akram-Lodhi, A.H. and Kay, C. (eds) (2012) *Peasants and globalisation: Political economy, agrarian transformation and development*, Abingdon: Routledge.

Alabab-Moser, J. (2021) 'Indigenous, rural Mexicans in Morelos fight against energy project that threatens their water supplies', *Latino Rebels*, 15 March, Available from: www.latinorebels.com/2021/03/15/fightagainstenergyproject

Alighieri, D. and Musa, M. (1971) *Dante's inferno*, Bloomington, IN: Indiana University Press.

Aloisio, G. (2009) 'Join the revolution just for the health of it: A comparison of Indigenous health in and outside of the Zapatista movement in Chiapas, Mexico', MA thesis, The Ohio State University, Available from: https://kb.osu.edu/handle/1811/37048

Altamirano-Jiménez, I. (2013) *Indigenous encounters with neoliberalism: Place, women, and the environment in Canada and Mexico*, Vancouver: UBC Press.

Altieri, M.A. and Toledo, V.M. (2011) 'The agroecological revolution in Latin America: Rescuing nature, ensuring food sovereignty and empowering peasants', *Journal of Peasant Studies*, 38(3): 587–612.

Amsler, S. and Motta, S. (2017) 'The marketised university and the politics of motherhood', *Gender and Education*, 31(1): 82–99. Available from: https://doi.org/10.1080/09540253.2017.1296116

Anderson, J., Raine, L. and Vogels, E.A. (2021) 'Experts say the "new normal" in 2025 will be far more tech-driven, presenting more big challenges', Pew Research Centre, 18 February, Available from: www.pewresearch.org/internet/2021/02/18/experts-say-the-new-normal-in-2025-will-be-far-more-tech-driven-presenting-more-big-challenges

Baaz, M., Lilja, M., Schulz, M. and Vinthagen, S. (2016) 'Defining and analyzing "resistance": Possible entrances to the study of subversive practices', *Alternatives*, 41(3): 137–53.

Bala, A. and Gheverghese, J. (2007) 'Indigenous knowledge and Western science: The possibility of dialogue', *Race and Class*, 49: 39–61.

Baltodano, M. (2012) 'Neoliberalism and the demise of public education: The corporatisation of schools of education', *International Journal of Qualitative Studies in Education*, 25(4): 487–507.

Bambra, C., Fox, D. and Scott-Samuel, A. (2005) 'Towards a politics of health promotion', *Health Promotion International*, 20: 187–9.

Barbosa, L.P. (2021) '*Lajan lajan'ayatik* or "walking in complementary pairs" in the Zapatista women's struggle', *Latin American Perspectives*, doi:0094582X211012645.

Barbosa, L.P. and Sollano, M.G. (2014) 'La educación autónoma Zapatista en la formación de los sujetos de la educación: Otras epistemes, otros horizontes', *Intersticios de la Política y la Cultura. Intervenciones Latinoamericanas*, 3(6): 67–89.

Barmeyer, N. (2003) 'The guerrilla movement as a project: An assessment of community involvement in the EZLN', *Latin American Perspectives*, 30(1): 122–38.

Baronnet, B. (2008) 'Rebel youth and Zapatista autonomous education', *Latin American Perspectives*, 35(4): 112–24.

Baronnet, B. (2012) *Autonomía y educación indígena: Las escuelas zapatistas de la Selva Lacandona de Chiapas, México*, Quito: Abya Yala.

Baronnet, B., Bayo, M.M. and Stahler-Sholk, R. (2011) *Luchas 'muy otras': Zapatismo y autonomía en las comunidades indígenas de Chiapas*, Juárez: CIESAS (Centro de Investigaciones y Estudios Superiores en Antropología Social).

Benería, L., Berik, G. and Floro, M. (2015) *Gender, development and globalisation: Economics as if all people mattered*, Abingdon: Routledge.

Bennett, K., Ingleton, D., Nah, A.M. and Savage, J. (2015) 'Critical perspectives on the security and protection of human rights defenders', *The International Journal of Human Rights*, 19(7): 883–95.

Berlin, E. and Berlin, B. (1996) *Medical ethnobotany of the highland Maya of Chiapas, Mexico*, Princeton, NJ: Princeton University Press.

Berman, E.P. (2012) *Creating the market university: How academic science became an economic engine*, Princeton, NJ: Princeton University Press.

Bhambra, G.K. Nisancioglu, K. and Gebrial, D. (2018) *Decolonising the university*, London: Pluto Press.

Bhattacharya, T. (ed) (2017) *Social reproduction theory: Remapping class, recentering oppression*, London: Pluto Press.

Birss, M. (2017) 'Criminalizing environmental activism', *NACLA Report on the Americas*, 49(3): 315–22.

Blaut, J.M. (1993) *The coloniser's model of the world: Geographical diffusionism and Eurocentric history*, New York: Guilford Press.

Bobrow-Strain, A. (2007) *Intimate enemies: Landowners, power, and violence in Chiapas*, London: Duke University Press.

Braedley, S. and Luxton, M. (eds) (2010) *Neoliberalism and everyday life*, Kingston: McGill-Queen's University Press.

Brown v Board of Education (1954) 347 US 483.

Brown, P. (2013) 'Maya mother seeds in resistance of highland Chiapas in defence of native corn', in V.D. Nazarea, R.E. Rhoades and J. Andrews-Swann (eds) *Seeds of resistance, seeds of hope: Place and agency in the conservation of biodiversity*, Tucson: University of Arizona Press, pp 151–77.

Butler, J. (2011) *Gender trouble: Feminism and the subversion of identity*, Abingdon: Routledge.

Büyüm, A.M., Keeney, C., Koris, A., Mkumba, L. and Raveendran, Y. (2020) 'Decolonising global health: If not now, when?', *BMJ Global Health*, 5: 1–4.

Cabezas, A.L., Reese, E. and Waller, M. (2015) *Wages of empire: Neoliberal policies, repression, and women's poverty*, Abingdon: Routledge.

Callaban, M. (2005) 'Why not share a dream? Zapatismo as political and cultural practice', *Humbolt Journal of Social Relations*, 29(1): 6–38.

Cantwell, B. (2016) 'The new prudent man: Financial-academic capitalism and inequality in higher education', in S. Slaughter and B.J. Taylor (eds) *Higher education, stratification, and workforce development: Competitive advantage in Europe, the US, and Canada*, Dordrecht: Springer, pp 173–92.

Care Collective (2020) *Care manifesto: The politics of interdependence*, London: Verso Books.

Carr, E.R. and Thompson, M.C. (2014) 'Gender and climate change adaptation in agrarian settings: Current thinking, new directions, and research frontiers', *Geography Compass*, 8(3): 182–97.

Case, A. and Deaton, A. (2020) *Deaths of despair and the future of capitalism*, Princeton, NJ: Princeton University Press.

Cerda García, A. (2006) 'Gobierno indígena: La disputa entre el ámbito local y la autonomía regional', *Espacios Públicos*, 9: 17.

Césaire, A. (2001) *Discourse on colonialism*, New York: NYU Press.

Chattopadhyay, S. (2014) 'Postcolonial development state, appropriation of nature, and social transformation of the ousted Adivasis in the Narmada Valley, India', *Capitalism Nature Socialism*, 25(4): 65–84.

Chomsky, N. (1999) *Profit over people: Neoliberalism and global order*, New York: Seven Stories Press.

Chomsky, N. (2021) *Consequences of capitalism: Manufacturing discontent and resistance*, Chicago: Haymarket Books.

Choudry, A. and Kapoor, D. (2013) *NGOisation: Complicity, contradictions and prospects*, London: Zed Books.

Choudry, A., Majavu, M. and Wood, L. (2013) 'Struggles, strategies and analysis of anti-colonial and postcolonial social movements', *Interface: A Journal for and about Social Movements*, 5(1): 1–10.

Claeys, P. (2015) *Human rights and the food sovereignty movement: Reclaiming control*, Abingdon: Routledge.

Clarke, A.E. (2014) 'Biomedicalization', in W.C. Cockerham, R. Dingwall and S.R. Quah (eds) *The Wiley Blackwell encyclopaedia of health, illness, behaviour and society*, London: Wiley-Blackwell, pp 136–42.

Clarke, B. and Ross, C. (1994) *Voice of fire: Communiqués and interviews from the Zapatista National Liberation Army*, San Francisco: Freedom Voices.

Clastres, P. (1987) *Society against the state: Essays in political anthropology* (trans R. Hurley, in collaboration with A. Stein). New York: Zone Books.

Cleaver Jr, H.M. (1998) 'The Zapatista effect: The internet and the rise of an alternative political fabric', *Journal of International Affairs*, 51(2): 621–40.

Code, L. (ed) (2002) *Encyclopedia of feminist theories*, Abingdon: Routledge.

Collier, G.A. and Quaratiello, E.L. (2005) *Basta! Land and the Zapatista rebellion in Chiapas*, New York: Food First Books.

Collins, P.H. (2002) *Black feminist thought: Knowledge, consciousness, and the politics of empowerment*, Abingdon: Routledge.

Collins, P.H. and Bilge, S. (2020) *Intersectionality*, Hoboken, NJ: John Wiley & Sons.

Collins, P.Y., Patel, V., Joestl, S., March, D., Insel, T., Daar, A. and Walport, M. (2011) 'Grand challenges in global mental health', *Nature*, 475: 27–30.

Comandanta (Major) Ana María (1994) 'Interview with Major Ana María of the EZLN', Available from: https://web.archive.org/web/20071007181504/http://www.struggle.ws/mexico/ezln/interview_annmaria_feb94.html

Comandanta (Major) Esther (2001) 'Words of Comandanta Ester at Milpa Alta', *Crises in Chiapas*, Available from: www.criscenzo.com/jaguarsun/chiapas/chiapas119.html

Comandanta (Major) Ramona (1997) 'Message from Comandante Ramona, to the students of University City', *The Struggle Site*, Available from: https://web.archive.org/web/20160421050628/http://struggle.ws/mexico/ezln/1997/romana_at_uni_mar.html

Commonwealth Fund, The (2019) 'Survey: 79 million Americans have problems with medical bills or debt', Available from: www.commonwealthfund.org/publications/newsletter-article/survey-79-million-americans-have-problems-medical-bills-or-debt

Conant, J. (2010) *A poetics of resistance: The revolutionary public relations of the Zapatista insurgency*, Oakland, CA: AK Press.

Connell, R.W. and Messerschmidt, J.W. (2005) 'Hegemonic masculinity: Rethinking the concept', *Gender and Society*, 19(6): 829–59.

Cooper, M. (2008) *Life as surplus: Biotechnology and capitalism in the neoliberal era*, Washington, DC: University of Washington Press.

Corntassel, J. and Bryce, C. (2012) 'Practicing sustainable Indigenous approaches to cultural restoration and revitalization', *The Brown Journal of World Affairs*, XVII(II): 151–62.

Cox, L. (2017) 'Pedagogy from and for social movements: A conversation between theory and practice', *Capitalism Nature Socialism*, 30(1): 70–88, doi:10.1080/10455752.2017.1360373.

Crass, C. (2013) *Towards collective liberation: Anti-racist organizing, feminist praxis, and movement building strategy*, Oakland, CA: PM Press.

Cuevas, J. (2007) *Health and autonomy: The case of Chiapas*, Available from: www.who.int/social_determinants/resources/csdh_media/autonomy_mexico_2007_en.pdf

Cusicanqui, S.R. (2010) 'The notion of "rights" and the paradoxes of postcolonial modernity', *Qui Parle: Critical Humanities and Social Sciences*, 18(2): 29–54.

Cusicanqui, S.R. (2012) '*Ch'ixinakax utxiwa*: A reflection on the practices and discourses of decolonisation', *The South Atlantic Quarterly*, 111(1): 95–109.

Davis, A. (2014) 'The prison industrial complex and transformative resistance', Lecture for Black History Month 2014: Civil Rights in America at the Southern Illinois University, Carbondale, 13 February.

Davis, K. (2005) *A girl like me*, short documentary, Reel Works Teen Filmmaking, Available from: www.youtube.com/watch?v=KkSDNxM1w58

Dawes, D. (2020) *The political determinants of health*, Baltimore, MD: Johns Hopkins University Press.

Deere, C.D. and De Leal, M.L. (2014) *Empowering women: Land and property rights in Latin America*, Pittsburgh: University of Pittsburgh Press.

Dei, G.J., Hall, B.L. and Goldin, R.D. (2000) *Indigenous knowledges in global contexts: Multiple readings of our world*, Toronto: University of Toronto Press.

de Leeuw, S. and Hunt, S. (2018) 'Unsettling decolonising geographies', *Geography Compass*, 12(7): e12376.

de Leeuw, S., Greenwood, M. and Lindsay, N. (2013) 'Troubling good intentions', *Settler Colonial Studies*, 3(3–4): 381–94.

Dinerstein, A.C. (2015) *The politics of autonomy in Latin America: The art of organising hope*, New York: Palgrave Macmillan.

Di Piramo, D. (2011) 'Beyond modernity: Irony, fantasy, and the challenge to grand narratives in Subcomandante Marcos's tales', *Mexican Studies/Estudios Mexicanos*, 27(1): 177 205.

Dirik, D. (2016) 'Building democracy without the state', *Reflections on a Revolution*. Issue # 1, Available from: https://roarmag.org/magazine/building-democracy-without-a-state

Duffy, A., Saunders, K.E., Malhi, G.S., Patten, S., Cipriani, A., McNevin, S.H., MacDonald, E. and Geddes, J. (2019) 'Mental health care for university students: A way forward?', *The Lancet Psychiatry*, 11: 885–87.

Durand, C. (2017) *Fictitious capital: How finance is appropriating our future*. London: Verso.

Dussel, E. (1993) 'Eurocentrism and modernity: Introduction to the Frankfurt lectures', *Boundary 2*, 20(3): 65–76.

Dussel, E. (1994) *1492: El encubrimiento del otro: Hacia el origen del mito de la modernidad*, La Paz: Plural Editores.

Dussel, E. (1998) 'Beyond Eurocentrism: The world-system and the limits of modernity', in F. Jameson and M. Miyoshi (eds) *The cultures of globalization*, Durham, NC: Duke University Press, pp 3–31.

Dussel, E. (2019) 'World-system and "trans"-modernity', in S. Dube and I. Banerjee-Dube (eds) *Unbecoming modern: Colonialism, modernity, colonial modernities* (2nd edn), London: Routledge, pp 165–88, Available from: https://doi.org/10.4324/9780429027239-9

Earle, D. and Simonelli, J. (2005) *Uprising of hope: Sharing the Zapatista journey to alternative development*, Oxford: Rowman & Littlefield.

Eber, C. and Kovic, C. (2003) *Women of Chiapas: Making history in times of struggle and hope*, New York: Routledge.

Edelman, M., Oya, C. and Borras Jr, S. M. (2013) 'Global land grabs: Historical processes, theoretical and methodological implications and current trajectories', *Third World Quarterly*, 34(9): 1517–31.

El-Khatib, Z., Jacobs, G.B., Ikomey, G.M. and Neogi, U. (2020) 'The disproportionate effect of COVID-19 mortality on ethnic minorities: Genetics or health inequalities?', *EClinicalMedicine*, 23: 1–2.

Emejulu, A. (2017) 'The university is not innocent: Speaking of universities', *Verso Books Blog*, 29 March, Available from: www.versobooks.com/blogs/3148-the-university-is-not-innocentspeaking-of-universities

Engels, F. (1887) *Condition of the working class in England*, Available from: www.marxists.org/archive/marx/works/download/pdf/condition-working-class-england.pdf

Erikson, S. (2019) 'Global health futures: Reckoning with a pandemic bond', *Medicine Anthropology Theory*, 6: 77–108.

Erikson, S. (2020) 'Betting on pandemic', *Medical Anthropology*, 39: 380–1.

Escobar, A. (2004) 'Beyond the Third World: Imperial globality, global coloniality, and anti-globalization social movements', *Third World Quarterly*, 25(1): 207–30.

Escobar, A. (2018) *Designs for the pluriverse: Radical interdependence, autonomy, and the making of worlds*, Durham, NC: Duke University Press.

EZLN (Ejército Zapatista de Liberación Nacional) (1998) *Zapatista encuentro: Documents from the 1996 encounter for humanity and against neoliberalism*, New York: Seven Stories Press.

EZLN (2005) 'Sexta Declaración de la Selva Lacandona', *Enlace Zapatista*, Available from: http://enlacezapatista.ezln.org.mx/2005/06/30/sexta-declaracion-de-la-selva-lacandona

EZLN (2012) 'EZLN announces the following steps', *Enlace Zapatista*, Available from: http://enlacezapatista.ezln.org.mx/2013/01/02/ ezln-announces-the-following-steps-communique-of-december-30-2012

EZLN (2015a) *Critical thought in the face of the capitalist hydra*, Durham, NC: Paperboat Press.

EZLN (2015b) 'The words of the EZLN on the 21st anniversary of the beginning of the war against oblivion', *Enlace Zapatista*, Available from: http://enlacezapatista.ezln.org.mx/2015/01/01/palabras-del-ezln-en-el-21-aniversario-del-inicio-de-la-guerra-contra-el-olvido

EZLN (2015c) 'On the elections: ORGANIZE', *Enlace Zapatista*, Available from: http://enlacezapatista.ezln.org.mx/2015/05/14/ on-the-elections-organize/

EZLN (2016a) 'May the earth tremble at its core', *Enlace Zapatista*, Available from: http://enlacezapatista.ezln.org.mx/2016/10/14/ que-retiemble-en-sus-centros-la-tierra

EZLN (2016b) 'Open letter on the aggressions against the people's movement in San Cristóbal de las Casas, Chiapas', *Enlace Zapatista*, Available from: http://enlacezapatista.ezln.org.mx/2016/07/23/open-letter-on-the-aggressions-against-the-peoples-movement-in-san-cristobal-de-las-casas-chiapas

EZLN (2017) 'The first of several', *Enlace Zapatista*, Available from: http:// enlacezapatista.ezln.org.mx/2017/03/17/the-first-of-many

EZLN (2018) 'Zapatista Women's opening address at the first International Gathering of Politics, Art, Sport, and Culture for Women in Struggle', *Enlaçe Zapatista*, Available from: http://enlacezapatista.ezln.org.mx/2018/ 03/26/zapatista-womens-opening-address-at-the-first-international-gathering-of-politics-art-sport-and-culture-for-women-in-struggle

EZLN (2019) 'Words of the EZLN's CCRI-CG to the Zapatista peoples on the 25th anniversary of the beginning of the war against oblivion', *Enlace Zapatista*, Available from: http://enlacezapatista.ezln.org.mx/2019/ 01/09/words-of-the-ezlns-ccri-cg-to-the-zapatista-peoples-on-the-25th-anniversary-of-the-beginning-of-the-war-against-oblivion

EZLN (2020a) 'Part Six: A mountain on the high seas', *Enlace Zapatista*, Available from: https://enlacezapatista.ezln.org.mx/2020/10/07/ part-six-a-mountain-on-the-high-seas

EZLN (2020b) 'Part Five: The gaze and the distance to the door', *Enlace Zapatista*, Available from: https://cnlacczapatista.czln.org.mx/2020/10/ 11/part-five-the-gaze-and-the-distance-to-the-door

EZLN (2020c) 'Part Four: Memory of what is to come', *Enlace Zapatista*, Available from: https://enlacezapatista.ezln.org.mx/2020/10/23/ part-four-memory-of-what-is-to-come

EZLN (2020d) 'Part Three: The mission', *Enlace Zapatista*, Available from: https://enlacezapatista.ezln.org.mx/2020/12/24/part-three-the-mission/

EZLN (2021) 'Part One: A declaration … for life', *Enlace Zapatista*, Available from: https://enlacezapatista.ezln.org.mx/2021/01/01/part-one-a-declaration-for-life

Fanjul, G. and Fraser, A. (2003) 'Dumping without borders: How US agricultural policies are destroying the livelihoods of Mexican corn farmers', Oxfam Briefing Paper 50, Available from: https://oxfamilibrary.openrepository.com/bitstream/handle/10546/114471/bp50-dumping-without-borders-010803-en.pdf?sequence=1

Fanon, F. (1963) *The wretched of the earth*, New York: Grove Press.

Fanon, F. (1967) *Black skin, white masks*, New York: Grove Press.

Fanon Project, The (2010) 'Beyond health disparities: Examining power disparities and industrial complexes from the views of Frantz Fanon (Part 1)', *Journal of Pan African Studies*, 3: 151–78.

Federici, S. (2004) *Caliban and the witch*, Brooklyn: Autonomedia.

Federici, S. (2012) *Revolution at point zero: Housework, reproduction, and feminist struggle*, Oakland, CA: PM Press.

Ferrell, J. (1998) 'Against the law: Anarchist criminology', in D. MacLean and D. Milovanovic (eds) *Thinking critically about crime*, Bloomington, IN: The Collective Press, pp 118–29.

Fitzwater, D.E. (2019) *Autonomy is in our hearts: Zapatista autonomous government through the lens of the Tsotsil language*, Oakland, CA: PM Press.

Flores Osorio, J.M. (2009) 'Praxis and liberation in the context of Latin American theory', in M. Montero and C. Sonn (eds) *Psychology of liberation: Theory and applications*, New York: Springer Publishing, pp 11–36.

Flynn, M.B. (2021) 'Global capitalism as a societal determinant of health: A conceptual framework', *Social Science & Medicine*, 268: 1–8.

Food First (2012) 'We already grow enough food for 10 billion people and still can't end hunger', Available from: https://foodfirst.org/publication/we-already-grow-enough-food-for-10-billion-people-and-still-cant-end-hunger/

Foucault, M. (2003) *Society must be defended*, New York: Picador.

Foucault, M. (2008) *The birth of biopolitics: Lectures at the Collège de France, 1978–79*, Basingstoke: Palgrave Macmillan.

Foucault, M. (edited by A.I. Davidson and G. Burchell) (2010) *The government of self and others: Lectures at the Collège de France 1982–1983*, London: Springer.

Fraser, A. (2019) 'Land grab/data grab: Precision agriculture and its new horizons', *The Journal of Peasant Studies*, 46: 893–912.

Fraser, N. and Pettifor, A. (2018) 'Understanding capitalism: Nancy Fraser in conversation with Ann Pettifor', *IPPR Progressive Review*, 25(2): 154–65.

Freire, P. (2018) *Pedagogy of the oppressed*, New York: Bloomsbury Publishing.

Friedman, M. (2019) 'Is the state of the world causing more mental illness? Social issues might affect a younger generation', *Medpage Today*, 25 March, Available from: www.medpagetoday.com/psychiatry/generalpsychiatry/78775

Gahman, L. (2016) 'Zapatismo versus the neoliberal university: Towards a pedagogy against oblivion', in S. Springer, M.L. de Souza and R.J. White (eds) *The radicalization of pedagogy: Anarchism, geography, and the spirit of revolt*, London: Rowman & Littlefeld International, pp 73–100.

Gahman, L. (2017) 'Building "a world where many worlds fit": Indigenous autonomy, mutual aid, and an (anti-capitalist) moral economy of the (rebel) peasant', in J. Duncan and M. Bailey (eds) *Sustainable food futures: Multidisciplinary solutions*, Abingdon: Routledge, pp 103–16.

Gahman, L. (2020a) 'Contra plantation, prison, and capitalist annihilation: Collective struggle, social reproduction, and the co-creation of lifegiving worlds', *The Journal of Peasant Studies*, 47(3): 503–24.

Gahman, L. (2020b) *Land, god, and guns: Settler colonialism and masculinity in the American Heartland*, London: Zed Books.

Gahman, L., Greenidge, A. and Mohamed, A. (2020) 'Plunder via violation of FPIC: Land grabbing, state negligence, and pathways to peace in Central America and the Caribbean', *Journal of Peacebuilding and Development*, 15(3): 372–6.

Gahman, L., Reyes, J.R., Miller, T., Gibbings, R., Cohen, A., Greenidge, A. and Chattopadhyay, S. (2019) 'Activist geographies', in A. Kobayashi (ed) *International encyclopedia of human geography*, Amsterdam: Elsevier, pp 23–31.

Gallegos, S. and Quinn, C. (2017) 'Epistemic injustice and resistance in the Chiapas Highlands: The Zapatista case', *Hypatia*, 32: 247–62.

Gibson-Graham, J.K. (1996) *The end of capitalism (as we knew it): A feminist critique of political economy*, Oxford: Blackwell.

Gibson-Graham, J.K. (2006) *A postcapitalist politics*, Minneapolis: University of Minnesota Press.

Gilly, A. (1997) *Chiapas: La razón ardiente: Ensayo sobre la rebelión del mundo encantado*, Mexico City: Ediciones Era.

Gilmore, R.W. (2002) 'Fatal couplings of power and difference: Notes on racism and geography', *The Professional Geographer*, 54(1): 15–24.

Gilroy, P. (2000) *Between camps: Race, identity and nationalism at the end of the colour line*, London: Allen Lane/Penguin Press

Giraldo, O.F. and Rosset, P.M. (2018) 'Agroecology as a territory in dispute: Between institutionality and social movements', *The Journal of Peasant Studies*, 45(3): 545–64.

Giroux, H.A. (2014) *Neoliberalism's war on higher education*, Chicago: Haymarket Books.

Glazebrook, T. and Opoku, E. (2018) 'Defending the defenders: Environmental protectors, climate change and human rights', *Ethics and the Environment*, 23(2): 83–109.

Global Burden of Disease Study (2019) 'Five insights from the Global Burden of Disease Study 2019', *The Lancet*, 396: 1135–59.

Good, B., Fischer, M., Willen, S. and DelVecchio Good, M.J. (2010) *A reader in medical anthropology: Theoretical trajectories, emergent realities*, Malden, MA: Wiley-Blackwell.

Goldberg, D.T. (2009) *The threat of race: Reflections on racial neoliberalism*, Hoboken, NJ: John Wiley & Sons.

Goldman, E. (1910) *Anarchism and other essays*, New York: Mother Earth Publishing.

Grassi, J., Lamberg, J. and Huyer, S. (2015) *Running out of time: The reduction of women's work burden in agricultural production*, Rome: Food and Agriculture Organization.

Gray, D.M., Anyane-Yeboa, A., Balzora, S., Issaka, R.B. and Folasade, P.M. (2020) 'COVID-19 and the other pandemic: Populations made vulnerable by systemic inequity', *Nature Reviews: Gastroenterology Hepatology*, 17: 520–2.

Green, L. (2011) 'The nobodies: Neoliberalism, violence, and migration', *Medical Anthropology*, 30(4): 366–85.

Greenwood, M., de Leeuw, S. and Lindsay, N.M. (2018) *Determinants of Indigenous people's health: Beyond the social*, Toronto: Canadian Scholars.

Grosfoguel, R. (2016) 'What is racism?', *Journal of World-Systems Research*, 22(1): 9–15.

Gunderson, C. (2019) 'Cycles of accumulation, cycles of struggle: The Zapatista revolt in world-systemic perspective', *Critical Sociology*, 45(4–5): 667–81.

Gutierrez, A. (1996) 'Codifying the past, erasing the future: NAFTA and the Zapatista uprising of 1994', *Hastings West-Northwest Journal of Environmental Law and Policy*, 4(2): 143–62.

Haiven, M. (2020) 'No return to normal: For a post-pandemic liberation', *ROAR: Reflections on a Revolution*, 23 March, Available from: https://roarmag.org/essays/no-return-to-normal-for-a-post-pandemic-liberation

Hall, R. and Bowles, K. (2016) 'Re-engineering higher education: The subsumption of academic labour and the exploitation of anxiety', *Workplace: A Journal for Academic Labour*, 28: 30–47.

Hall, S. and Massey, D. (2010) 'Interpreting the crisis', *Soundings*, 44: 57–71.

Hammelman, C., Reynolds, K. and Levkoe, C.Z. (2020) 'Toward a radical food geography praxis: Integrating theory, action, and geographic analysis in pursuit of more equitable and sustainable food systems', *Human Geography*, 13(3): 211–27.

Haraway, D.J. (2009) 'Situated knowledges: The science question in feminism of partial and the privilege', *Feminist Studies*, 14(3): 575–99.

Harding, S. (1992) 'Rethinking standpoint epistemology: What is strong objectivity?', *The Centennial Review*, 36(3): 437–70.

Harris, S. (2020) 'Traveling for treatment: Psychedelics and addiction care in Mexico: Hot spots, fieldsights', *Society for Cultural Anthropology*, 21 July, Available from: https://culanth.org/fieldsights/traveling-for-treatment-psychedelics-and-addiction-care-in-mexico

Harvey, D. (2001) 'Globalization and the "spatial fix"', *Geographische Revue*, 2: 23–30.

Harvey, D. (2004) 'The "new" imperialism: Accumulation by dispossession', *Socialist Register*, 40: 63–87.

Harvey, D. (2007) *A brief history of neoliberalism*, Oxford: Oxford University Press.

Harvey, N. (1998) *The Chiapas rebellion: The struggle for land and democracy*, Durham, NC: Duke University Press.

Harvey, N. (2005) 'Inclusion through autonomy: Zapatistas and dissent', *NACLA Report on the Americas*, 39(2): 12–17.

Harvey, N. (2016) 'Practicing autonomy: Zapatismo and decolonial liberation', *Latin American and Caribbean Ethnic Studies*, 11(1): 1–24.

Henck, N. (2007) *Subcommander Marcos: The man and the mask*, Durham, NC: Duke University Press.

Hernández, C., Perales, H. and Jaffee, D. (2020) 'Without food there is no resistance: The impact of the Zapatista conflict on agrobiodiversity and seed sovereignty in Chiapas, Mexico', *Geoforum*, Available from: https://doi.org/10.1016/j.geoforum.2020.08.016

Hernández Castillo, R.A. (2010) 'The emergence of indigenous feminism in Latin America', *Signs: Journal of Women in Culture and Society*, 35(3): 539–45.

Heynen, N., McCarthy, J., Prudham, S. and Robbins, P. (eds) (2007) *Neoliberal environments: False promises and unnatural consequences*, Abingdon: Routledge.

Hickel, J. and Khan, A. (2012) 'The culture of capitalism and the critique of crisis', *Anthropological Quarterly*, 85: 203–28.

Holloway, J. (2002a) *Change the world without taking power: The meaning of revolution today*, London: Pluto Press.

Holloway, J. (2002b) 'Zapatismo and the social sciences', *Capital and Class*, 26(3): 153–60.

Holloway, J. (2010) *Crack capitalism*, London: Pluto Press.

Holloway, J. and Peláez, E. (1998) *Zapatista! Reinventing revolution in Mexico*, London: Pluto Press.

hooks, b. (1990) *Yearning: Race, gender, and cultural politics*, Boston, MA: South End Press.

hooks, b. (2014a) *Talking back: Thinking feminist, Thinking Black*, Abingdon: Routledge.

hooks, b. (2014b) *Teaching to transgress*, Abingdon: Routledge.

IFAD (International Fund for Agricultural Development) (2016) 'Reducing rural women's domestic workload through labour-saving technologies and practices', Available from: www.ifad.org/documents/10180/c86179dd-ad6d-4622-864a-ed590016250d

Jameson, F. (2003) 'Future city', *New Left Review*, 21: 65–79.

JBG (Juntas de Buen Gobierno Zapatistas) (2013a) *Gobierno Autonomo I: Cuaderno de texto de primer grado del curso 'La Libertad Según l@s Zapatistas'*, Chiapas, Mexico, Available from: http://anarquiacoronada.blogspot.mx/2013/09/primera-escuela-zapatista-descarga-sus.html

JBG (2013b) *Gobierno Autonomo II: Cuaderno de texto de primer grado del curso 'La Libertad Según l@s Zapatistas'*, Chiapas, Mexico, Available from: https://radiozapatista.org/?page_id=20294

JBG (2013c) *Participación de las mujeres en el Gobierno Autónomo: Cuaderno de texto de primer grado del curso 'La Libertad Según l@s Zapatistas'*, Chiapas, Mexico, Available from: https://radiozapatista.org/?page_id=20294

JBG (2013d) *Resistencia autónoma: Cuaderno de texto de primer grado del curso 'La Libertad Según l@s Zapatistas'*, Chiapas, Mexico, Available from: https://radiozapatista.org/?page_id=20294

Jones, C. (1949) *To end the neglect of the problems of the negro woman!*, New York: National Women's Commission (Originally published in *Political Affairs*).

Jordaan, J.A. (2012) *Foreign direct investment, agglomeration and externalities: Empirical evidence from Mexican manufacturing industries*, Farnham: Ashgate Publishing.

Kallis, G. (2011) 'In defence of degrowth', *Ecological economics*, 70(5): 873–80.

Katzenberger, E. (ed) (1995) *First world, ha, ha, ha! The Zapatista challenge*, San Francisco: City Lights Books.

Kawano, E. (2013) 'Social solidarity economy: Toward convergence across continental divides', United Nations Research Institute for Social Development 'Think Piece', Available from: www.unrisd.org/80256B3C005BE6B5/search/F1E9214CF8EA21A8C1257B1E003B4F65?OpenDocument

Kelly, M. and Griffin, C. (2010) 'Curanderism', in C. Clauss-Ehlers (ed) *Encyclopaedia of cross-cultural school psychology*, New York: Springer Publishing, pp 354–55.

Khasnabish, A. (2011) 'Anarch@- Zapatismo: Anti-capitalism, anti-power, and the insurgent imagination', *Affinities: A Journal of Radical Theory, Culture, and Action*, 5 (1): 70–95.

Khasnabish, A. (2013) *Zapatistas: Rebellion from the grassroots to the global*, London: Zed Books.

Kickbusch, I. (2015) 'The political determinants of health – 10 years on', *BMJ*, 350: 1–2.

Kierans, C. (2019) *Chronic failures: Kidneys, regimes of care and the Mexican state*, New Brunswick, NJ: Rutgers University Press.

Kilombo Women's Delegation (2018) 'What does it mean to live?', *Viewpoint Magazine*, 7 June, Available from: www.viewpointmag.com/2018/06/07/what-does-it-mean-to-live-notes-from-the-zapatistas-first-international-gathering-of-politics-art-sport-and-culture-for-women-in-struggle

Kipling, R. (1998 [1899]) 'The white man's burden', *Peace Review: A Journal of Social Justice*, 10(3): 311–12.

Klein, E. (2016) *Developing minds: Psychology, neoliberalism, and power*, Abingdon: Routledge.

Klein, H. (2015) *Compañeras: Zapatista women's stories*, New York: Seven Stories Press.

Klein, N. (2014) *This changes everything: Capitalism vs the climate*, New York: Simon & Schuster.

Kropotkin, P. (1975) *The essential Kropotkin*, London: Palgrave Macmillan.

Kuhlmann, E. and Annandale, E. (eds) (2012) *The Palgrave handbook of gender and healthcare*, Basingstoke: Palgrave Macmillan.

Kwan, M.P. (2016) *Geographies of health, disease and wellbeing: Recent advances in theory and method*, New York: Routledge.

Lambrou, Y. and Nelson, S. (2010) *Farmers in a changing climate: Does gender matter? Food security in Andhra Pradesh, India*, Rome: Food and Agriculture Organization.

La Via Campesina (2007) 'Declaration of Nyéléni', Available from: https://nyeleni.org/spip.php?article290

La Via Campesina (2013) 'Women of *Via Campesina* international manifesto', *La Via Campesina*, Available from: https://viacampesina.org/en/women-of-via-campesina-international-manifesto-2

Lawrence, M. and Laybourn-Langton, L. (2021) *Planet on fire: A manifesto for the age of environmental breakdown*, London: Verso Books.

López, E. and Vértiz, F. (2015) 'Extractivism, transnational capital, and subaltern struggles in Latin America', *Latin American Perspectives*, 42(5): 152–68.

Lopez-Calvo, I. (2016) '"Coloniality is not over, it is all over": Interview with Dr Walter Mignolo (Part I)', *Transmodernity*, 6: 175–84.

Lopez y Rivas, G. (2019) 'The peoples will continue in struggle against the Morelos Integral Project', The Chiapas Support Committee, Available from: https://chiapas-support.org/2019/03/17/the peoples will continue-in-struggle-against-the-morelos-integral-project

Lorde, A. (2018) *The master's tools will never dismantle the master's house*, London: Penguin.

Lorenzano, L. (1998) 'Zapatismo: Recomposition of labour, radical democracy, and revolutionary project', in J. Holloway and E. Peláez (eds) *Zapatista!*, London: Pluto Press, pp 126–58.

Los Tercios Compas (2014) 'First report on reconstruction progress in Zapatista La Realidad', Available from: http://enlacezapatista.ezln.org.mx/2014/08/13/first-report-on-reconstruction-progress-in-zapatista-la-realidad

Loveday, V. (2018) 'The neurotic academic: Anxiety, casualisation, and governance in the neoliberalising university', *Journal of Cultural Economy*, 11(2): 154–66.

Lugones, M. (2008) 'Coloniality and gender', *Tabula Rasa*, 9: 73–102.

Luxton, M. and K. Bezanson, K. (eds) (2006) *Social reproduction: Feminist political economy challenges neo-liberalism*, Montreal: McGill-Queen's Press.

Lyon, S., Mutersbaugh, T. and Worthen, H. (2017) 'The triple burden: The impact of time poverty on women's participation in coffee producer organisational governance in Mexico', *Agriculture and Human Values*, 34(2): 317–31.

Mackey, K., Ayers, C., Kondo, K., Saha, S., Advani, S., Young, S. and Kansagara, D. (2021) 'Racial and ethnic disparities in COVID-19-related infections, hospitalizations, and deaths', *Annals of Internal Medicine*, 174: 362–73.

Mair, S. (2020) 'Neoliberal economics, planetary health, and the COVID-19 pandemic: A Marxist ecofeminist analysis', *The Lancet Planet Health*, 4.

Maldonado-Torres, N. (2007) 'On the coloniality of being: Contributions to the development of a concept', *Cultural Studies*, 21(2–3): 240–70.

Manji, F. and Fletcher Jr, B. (2013) *Claim no easy victories: The legacy of Amílcar Cabral*, Cantley: Daraja Press.

Marcos, S. (2005) 'The borders within: The Indigenous women's movement and feminism in Mexico', in M.R. Waller and S. Marcos (eds) *Dialog and difference*, New York: Palgrave, pp 81–112.

Marcos, S. (2014) 'The Zapatista Women's Revolutionary Law as it is lived today', *Open Democracy*, 22 July, Available from: www.opendemocracy.net/sylvia-marcos/zapatista-women%E2%80%99s-revolutionary-law-as-it-is-lived-today

Marcos, S. (2018) 'Reconceiving rights: An analysis on their declarations, proposals and demands', in Ú. Spring and S. Oswald (eds) *Risks, violence, security and peace in Latin America*, Cham: Springer, pp 283–96.

Marcos, S.I. (1994) 'The first uprising', *La Jornada*, 26 January.

Marcos, S.I. (2001) 'The roads of dignity: Indigenous rights, memory and culture patrimony', *Synthesis/Regeneration*, 25 (Summer), Available from: www.greens.org/s-r/25/25-11.html

Marcos, S.I. (2005) *Conversations with Durito: Stories of the Zapatistas and neoliberalism*, New York: Autonomedia.

Marcos, S.I. and de Leon, J.P. (2002) *Our word is our weapon: Selected writings*, New York: Seven Stories Press.

Marley, B. (1980) 'Redemption song', *Uprising*, Tuff Gong/Island Records.

Martín, D.A. (2004) ' "Excuse the inconvenience, but this is a revolution": Zapatista paradox and the rhetoric of tourism', *South Central Review*, 21(3): 107–28.

Martín-Baró, I. (1991) 'Developing a critical consciousness through the university curriculum', in J. Hasset and H. Lacey (eds) *Towards a society that serves its people: The intellectual contributions of El Salvador's murdered Jesuits*, Washington, DC: Georgetown University Press, pp 220–44.

Martín-Baró, I. (1996) *Writings for a liberation psychology*, New York: Harvard University Press.

Martínez-Torres, M.E. and Rosset, P.M. (2010) 'La Via Campesina: The birth and evolution of a transnational social movement', *The Journal of Peasant Studies*, 37(1): 149–75.

Matsushita, M., Schoenbaum, T.J., Mavroidis, P.C. and Hahn, M. (2015) *The World Trade Organization: Law, practice, and policy*, Oxford: Oxford University Press.

Mbah, S. and Igariwey, I.E. (2001) *African anarchism: The history of a movement*, Chicago: Sharp Press.

McClure, E.S., Vasudevan, P., Bailey, Z., Patel, S. and Robinson, W.R. (2020) 'Racial capitalism within public health – How occupational settings drive COVID-19 disparities', *American Journal of Epidemiology*, 18: 1244–53.

McMichael, P. (2005) *Global development and the corporate food regime*, Bingley: Emerald Group Publishing Limited.

Menton, M., and Le Billon, P. (Eds.) (2021) *Environmental defenders: Deadly strggles for life and territory*. London: Routledge.

Miedzian, M. (2002) *Boys will be boys: Breaking the link between masculinity and violence*, Brooklyn: Lantern Books.

Mies, M. (1998) *Patriarchy and accumulation on a world scale: Women in the international division of labour*, London: Palgrave Macmillan.

Mignolo, W. (2000) *Local histories/global designs: Coloniality, subaltern knowledges and border thinking*, Princeton, NJ: Princeton University Press.

Mignolo, W. (2011) *The darker side of Western modernity: Global futures, decolonial options*, Durham, NC: Duke University Press.

Miller, V., VeneKlasen, L., Reilly, M. and Clark, C. (2006) *Making change happen 3: power. Concepts for revisioning power for justice, equality and peace.* Washington, DC: Just Associates.

Mishra, D.K. (2020) 'Agrarian crisis and neoliberalism in India', *Human Geography*, 13(2). 183–6.

Moerman, D.E. (1983) 'Physiology and symbols: The anthropological implications of the placebo effect', in L. Romanucci-Ross, D.E. Moerman and L.R. Tancredi (eds) *The Anthropology of medicine: From culture to method*, New York: Praeger, pp 240–53.

Mohanty, C.T. (2003) *Feminism without borders*, Durham, NC: Duke University Press.

Mohanty, C.T. (2013) 'Transnational feminist crossings: On neoliberalism and radical critique', *Signs*, 38(4): 967–91.

Mora, M. (2015) 'The politics of justice: Zapatista autonomy at the margins of the neoliberal Mexican state', *Latin American and Caribbean Ethnic Studies*, 10(1): 87–106.

Mora, M. (2017) *Kuxlejal politics: Indigenous autonomy, race, and decolonising research in Zapatista communities*, Austin: University of Texas Press.

Morales, H. (2021) 'Agroecological feminism', *Agroecology and Sustainable Food Systems*, 45(7): 955–6.

Moreman, C.M. and Rushton, C.J. (2011) *Race, oppression and the zombie: Essays on cross-cultural appropriations of the Caribbean tradition*, Jefferson, NC: McFarland & Company.

Morrison, T. (1988) 'Unspeakable things unspoken: The Afro-American presence in American literature', in *The Tanner Lectures*, Ann Arbor, MI: University of Michigan Press.

Morvaridi, B. (2012) 'Capitalist philanthropy and the new green revolution for food security', *The International Journal of Sociology of Agriculture and Food*, 19(2): 243–56.

Mountz, A., Bonds, A., Mansfield, B., Lloyd, J.M., Hyndman, J., Walton-Roberts, M., Basu, R., Whison, R., Hawkings, R., Hamilton, T. and Curran, W. (2015) 'For slow scholarship: A feminist politics of resistance through collective action in the neoliberal university', *ACME: An International Journal for Critical Geographies*, 14(4): 1235–59.

Mullaly, R.P. (2010) *Challenging oppression and confronting privilege: A critical social work approach*, Oxford: Oxford University Press.

Narayan Y. (2012) 'The cultural turn, racialisation and postcoloniality', in S. Roseneil and S. Frosh (eds) *Social research after the cultural turn*, London: Palgrave Macmillan, pp 144–59.

Neary, M. and Winn, J. (2009) 'The student as producer: Reinventing the student experience in higher education', in L. Bell, H. Stevenson and M. Neary (eds) *The future of higher education: Policy, pedagogy and the student experience*, London: Continuum, pp 192–201.

Newdick, V. (2005) 'The Indigenous woman as victim of her culture in neoliberal Mexico', *Cultural Dynamics*, 17(1): 73–92.

Nirmal, P. and Rocheleau, D. (2019) 'Decolonizing degrowth in the post-development convergence: Questions, experiences, and proposals from two Indigenous territories', *Environment and Planning E: Nature and Space*, 2(3): 465–92.

Nixon, R. (2011) *Slow violence and the environmentalism of the poor*, Cambridge, MA: Harvard University Press.

Nuijten, M. (2003) 'Family property and the limits of intervention: The Article 27 reforms and the PROCEDE programme in Mexico', *Development and Change*, 34(3): 475–97.

Nyéléni Newsletter (2020) 'Beyond land: Territory and food sovereignty', Available from: https://nyeleni.org/DOWNLOADS/newsletters/Nyeleni_Newsletter_Num_41_EN.pdf

Oikonomakis, L. (2019) *Political strategies and social movements in Latin America*, Cham: Palgrave Macmillan.

Olesen, T. (2007) 'The funny side of globalisation: Humour and humanity in Zapatista framing', *International Review of Social History*, 52(S15): 21–34.

Olivera, M. (2005) 'Subordination and rebellion: Indigenous peasant women in Chiapas ten years after the Zapatista uprising', *The Journal of Peasant Studies*, 32(3–4): 608–28.

Oropeza, D. (2021) 'Samir Flores: The ahuehuete that blossoms', *Schools for Chiapas*, 18 February, Available from: https://schoolsforchiapas.org/samir-flores-the-ahuehuete-that-blooms

Otero, G. (2011) 'Neoliberal globalisation, NAFTA, and migration: Mexico's loss of food and labor sovereignty', *Journal of Poverty*, 15(4): 384–402.

Padilla-Altamira, C. (2017) 'Healthcare at the margins: An ethnography of chronic kidney disease and peritoneal dialysis in Mexico', Doctoral thesis, University of Liverpool, Available from: https://livrepository.liverpool.ac.uk/3007309

Palley, T.I. (2013) *Financialization: What it is and why it matters*, London: Palgrave Macmillan.

Patel, R. (2009) 'Food sovereignty', *The Journal of Peasant Studies*, 36(3): 663–706.

Peake, L. and Mullings, B. (2017) 'Critical reflections on mental and emotional distress in the academy', *ACME: An International Journal for Critical Geographies*, 15(2): 253–84.

Peluso, N.L. and Lund, C. (2011) 'New frontiers of land control: Introduction', *Journal of Peasant Studies*, 38(4): 667–81.

Penados, F. (1999) 'Trusting teachers and encountering professional development', PhD thesis, University of Otago.

Penados, F. (2018) 'Governance and Indigenous education in Belize: Lessons from the Maya land rights struggle and Indigenous education initiatives', in E. Mckinley and L. Tuhiwai Smith (eds) *Handbook of Indigenous education*, Singapore: Springer, pp 207–28.

Phipps, A. (2020) *Me, not you: The trouble with mainstream feminism*, Manchester: Manchester University Press.

Pilecki, B., Luoma, J.B., Bathje, G.J., Rhea, J. and Fraguada Narloch, V. (2021) 'Ethical and legal issues in psychedelic harm reduction and integration therapy', *Harm Reduction Journal*, 18.

Press, B. and Carothers, T. (2020) 'Worldwide protests in 2020: A year in review', Carnegie Endowment for International Peace, Available from: https://carnegieendowment.org/2020/12/21/worldwide-protests-in-2020-year-in-review-pub-83445

Quijano, A. (2000) 'Coloniality of power and Eurocentrism in Latin America', *International Sociology*, 15(2): 215–32.

Quijano, A. (2007) 'Coloniality and modernity/rationality', *Cultural Studies*, 21(768980396): 168–78.

Ramírez, G.M., Carlsen, L. and Arias, A.R. (2008) *The fire and the word: A history of the Zapatista movement*, San Francisco, CA: City Lights Publishers.

Razack, S., Thobani, S. and Smith, M. (eds) (2010). *States of race: Critical race feminism for the 21st century*, Toronto: Between the Lines.

Razai, M.S., Kankam, H.K.N., Majeed, A., Esmail, A. and Williams, D.R. (2021) 'Mitigating ethnic disparities in COVID-19 and beyond', *BMJ*, 372.

Robbins, R.H. and Dowty, R. (2008) *Global problems and the culture of capitalism*, Boston, MA: Pearson/Allyn & Bacon.

Rockenbauch, T. and Sakdapolrak, P. (2017) 'Social networks and the resilience of rural communities in the Global South: A critical review and conceptual reflections', Ecology and Society, 22(1), doi:10.5751/es09009-220110.

Rodney, W. (2018) *How Europe underdeveloped Africa*, London: Verso Trade.

Ross, J. (2000) *The war against oblivion: Zapatista chronicles, 1994–2000*, Monroe, ME: Common Courage Press.

Ross, J. (2006) *¡Zapatistas! Making another world possible: Chronicles of resistance, 2000–2006*, New York: Nation Books.

Rosset, P. (2014) 'Zapatista uprising 20 years later: How Indigenous Mexicans stood up against NAFTA "death sentence"', *Democracy Now!*, 20 January, Available from: www.democracynow.org/2014/1/3/zapatista_uprising_20_years_later_how

Rosset, P. and Martínez-Torres, M. (2012) 'Rural social movements and agroecology: Context, theory, and process', *Ecology and Society*, 17(3): 17.

Rosset, P., Patel, R. and Courville, M. (eds) (2006) *Promised land: Competing visions of agrarian reform*, Oakland, CA: Food First Books.

Roy, A. (2003) *War talk*, Boston, MA: South End Press.

Roy, A. (2004) *Public power in the age of empire*, San Francisco: Seven Stories Press.

Rus, J. (2010) 'The end of the plantations and the transformation of Indigenous society in highland Chiapas, Mexico, 1974–2009', Doctoral dissertation, UC Riverside.

Rus, J., Hernández, R.A. and Mattiace, S.L. (eds) (2003) *Mayan lives, Mayan utopias: The Indigenous peoples of Chiapas and the Zapatista rebellion*, Lanham, MD: Rowman & Littlefield.

Said, E.W. (2012) *Culture and imperialism*, London: Chatto & Windus.

Sakellariou, D. and Rotarou, E.S. (2017) 'The effects of neoliberal policies on access to healthcare for people with disabilities', *International Journal for Equity in Health*, 16: 199.

Saxena, S., Thornicroft, G., Knapp, M. and Whiteford, H. (2007) 'Resources for mental health: Scarcity, inequity, and inefficiency', *The Lancet*, 370(9590): 878–89.

Scharff, C. (2016) 'The psychic life of neoliberalism: Mapping the contours of entrepreneurial subjectivity', *Theory, Culture & Society*, 33(6): 107–22.

Scoones, I., Edelman, M., Borras Jr, S.M., Hall, R., Wolford, W. and White, B. (2017) 'Emancipatory rural politics: Confronting authoritarian populism', *The Journal of Peasant Studies*, 1–20, doi:10.1080/03066150.2017.1339693.

Sell, S. and Williams, O. (2020) 'Health under capitalism: A global political economy of structural pathogenesis', *Review of International Political Economy*, 27: 1–25.

Sessa, B. (2012) *The psychedelic renaissance: Reassessing the role of psychedelic drugs in 21st century psychiatry and society*, London: Muswell Hill Press.

Sevilla Guzmán, E. and Woodgate, G. (2013) 'Agroecology: Foundations in agrarian social thought and sociological theory', *Agroecology and Sustainable Food Systems*, 37(1): 32–44.

Shenker, S.D. (2012) 'Towards a world in which many worlds fit? Zapatista autonomous education as an alternative means of development', *International journal of educational development*, 32(3): 432–43.

Shiva, V. (2001) *Stolen harvest: The hijacking of the global food supply*, London: Zed Books.

Shiva, V. (2005) *Earth democracy: Justice, sustainability, and peace*, Cambridge: South End Press.

Sierra, M.T. (2004) 'Diálogos y prácticas interculturales: Derechos humanos, derechos de las mujeres y políticas de identidad', *Desacatos*, (15-16): 126–47.

Silva Montes, C. (2019) 'The Zapatista school: Educating for autonomy and emancipation', *Alteridad: Revista de Educación*, 14(1): 109–21.

Simpson, A. (2007) 'On ethnographic refusal: Indigeneity, "voice" and colonial citizenship', *Junctures: The Journal for Thematic Dialogue*, 9: 67–80.

Simpson, L. (2008) 'Our elder brothers: The lifeblood of resurgences', in L. Simpson (ed) *Lighting the eighth fire: The liberation, resurgence, and protection of Indigenous nations*, Winnipeg, MB: Arbeiter Ring Publishing, pp 73–87.

Soriano González, M. (2012) 'La revolución Zapatista de Chiapas. Guerra, paz y conflicto (desde la perspectiva de sus protagonistas)', *Revista Internacional de Pensamiento Político*, 7: 391–408.

Sparke, M. (2013) *Introducing globalization: Ties, tensions, and uneven integration*, Hoboken, NJ: John Wiley & Sons.

Speed, S. and Forbis, M. (2005) 'Embodying alternative knowledges: Everyday leaders and the diffusion of power in Zapatista autonomous regions', *LASA Forum*, 36(1): 17–18.

Speed, S. and Reyes, A. (2002) '"In our own defense": Rights and resistance in Chiapas', *PoLAR: Political and Legal Anthropology Review*, 25(1): 69–89.

Speed, S., Castillo, R.A.H. and Stephen, L. (eds) (2006) *Dissident women: Gender and cultural politics in Chiapas*, Austin: University of Texas Press.

Springer, S. (2016a) 'Fuck neoliberalism', *ACME: An International Journal for Critical Geographies*, 15(2): 285–92.

Springer, S. (2016b) *The discourse of neoliberalism: An anatomy of a powerful idea*, Lanham, MD: Rowman & Littlefield.

Springer, S., Birch, K. and MacLeavy, J. (eds) (2016) *Handbook of neoliberalism*, New York: Routledge.

Springer, S., De Souza, M.L. and White, R. (2016) *The radicalisation of pedagogy: Anarchism, geography, and the spirit of revolt*, Lanham, MD: Rowman & Littlefield.

Stahler-Sholk, R. (2007) 'Resisting neoliberal homogenisation: The Zapatista autonomy movement', *Latin American Perspectives*, 34(2): 48–63.

Stahler-Sholk, R. (2019) 'Zapatistas and new ways of doing politics', *Oxford Research Encyclopedia of Politics*, Available from: https://doi.org/10.1093/acrefore/9780190228637.013.1724

Stephen, L. (2002) *Zapata lives! Histories and cultural politics in southern Mexico*, Berkeley, CA: University of California Press.

Stephens, E.C., Jones, A.D. and Parsons, D. (2018) 'Agricultural systems research and global food security in the 21st century: An overview and roadmap for future opportunities', *Agricultural Systems*, 163: 1–6.

Sunder Rajan, K. (2006) *Biocapital: The constitution of postgenomic life*, Durham, NC: Duke University Press.

Sunder Rajan, K. (2012) *Lively capital: Biotechnologies, ethics, and governance in global markets*, Durham, NC: Duke University Press.

Surviving Society (2019) *A note on hope*, Available from: www.patreon.com/posts/note-on-hope-in-45560579?utm_medium=clipboard_copy&utm_source=copy_to_clipboard&utm_campaign=postshare

Tate, K.A., Torres Rivera, E., Brown, E. and Skaistis, L. (2013) 'Foundations for liberation: Social justice, liberation psychology, and counselling', *InterAmerican Journal of Psychology*, 47: 373–82.

Taylor, K.Y. (2016) *From #BlackLivesMatter to Black liberation*, Chicago: Haymarket Books.

Thatcher, M. (1987) 'Interview in *Women's Own*', Available from: www.theguardian.com/politics/2013/apr/08/margaret-thatcher-quotes

Thieme, T.A. (2018) 'The hustle economy: Informality, uncertainty and the geographies of getting by', *Progress in Human Geography*, 42(4): 529–48.

Torres, E. and Sawyer, T. (2005) *Curandero: A life in Mexican folk healing*, New Albuquerque, NM: University of New Mexico Press.

Tran, D., Martinez-Alier, J., Navas, G. and Mingorria, S. (2020) 'Gendered geographies of violence: A multiple case study analysis of murdered women environmental defenders', *Journal of Political Ecology*, 27(1): 1189–212.

Tuck, E. and Yang, K.W. (2012) 'Decolonisation is not a metaphor', *Decolonisation: Indigeneity, Education and Society*, 1(1): 1–40.

Tupper, K.W. and Labate, B.C. (2014) 'Ayahuasca, psychedelic studies and health sciences: The politics of knowledge and inquiry into an Amazonian plant brew', *Current Drug Abuse Reviews*, 7: 71–80.

UN News (2021) '"COVID-19 doesn't discriminate, but societies do"', say women frontliners', March, Available from: https://news.un.org/en/story/2021/03/1086692

van de Sande, M. (2015) 'Fighting with tools: Prefiguration and radical politics in the twenty-first century', *Rethinking Marxism*, 27(2): 177–94.

Vergara-Camus, L. (2007) 'The MST and the EZLN struggle for land: New forms of peasant rebellions', *Journal of Agrarian Change*, 9(3): 365–91.

Vergara-Camus, L. (2014) *Land and freedom: The MST, the Zapatistas and peasant alternatives to neoliberalism*, London: Zed Books.

Vostal, F. (2016) *Accelerating academia: The changing structure of academic time*, Basingstoke: Palgrave Macmillan.

Waitzkin, H. (2018) *Health care under the knife: Moving beyond capitalism for our health*, New York: NYU Press.

Walia, H. (2021) *Border and rule: Global migration, capitalism, and the rise of racist nationalism*, Chicago: Haymarket Books.

Watkins, M. and Shulman, L. (2008) *Toward psychologies of liberation*, New York: Palgrave Macmillan.

Wattenbarger, H. (2020) 'The legacy of Samir Flores, one year later', NACLA, 18 February, Available from: https://nacla.org/news/2020/02/18/legacy-samir-flores-one-year-later

Weinberg, B. and Weinberg, W.J. (2000) *Homage to Chiapas: The new Indigenous struggles in Mexico*, London: Verso.

Weiner, L. and Compton, M. (eds) (2008) *The global assault on teaching, teachers, and their unions: Stories for resistance*, New York: Springer.

WHO (World Health Organization) (2008) *Closing the gap in a generation: Health equity through action on the social determinants of health*, Final Report of the Commission on the Social Determinants of Health. Geneva: WHO.

WomenWatch (2012) 'Facts and figures: Rural women and the millennium development goals', United Nations Inter-Agency Task Force on Rural Women, Available from: www.un.org/womenwatch/feature/ruralwomen/facts-figures.html#footnote1

World Bank, The (2020) *Fact sheet: Pandemic emergency financial facility*, Available from: www.worldbank.org/en/topic/pandemics/brief/fact-sheet-pandemic-emergency-financing-facility

Zapatista Squadron 421 (2021) 'Only 500 years later: Words of the Zapatista peoples', Available from: https:// enlacezapatista.ezln.org.mx/2021/08/17/only-500-years-later/

Zapatista Women (2018) 'Opening address at the First International Gathering of Politics, Art, Sport, and Culture for Women in Struggle', *Enlace Zapatista*, Available from: http://enlacezapatista.ezln.org.mx/2018/03/26/zapatista-womens-opening-address-at-the-first-international-gathering-of-politics-art-sport-and-culture-for-women-in-struggle

Zapatista Women (2019) 'Letter from the Zapatista Women to women in struggle around the world', *Enlace Zapatista*, Available from: https://enlacezapatista.ezln.org.mx/2019/02/13/letter-from-the-zapatista-women-to-women-in-struggle-around-the-world

Zapatista Women (2021) 'The women who are no longer with us', Enlace Zapatista, Available from: https://enlacezapatista.ezln.org.mx/2021/03/08/the-women-who-are-no-longer-with-us/

Zibechi, R. (2012) *Territories in resistance: A cartography of Latin American social movements*, Oakland, CA: AK Press.

Zibechi, R. (2013) 'The art of building a new world: Freedom according to the Zapatistas', *Americas Program*, 5 September, Available from: https://web.archive.org/web/20140219115121/http://www.cipamericas.org:80/archives/10603

Zibechi, R. (2019) 'The decolonizing Zapatista revolution', in R. McGee and J. Pettit (eds) *Power, empowerment, and social change*, Abingdon: Routledge, pp 199–212.

Zoomers, A. (2010) 'Globalisation and the foreignisation of space: Seven processes driving the current global land grab', *Journal of Peasant Studies*, 37: 429–47.

Zournazi, M. (2002) *Hope: New philosophies for change*, London: Pluto Press.

Index

References to figures appear in *italic* type.
References to endnotes show the
page number and note number (157n8).